Formosa

1895-1945

Government-General building, Taipei, completed by the Japanese in 1918, surrendered to the Chinese in 1945, and in 1949 declared by Chiang Kai-shek to be the "Temporary Headquarters of the Government of the Republic of China." [Naito Hideo, *Taiwan—a Unique Colonial Record, 1937–8 Edition* (Tokyo, 1938), frontispiece]

Formosa

Licensed Revolution
and the
Home Rule Movement
1895-1945

George H. Kerr

The University Press of Hawaii
Honolulu

For P. C. B.

Contents

Acknowledgments

$\mathcal{I}$T GIVES me pleasure first to thank Dr. Gengo Suzuki who was my teaching colleague at Taipei in 1937–1940. He was at that time an editor of important journals having to do with the economic and social development of Formosa. At the war's end, as I went about collecting research materials in Taipei, he gave me authoritative bibliographic advice and added substantially to my collection on the eve of his return to Japan. In prewar Formosa and at Tokyo my Formosan friends were always most helpful, and ready always to explain the Formosan point of view, or to tell of their lives as colonial subjects under the Japanese administration.

In 1944, while on navy duty, I developed a Formosa Research Unit for the U.S. Naval School for Military Government and Administration at Columbia University in New York. In preparing our Civil Affairs Handbook series, we relied principally upon Japanese-language sources selected and translated under the supervision of Dr. Francis W. Cleaves of Harvard University, who was then Lieutenant Commander Cleaves, USNR. In preparing this review, I have drawn heavily upon the Research Unit materials, and my appreciation of loyal staff support in 1944 remains undiminished.

A major portion of my own research collection is now at the East Asiatic Library of the University of California at Berkeley. In recording my thanks to Dr. Elizabeth Huff, the Library's former Director, and to Mr. Charles Hamilton, Curator of the Japanese Collection there, I should like to acknowledge my indebtedness to the entire Library staff.

ACKNOWLEDGMENTS

My indebtedness to the work of Dr. Edward I-te Chen and Dr. Harry J. Lamley is noted elsewhere in the text. In solving special problems I have called upon Dr. Ng Yuzin Chau-tong and Professor Ong Yok-tek, of Tokyo, and Messrs. Osamu Iiyama, Kazuo Kajimura, and Yoshimasa Kato, at Berkeley. Messrs. Neal Y. Goya, Nobuyuki Kato and George Sasaki have helped prepare the illustrations.

Among the friends who have read parts or all of the manuscript at different periods in its development are Mr. John S. Service, Mrs. R. A. Vitousek, Mr. Paul C. Blum, Dr. Cheng-mei Shaw and Dr. Wu-hao Tu. I am indebted to them all for criticism and advice, but of course I alone am to be held responsible for interpretations placed upon events recorded here.

Preface

ON DECEMBER 1, 1943, three Allied leaders—
Roosevelt, Churchill, and Chiang—having met at Cairo, declared publicly that at the war's end Japan would be stripped of
all "stolen" territories, and that the Pescadores and Formosa
would be restored to the Republic of China. That pledge was
reaffirmed at Potsdam in 1945 by the United States, Britain,
and Russia. Thirty years later the restoration was still in-
complete; it had proved much easier to make the pledge than to
carry it out.

When Japan at last surrendered, Washington arranged that
Formosa should be promptly handed over to Chiang Kai-shek's
Nationalist administration. There was no attempt to reserve
temporary Allied interests and no guarantee whatsoever of the
rights and interests of the island people pending a formal
transfer of sovereignty by treaty. It was an attempt to paste
Formosa back upon the map of China without delay. The results were disastrous.

We may be sure that at Cairo neither Prime Minister
Churchill nor President Roosevelt knew anything substantially
detailed concerning Formosa's past. That is to say they knew
nothing of the manner in which the continental Chinese first established a claim upon Formosa by conquest, and nothing of
the unhappy relationship that developed between the Formosan
people and the continental Chinese sent out to govern them.
After two centuries of rasping conflict, Peking ceded Formosa
to Japan "in perpetuity" by terms of the Treaty of Shimonoseki

in 1895. At that time a confused, ill-organized and hopeless attempt was made to declare the island independent and to block the oncoming Japanese. This move failed entirely, and for the next half-century the island and its people underwent a remarkable technological, social, and economic revolution. The record of this transformation becomes the principal theme of our present review.

It is a record which a majority of the State Department's China experts chose deliberately to ignore. It embarrassed them. They were determined that no "Formosa Question" should rise to complicate swift adjustment of postwar Sino-American relations. They were eager to foster China's postwar recovery under a strong, effective government, whatever its political coloration might be. Formosan-Chinese minority interests could not be allowed to stand in the way.

In private conversations on the subject, the lofty principles of the Atlantic Charter and the charter of the United Nations were sometimes shrugged off, becoming, by implication, no more than stale propaganda themes that had served their purpose late in the war, and now should be forgotten. Senior officers, however well informed, preferred not to disturb their superiors, the principal policymakers, by reminding them of troublesome postwar possibilities in Formosa, or by forewarning them that a reconciliation of the Formosan people with the continental Chinese would be no easy task after all that had taken place during the preceding Japanese half-century. A few officers—very few—were prepared to admit that a hasty, unqualified transfer might cause hardship, be unjust, and be in violation of principles Americans professed to value. But Realpolitik required a sacrifice of the Formosan-Chinese minority interest to the greater interest and importance of adjusting overall Sino-American relations. The Chinese had demanded immediate control of Formosa and we had promised it to Chiang.

Unfortunately for these State Department "realists," the Formosa Question would not vanish simply because bureaucrats in Washington would have it so. There were too many problems inherent in Formosa's geographical position, the historical tradition, and the temperament of its people. By late 1944 few China specialists in Washington believed that Chiang

Kai-shek's organization could survive without massive reform of a corrupt administration, a thorough revision of the political structure, and a sweeping rehabilitation of the armed forces. None of these seemed likely, and few State Department officers expected it. Occasionally it was pointed out that if Formosa were turned over to Chiang without reservation of any Allied interest, Washington was probably providing him a safe retreat in which he could indefinitely prolong the life of his unhealthy and embarrassing regime. The international complications rising then would be far greater than if Formosa were to be placed under a temporary trusteeship, pending a resolution of the continental civil war.

This argument was dismissed as merely a hypothetical possibility, a long-range guess, not to be taken seriously at that time. The historical separatist tradition, however, was a matter of record and a potential source of great trouble. The first Chinese to settle in Formosa had been emigrants who left the continent in the seventeenth century to escape conditions of desperate poverty and official exploitation. Subsequently four bloody "conquests" by continental expeditionary forces, three great rebellions, and innumerable local uprisings had marked Formosa's relations with China before Peking ceded the island to Japan. These troubled years had given rise to a strong separatist tradition, but this was dismissed as inconsequential by Washington's China specialists; many regions of China were noted for their restless and rebellious place in history. They refused to give sufficient weight to the importance of the *Japanese* half-century in Formosa's past.

Of the facts of geography and history there could be no dispute; on the temperament and character of the island people there can be less agreement, nevertheless personal observations may be useful. At Tokyo and Taipei in the period 1935 to 1940, I became well acquainted with many foreign students from Southeast Asia and the Indies, and with students from the Ryukyu Islands (Okinawa Prefecture) and Japan's colonies (Korea and Formosa). Individually and collectively they showed marked personality differences and exhibited a wide range of political interests and aspirations. From time to time all expressed grievances of some sort, reacting to colonial and semicolonial status. The Koreans, like the Indians, Indonesians, and Indo-Chinese, often revealed depths of irreconcilable bitterness. They were determined to achieve independence at whatever cost, and were ready to accept help from any quarter to reach that goal. The mild and notably patient Okinawans, on the other hand, clearly considered themselves Japanese, although sometimes irritated and offended by instances of crass discrimination they suffered at the hands of Japanese from other prefectures.

Between the Koreans (who lost their king and independence in 1910), and the Okinawans (who had lost theirs in 1878) stood the Formosan Chinese. Their ancestral island-home had been a maritime dependency of China since 1683. Japanese forces had occupied both Korea and Okinawa before final acts of annexation had taken place. Peking, on the other hand, had agreed to cede Formosa to Japan as part of a price to be paid for Japanese withdrawal from Manchuria and the continental road to Peking. Formosan leaders, who felt the island people had been betrayed, held that obligations of loyalty to China had been dissolved by such betrayal.

On the eve of the Pacific War the position of the young Formosans stood in marked contrast with that of the Koreans and the young men and women from European colonies in Asia. They did not like the Japanese en masse, to be sure, and deeply resented the arrogance of petty bureaucrats and hard-nosed police who served Tokyo in the colony, but there was no prospect of independence whatsoever, and no clamor for it. Instead, Formosan leaders argued for a special place within the Japanese empire. They asked for full participation in an elective island administration and just representation of Formosan interests in the National Diet at Tokyo. They asked the Japanese to respect island traditions and local customs, and to grant Formosans full recognition as political, social, and economic equals with the emperor's subjects everywhere within the empire.

There was no call for a "return to China." During this period of residence in Japan and Formosa I had occasion to travel through Korea, Manchuria, and North China. It took no great effort of the imagination to understand why the island people sought, instead, an improved position within the Japanese empire frame of reference. The contrasts in opportunity were too great. At that time Formosa had a population of fewer than six millions, the island was richly productive, and in all of Asia it was second only to Japan proper in general standards of living. This they recognized, and these benefits they did not want to lose.

In that last decade preceding World War II, "old China" held little appeal; the island people were identified with the most modern and most powerful nation in Asia, "young Japan," and through Japan the young Formosan looked to the maritime world and the West.

When toward the war's end Japan was exhausted and faced defeat, American propaganda poured into the island, promising Formosans an end to Japanese police rule and the prospect of new life and dignity in a democratic postwar China. Island leaders believed in this propaganda and imagined themselves welcomed by this new China, sponsored by the United States of America, guarantor of freedom and the richest and most powerful nation on earth.

The war's end was greeted in Formosa with deep but mixed emotions. Some Japanese military men wanted to refuse the terms of surrender, and a few committed suicide. Civilians—Japanese and Formosans alike—welcomed peace. The Japanese prepared to return to the home country. The Formosan Chinese and the aborigines in the hills were happy to be rid of the ubiquitous Japanese policeman, and thanked the United States—not China—for it; for the rest, they were not unhappy to see the Japanese withdraw, but neither did they rejoice immoderately.

Beginning in October 1945, American ships and planes transported thousands of Chinese troops from the continent, together with Nationalist administrative officers, their relatives and their friends. A host of rapacious carpetbaggers had soon come in, eager for the spoils of war. The Formosan welcome was reserved. Within six weeks it had worn away. Within six months Formosan leaders were angrily protesting to the local administration and vainly attempting to invoke the attention of the Generalissimo. By the end of 1946 the American consulate had to warn the ambassador at Nanking and the State Department at Washington that the Formosans were on the point of rebellion. They felt that they had been thrust back fifty years, back into the turbulent nineteenth century. They feared that all the gains made under the long Japanese administration would soon be lost.

These Formosan appeals begged the United States to remember that Japan had surrendered Formosa to all the Allies and not to China alone, and that all bore a share of responsibility for what was then taking place. Washington's response was cold. At Taipei the consul, personally contemptuous of the Formosans, dismissed petitioning Formosan leaders curtly, saying, "This is China now."

On February 28, 1947, Formosans throughout the island began to rise in unarmed protest, demanding sweeping reforms in the Taipei administration. Some attempted to petition the Generalissimo for corrective action and others sought some form of foreign intervention to ensure reform and to keep Formosa clear from the mounting civil war on the continent.

In the eyes of continental Chinese—Nationalist and Communist alike—this was treasonable behavior. The Formosans were condemned as being not true Chinese, an island people spoiled by a tradition of rebellion and by fifty years of Japanese administration. Chiang Kai-shek's response to the Formosan reform demands was swift and brutal. A Chinese Nationalist expeditionary force of some fifty thousand well-armed men was sent out to the island. At least ten thousand Formosans were killed or imprisoned, and thousands were forced to seek safety overseas. A generation of well-educated Formosan leaders disappeared.

With this 1947 uprising and its bloody suppression, the island people resumed the tradition of rebellion, and continental authority resumed the pattern of military reconquest. This is not an appropriate place for detailed review of events in Formosa or related to it during the ensuing quarter-century. Washington's policies twisted and turned in confusing efforts to dissociate the United States from the "Formosa problem." The original premises upon which these policies were based were unreal; during World War II it had been assumed by the leading China specialists that because the Formosan majority was Chinese by race and cultural heritage and had been under the alien Japanese for fifty years, it followed that they must ipso facto now accept continental Chinese politics, government, and nationality. Other and more cynical explanations might be offered to explain an adamant refusal to consider seriously the facts of geography, the lessons of history, or the theoretical rights and interests of the island people who have been so long the victims of Great Power politics.

It will suffice to say that from 1942 until June 1950, Washington attempted to treat Formosa, unrealistically, as just another Chinese province, only lately overrun by the Japanese. Events in Korea suddenly modified this simplistic view. Now the facts of geography intruded themselves. Formosa's strategic importance as an island on the Western Pacific frontier had to be admitted, and from 1950 until 1970 Washington had perforce to treat it in economic and military terms as an independent maritime principality. Once cut off from the continent and the convulsions of social revolution there, the Formosan economy flourished to an extraordinary degree, sustained by a worldwide maritime trade. But under the misshapen and cynical "Dulles' policies," Washington continued to treat the island politically as if it were a province of continental China and as if Chiang's pretentious "government of China" at Taipei were real. This flawed policy asked the world to recognize Formosa as "Free China" when, throughout the decades, the island remained a police state. Under martial law, the prisons continued to be filled with dissidents and "traitors" who had agitated for reform or had called for foreign intervention if not for independence. Formosans held no effective place in the Taipei government. The voices proclaiming Formosa to be "Free China" and a strong democratic ally began notably to falter when at last the Nationalists were expelled from the United Nations and Peking's representatives took their place. Throughout these years all continental Chinese—Communists and Nationalists alike— were agreed that Formosa must be returned to Chinese administration from which it had been removed in 1895. Washington accepted this. It had become clear that the bitter Sino-American confrontation could not be resolved nor détente achieved until the Formosa problem was dealt with. In Washington's view the island people had been a continuously troublesome Chinese minority whose ultimate fate must be decided among the Chinese themselves. If this meant invasion, repression, concentration camps, executions, or forced migrations on a massive scale, it would be regrettable, but would constitute a moral responsibility that the Chinese must assume for themselves. Perhaps, on the other hand, if the principle of China's sovereignty were at last recognized universally, a lenient continental administration would tolerate an autonomous island dependency and develop an elaborate offshore base for intercourse with the Western world and Japan—an enlarged Hongkong, as it were—that would enable Peking to minimize unsettling foreign contacts with the other, continental provinces.

When the American President, Richard Nixon, determined to break through the impasse in Sino-American relations, Peking welcomed this major change in Washington's policies. It was made indisputably clear, however, that before any other Sino-American problems were resolved, the United States must publicly recognize continental China's claim to sovereignty in Formosa. The President agreed to this and made the necessary public avowal in the Nixon-Chou Communiqué, issued at Shanghai on February 27, 1972.

Two years later (in May 1974) the despatch of yet another American ambassador to Taipei, rather than to Peking, seemed to nullify the Communiqué and to call into question the President's sincerity. Had the Nixon trip to China been nothing more than an exercise in public relations, or was this 1974 appointment a move, understood at Peking, to preclude the possibility of a Taipei invitation to Russia to replace the United States as guarantor for the security of Chiang Ching-kuo's inherited island principality? On behalf of Washington the new ambassador assured the Nationalists of a continuing American commitment "to safeguard the security of Taiwan."

The Allied directive transferring Formosa to continental Chinese control in 1945 and the 1972 Communiqué made no mention of inherent Formosan Chinese rights and interests. It was as if nothing significant had occurred during the seventy-seven years following Peking's cession of Formosa to Japan in 1895. It was left to the future to disclose how soon Peking might move to occupy and govern the island, and to disclose what methods might be adopted thereafter to cope with the traditional Formosan Chinese desire for autonomy.

1. Formosa and Continental China before 1895

AN ISLAND FRONTIER

*L*IKE the popes at Rome, Chinese emperors long claimed "all under Heaven." Until late in the nineteenth century this idea of universal dominion prompted Peking to refer to England, France, the Papacy, and other European states as "tributaries" subordinate to China. Small countries nearby which were wise enough to adopt Chinese as the language of diplomatic intercourse and to pay periodical formal tribute, in exchange received permission to trade with China and were sometimes honored by the dispatch of Chinese ambassadors to confirm the tributary rulers in office. These peripheral nations included Korea and Tibet, the small states of Indo-China, and the island kingdom of Liu-ch'iu (Ryukyu). Only Japan refused to call itself a tributary, and even dared to claim equality with Great China. Traditionally, when speaking of Japan, the Chinese referred to the Japanese people contemptuously as "dwarf slaves," but in Chinese eyes they had at least the grace to adopt the Chinese language for diplomatic and literary purposes.

Formosa offered a different problem. Chinese governments had known of a great island lying in the seas east of Fukien for at least a thousand years before European navigators first came upon it in the sixteenth century. At that time the Chinese called it sometimes Pakkan-tao ("Pakkan Island") and sometimes Hsiao Liu-ch'iu, or "Little Liu-ch'iu." To this magnificent discovery the Europeans gave the name *Ilha Formosa* or "Beautiful Island."

Pakkan-tao (or Formosa) was then a formidable wilderness throughout, sparsely inhabited by headhunting tribesmen who had no government with which the Chinese could communicate. They had no established trade of value, they were unprepared to pay tribute, and they showed no proper desire to learn the Chinese language. In brief, Formosa was distinctly not "part of China" when the Spanish, the Japanese, and the Dutch in turn undertook to chart its coasts and to establish settlements ashore.

The Europeans and the Japanese found a few Chinese fishermen, pirates, and lawless adventurers living on small offshore islands or settled at rivermouth anchorages. For a brief time the Japanese maintained a hamlet on a sandy southwestern coastal islet near the entrance to a wide lagoon. This was a shelter for merchantmen and buccaneers who made passage between Japan and China's forbidden coastal ports, or the long run to ports in Southeast Asia and the Philippines. Spaniards, based at Manila, were the first to chart Formosa's coasts in the late sixteenth century. At last, in 1628, they settled a garrison, a mission outpost, and a trading depot in the northern region. There Manila proposed to use the Tamsui and Keelung anchorages as a base for military, mercantile, and evangelical campaigns westward into China and northward through Okinawa into Japan.

The Dutch, based on Java, landed first in the Pescadores in 1622 where they found a Chinese fishing village long established beside a splendid harbor. This anchorage had been used for centuries as a refuge for Chinese and Japanese pirate fleets. It was now lightly garrisoned and governed as a dependency of Fukien Province across the Strait. After two years of ruthless Dutch occupation the Fukien authorities organized an expeditionary force with which to destroy the foreign barbarians. At the same time they suggested that perhaps the Europeans might prefer to move on *beyond* Chinese territory to the shores of wild Pakkan-tao. This the Dutch did in 1624, settling near the Japanese hamlet known as Takasago. On their own sandy islet at the mouth of the lagoon the Dutch then built a castle, a colonial town, and a shipyard, making the settlement a way-station for Dutch shipping passing from the Netherlands East Indies to the ports of China and Japan.

The fort and town, which they named Zelandia, stood on an islet named T'aiwan. This latter the Dutch spelt in various ways and soon extended the name to include all the interior lands nearby as they brought them under control. Within a hundred years *Pakkan-tao* faded from common use in China, and the Chinese too, extended the name T'aiwan to include all of Formosa. The Japanese Takasago hamlet was abandoned soon after the Dutch established themselves nearby, but Japanese maps and texts continued to refer to Formosa interchangeably as Taiwan or Takasago until the midnineteenth century.

The Dutch—not the Chinese—opened Formosa to plantation settlement, explored the interior lowland, brought scores of aboriginal villages under control, and gave them a village council system. Company clerks and Protestant missionaries reduced the local languages to written form, introduced schools and mission chapels, and made many converts. As they introduced new food-plants, trees, oxen, poultry, and European farm utensils, they took out sugar, rice, deerhides, rattan, camphor, sulphur, and forge coal for shipment to Japan, China, Southeast Asia, the Indies, the Middle East, and Europe. To obtain cheap labor the Dutch recruited thousands of tough, quarrelsome but hardworking peasants and fishermen from the impoverished coastal districts of Fukien, across the Strait. Thousands more defied Peking's ban on migration, crossing over on their own initiative as soon as it became known along the China coast that the foreign barbarians—the Dutch—had brought the fierce Formosan aborigines under some control on Pakkan-tao. Like the European migrants entering the North American colonies at that time, these émigré Chinese pioneers sought to escape intolerable conditions in their homeland, or were lured by the prospect of pioneer homesteading on the wilderness frontier. They were ready to take risks and they had to be inventive in order to survive. The majority were men, traveling on their own, who soon found wives among the aboriginal population.

The Dutch steadily developed Formosa during a period of

nearly forty years. Teas, silks, lacquer, and porcelain from the China ports were transshipped through Zelandia to Java and onward to Europe. Dutch ships passing to and from Japan made this a sheltering way-station, and the colony itself exported products of its own fields, mines, and forests, principally to Japan. Soon after the Japanese withdrew from near Zelandia, the Dutch drove their Spanish rivals from Formosa and added the northern region to their own.

Dutch policy actively encouraged intermarriage among the Europeans, the aborigines, and the incoming Chinese pioneers, producing a rugged society on a wilderness frontier, a rising generation of farmers, fishermen, and hunters who knew only Formosa as their home. This intermixture of races in the seventeenth century created a gene-pool drawn upon by all subsequent generations. The energetic Dutchmen brought about Formosa's first technological and social revolution, a magnitude of change not to be experienced again until the close of the nineteenth century when the Japanese assumed control. This "European period" came to a sudden end in 1663. The Dutch had made Formosa too attractive. While the Dutch were opening up the island, the Ming dynastic government in China had collapsed. On the continent, between 1644 and 1681, the incoming Manchus and their Chinese collaborators gradually brought all the Chinese provinces under firm control. The last resistance was put down in the coastal districts of Fukien Province. There a slightly mad adventurer named Cheng Ch'eng-kung had recruited a small army and developed a fleet with which he ostentatiously proposed to destroy the "bandit" Manchus at Peking and to restore the old regime. This ambitious and interesting sea baron, known to the Western world as "Koxinga the Pirate," had been born in Japan, the son of a Japanese mother and an immensely wealthy Chinese father. The father was in turn pirate, buccaneer, and legitimate trader. Koxinga's childhood had been spent in the busy international port of Hirado, in Japan, and his youth was spent near the port of Amoy, and at Nanking. Thus his world was essentially a maritime world; he had traveled nowhere beyond Nanking and knew little of the vast extent and resources of interior China. Although his fleets could control coastal shipping in the Strait, his troops ashore were no more than an irritating local nuisance to the new imperial government.

By 1662 Koxinga and his son had been driven from Fukien. They held only Quemoy Island in the mouth of Amoy Harbor, and a few offshore islets along the coast nearby. Looking for a place of further retreat and safety they considered the Pescadores and the Dutch colony on Formosa. Koxinga's agents informed him that the Europeans there were quarreling bitterly among themselves on matters of policy, that the governor had no more than twelve hundred men ready to hold the principal fort, Zelandia, and that he could expect no early reenforcements from Java. With a body of some twelve thousand well-armed, well-trained men, Koxinga sailed from Quemoy, surprised the Dutch, and after a siege lasting eight months, took Zelandia and compelled the Europeans to leave the island. The Dutch, who had found Formosa a true wilderness, left it a productive colony, a rich prize for the Koxingan refugees.

The "Koxingan period" was brief but important. On entering the Dutch settlement Koxinga took with him hundreds of former Ming courtiers and scholars, clerks, craftsmen, and farmers with their gear, including plows and seeds. These newcomers displaced or dispossessed not only the Europeans but the earlier pioneer Chinese émigrés, the "tamed" aborigines, and the children and grandchildren of mixed blood. The courtiers and new administrators settled in the Dutch villages which they soon enlarged into proper Chinese towns. After the incoming troops had been settled on lands assigned to them near the edge of the wilderness they were obliged to alternate periods of military service with months of farming, and within the next twenty years they too had found local wives and fathered a generation of children of mixed blood who knew only Formosa as home.

Under Koxinga's son Formosa became in effect an independent principality, cut off from continental China and sustained by a wide-ranging seaborne commerce with Japan, Southeast Asia, and the Philippines. Like Chiang Kai-shek and his fellow refugees in a later age, this "Prince of Tung-t'u" and his associates formed an élite court and government imposed upon the earlier Chinese pioneers and the aboriginal population—the whole regime sustained by a refugee army and an overseas trade. And also like Chiang and the latter-day Nationalists, the Koxingans insisted that they would return to China, overthrow the "bandits" at Peking and restore the old order. Nor would they give up the Quemoy base and the offshore islets. Year after year they made ineffectual but irritating hit-and-run buccaneering raids along the Fukien coast, bidding meanwhile for military help from foreign barbarians—the British, the Dutch, and the Japanese.

Having slowly brought all the provinces of continental China under firm control, Peking decided to rid itself of this intolerable Koxingan nuisance. In 1683 an imperial expeditionary force crossed the channel, occupied the Pescadores, and overwhelmed the little principality. The Koxingan officers and aristocracy were dispossessed as the Dutch had been, Koxingan soldiers were forbidden to return to their continental homes, and Peking renewed the old Ming edicts banning unrestricted Chinese migration to Formosa. A garrison was established at Tainan to enforce Peking's will. All who attempted to resist this First Conquest suffered bloody reprisals, prompting a movement of people from the old Koxingan capital (now called Taiwan-fu) to regions near or beyond the old frontier.

Peking declared the Pescadores and the island of Formosa to be dependencies of the Chinese province of Fukien and so they remained until 1887. The area once controlled by the Dutch and their successors, the Koxingans, was substantially reduced by drawing back the official borderline. New laws and regulations, promulgated at Peking, forbade further agricultural expansion on Formosa and banned Formosan-Chinese intercourse with the aborigines beyond the new frontier. Cruel punishments were prescribed for any continental Chinese found attempting to evade restrictions upon migration to the island. Peking was determined that Formosa must never again become a base for dynastic rebels and dissidents, and never again be used by foreign barbarians. In brief, throughout the next two hundred years, China's scholar-bureaucrats pursued a decidedly negative policy toward the maritime dependency, so distant from Peking and, in their eyes, a decided liability.

The ban on cross-channel migration was exploited by venal port officials who took bribes from emigrants and squeezed the commerce slowly developing between Fukien and the dependency. Within the island a weak garrison government was unable to check expansion of frontier agricultural settlements and trade with the aborigines in the hills. Imperial authority was very slight in the lowlands and reached not at all to the high mountains and the eastern coast. Villages that developed beyond the official frontiers were for the most part a law unto themselves. Aggressive clan leaders paid scant attention to sententious imperial edicts and regulations renewed from time to time. Village rivalries and incessant clan warfare gave Formosa the reputation of a lawless island where life was dangerous and where an official sent out on temporary assignment (usually for a three-year term) was expected to enrich himself as speedily as possible.

Too many mandarins from the continent looked disdainfully upon the Formosan Chinese as unruly cultural renegades who could not be considered "true Chinese." They considered the mountain aborigines—the "raw savages"—to be nothing more than wild beasts of the interior, and the Pepohuan or "plains barbarians" to be little better. These latter for the most part were a feckless people of mixed aboriginal and Chinese blood, adopting some modes of Chinese life and dress, yet retaining elements of their Malayo-Polynesian past. They were without security in either world, living in hopeless poverty in scattered foothill villages. Having lost much of the cunning of their ancestors, they were too easily intimidated and outwitted by the better-organized Chinese.

The never-ending conflict between agents of continental authority and the island people gave each a jaundiced view of the other. There could be little mutual trust; in Formosan-Chinese eyes the distant imperial government had to be obeyed perforce, but it deserved little genuine respect.

Between 1683, the year of the First Conquest, and the decade of the 1850s, when foreigners again returned as traders, consuls, and missionaries, Formosa experienced three "Great Rebellions" and innumerable riots and uprisings against continental Chinese authority. Each major rebellion was followed by a new conquest and the uprisings were put down with utmost savagery. Here in these centuries of mutual dislike, mistrust, and violence lay the roots of a flourishing Formosan separatist tradition. But then (as now) the island people lacked an essential social cohesion and a distinguished, far-seeing leadership.

It was a fragmented society. Formosans quarreled not only with the continental Chinese sent out to govern them, but endlessly among themselves. There were three noteworthy divisions within the island's Chinese population, each based upon ancestral continental heritage. Emigrants from coastal Fukien villages formed the first of these divisions and represented the great majority. During the seventeenth and eighteenth centuries they had settled along Formosa's western coast and in lowland farming communities. They were known as the "Hoklo" people, speaking related Fukien dialects and living according to traditional Fukien custom. Within these Fukien groups clan rivalries were persistent and strong.

The second noteworthy division embraced the Hakka people, physically a larger, tougher type with bolder more aggressive character. Their distant origins are obscure; the ancestors appear to have migrated from northern China into the uplands and mountains of hinterland Kwangtung Province and there, during the passing centuries, preserved their own distinct dialects and the many peculiar characteristics of dress and work habits that set them apart. For this reason they became known as "Hakka" or "Guest People" (that is, strangers). The name itself helped to perpetuate a sense of separateness, a community apart. These marked differences were of course carried over into Formosa in the eighteenth and nineteenth centuries and so, too, was the discrimination the Hakka had experienced on the continent. Upon entering through the Formosan coastal anchorages these latecomers found the more desirable lowland farm country already well settled. (There were quarrels and riots, for example, when Hakka immigrants attempted to settle near the mouth of the Tamsui River.) In consequence they were obliged to push on to the less productive foothills and to the mountain frontiers. There they became woodsmen and camphor workers, mingling and intermarrying with the aboriginal tribesmen much more freely than the Hok-lo were accustomed to do.

In the nineteenth century the distribution pattern of Hakka settlements was unmistakable: Hakka villages and outpost farms were found principally in Hsinchu, where the hills and mountain spurs reached to the northwestern coast. Hakka settlements dotted the northeastern valleys southward from Keelung. A line of Hakka settlements from north to south in the high foothills marked the forest frontier, separating the lowland Hok-lo farmlands from the interior jungle occupied then by the untamed aborigines. From Kaohsiung (Takao) southward to the tip of the island Hakka frontiersmen probably formed a majority. Although no exact figures exist and no estimates are reliable, it may be presumed that the Hakka represented roughly one-fourth of the total Formosan-Chinese population. Cantonese immigrants, settled principally in the port towns, formed the third population division, but were always a distinct and a not very consequential minority.

No love was lost between the Hakka and the Hok-lo. Incoming Europeans and Japanese were quick to observe that, given equal opportunities, the assertive Hakka proved the better soldiers and provided an aggressive leadership and competition in every field of action.

When the Western maritime powers reentered Far Eastern waters after 1800, they found undisciplined Formosa a most serious hazard to international shipping. It lay in the principal sea-lanes on the approach to China's ports and the surrounding seas were notoriously rough. The treacherous coasts were unlighted and unmarked, and pirates and lawless seaside-village "wreckers" were ready and eager to prey upon any stranded ship. Castaways so unfortunate as to come ashore in territory occupied by the headhunting aborigines had scant chance for survival; if they came ashore elsewhere they risked enslavement. China's mandarins and magistrates stationed along the western shore were not only contemptuously indifferent to the fate of "foreign barbarians" but often helpless as well, quite unable to control local bandits, pirates, or headhunters. The Europeans and the Japanese, now again coming upon the scene, soon discovered that the mandarins sometimes protected these lawless Formosan elements and shared booty with them.

The nineteenth-century governments of England, France, Germany, and the United States each in turn pressed China to "do something" to improve the situation, but Peking did nothing. France and Prussia each considered taking Formosa as a new colonial possession, and London considered proposals to make it a penal colony following the Australian pattern. The American Commodore Perry recommended a joint Sino-American economic development program, with an American settlement established at Keelung, all conceived with the idea that this would lead on to a break away from China and an ultimate appeal for annexation by the United States. His contemporary, Townsend Harris (Washington's first envoy to Japan) recommended outright purchase from the Chinese government.

Peking reacted to these international pressures first by disclaiming all responsibility for Formosan territory lying beyond the official lowland borders, in other words refusing responsibility for some two-thirds of the total area of Formosa. Taking this as a cue, Tokyo sent an expeditionary force to South Cape in 1874, ostensibly to punish the aborigines who had murdered castaways there in 1871. When Peking protested that this was an unfriendly act, Tokyo demanded a statement in writing of China's claim to sovereignty throughout the island. If this were produced, Peking would then be called upon to meet the obligations inherent in sovereignty, and would thereafter be held responsible for the actions of aborigines and Formosan Chinese alike throughout the island and in territorial waters. As an alternative, Tokyo threatened to occupy the ungoverned two-thirds of Formosa, after which Japan would offer to purchase the remaining one-third, the settled western lowland region.

Japan had sufficient reason to fear that a predatory Western colonial power might take the island from China and establish itself on Japan's southern frontier. England, on the other hand, having acquired Hongkong and having considered Formosa, was not happy with the prospect of a Japanese occupation of this great island lying along the sea-lanes leading into China's ports. The British Minister at Peking therefore brought his influence to bear, and Peking chose to claim full sovereignty throughout Formosa and to pay costs of the Japanese expedition to South Cape. In consequence Japan withdrew its forces in December 1874, and for the moment the threat of foreign occupation was removed.

By now it was evident to the few progressive officers at Peking that the traditional passive or negative policies in Formosa would no longer suffice. Who next among the foreign barbarians would seek to occupy Formosa, and when? It was imperative to make a show of reform on the island and if possible to remove any excuse for foreign intrusion on any pretext. In 1875, therefore, the imperial edicts prohibiting unrestricted Chinese migration to Formosa were at last canceled. The ban upon local economic development was lifted, and an unusually progressive officer, Ting Chih-chang, was sent out to govern and to improve the administration. But having sent him to the island, Peking gave him no real support. He found the inefficient, venal mandarin bureaucracy too much to manage, reported this to the Throne in bitter terms, and resigned in ill health and hopeless discouragement. The short-lived reform program was abandoned.

In 1884, as France seized the Pescadores, blockaded Formosa and occupied Keelung, Peking was again stirred to action and again sent out a progressive officer to retrieve the situation if he could. The French withdrew in the following year, making it possible for the new governor (General Liu Ming-ch'üan) to attempt many innovations. In 1887 Formosa was detached from the Fukien administration and declared to be a full-fledged new province of China. Foreign barbarians might find it a little more difficult to detach a province than a mere dependency.

Governor Liu then fostered the introduction of a railroad and postal and telegraph systems. He developed modern mines, improved harbor works, and established steamship and cable connections overseas. He built a new and comparatively modern capital city, Taipei, and for a brief time Formosa was beyond doubt the most progressive province in all of China. This was at a moment when the continental provinces were being swept by passionate antiforeign sentiment and moving toward the excesses of the Boxer Uprising soon to take place at Peking.

Liu's comparatively great success could be attributed in part to the fact that he was working with an island people less tradition-bound than the Chinese masses on the continent. They were frontiersmen and pioneers by tradition, obliged to experiment in new situations and already aware of great economic advantage through intercourse with foreign barbarians. They were beginning to look away from the continent to a world beyond China. Foreign merchants settling at the Formosan ports after 1855 had become entrepreneurs stimulating production and export of sugar, tea, and camphor in unprecedented quantities, and foreign consuls were attempting to advertise Formosan products overseas, something never done before. Between 1870 and 1890 there had been spectacular economic growth, bringing a harvest of silver dollars into Formosan hands. Moreover the Christian missionaries had opened schools, clinics, and hospitals, and had made thousands of converts. All these changes, presaging a second ideological and technological revolution in Formosa, drew Formosan eyes away from traditional China to the new world and to other governments overseas. Many Formosans who remained indifferent to Christianity, as such, were influenced nevertheless by the unprecedented Christian social-service programs. They were conscious, too, that in Formosa's rasping confrontations with continental Chinese mandarins, these bold and forthright foreigners tended to support Formosan rights and interests. As antiforeign passions mounted toward a crisis on the continent, Formosan-Chinese antipathy to foreign barbarians gradually died away.

General Liu Ming-ch'üan had encouraged foreign enterprise, had employed many foreigners in his administration, and had founded schools for foreign languages and technology, but like his reforming predecessor, Governor Ting, he was defeated by the reactionary mandarinate serving under him. In 1891 he too returned to the continent, discouraged and in ill health.

His successor, a man named Shao, promptly abandoned Liu's progressive institutions and programs, choosing instead to devote himself to intensive cultivation of his private fortune and the fortunes of his colleagues from the continent. Since this was done at public expense, Formosan leaders and foreign residents alike suffered loss. The island people had briefly experienced progressive and economically rewarding reform under Governor Ting and General Liu. They resented this retreat to the past.

China and Japan went to war with one another in 1894. The quarrel concerned Korea and the fighting took place principally in Manchuria, far from Formosa. China sued for peace. While preliminary negotiations were in progress, however, Tokyo discovered that Peking was secretly appealing to Russia,

Germany, and France to intervene on China's behalf, and that there was a Chinese proposal to hand the Pescadores over to France on a "temporary" basis.

A Japanese naval force moved in to forestall this, but there was no military action involving Formosa proper before China signed the Shimonoseki Treaty on April 17, 1895. This brought peace. Treaty terms provided for an indemnity paid by China to Japan, and the cession of the Liaotung Peninsula (in southern Manchuria), the Pescadores, and Formosa.

Within the week the Japanese nation suffered a traumatic blow, never to be forgotten or forgiven. Russia, France, and Germany "advised" Tokyo to renounce her claim upon the Liaotung Peninsula before midnight, May 8. At the same time the Russian, French, and German warships in adjacent waters cleared for battle action. The menace was clear, for they were in a position to cut Japan's lines of communication with her victorious armies in Manchuria. Having no choice, Tokyo bowed to this Triple Intervention. In exchange for Liaotung, snatched from her grasp, Japan was to receive a greatly increased indemnity. As the cynical interventionists foresaw, Peking was then obliged to borrow heavily from a European bank consortium to meet the bill.

Japan thereafter was left in unchallenged possession of Formosa and the Pescadores until World War II.

Neither the Chinese nor the Japanese envoys at Shimonoseki had been obliged to consider the wishes of the Formosan people when the cession was agreed upon; nevertheless Japan rather generously provided a two-year grace period in which a choice of nationality might be made and registered. Those who wished to take up their movable property and cross the Strait were free to do so. Those who wished to remain on the island but to retain Chinese nationality were allowed to register as resident aliens. All who had not made a choice by May 1, 1898, were then automatically to be considered subjects of the Emperor of Japan.

Two days after the Shimonoseki Treaty had been signed, Taipei received from Peking a terse telegraphic notice that Formosa had been ceded to Japan and was no longer Chinese territory. Chinese officers were directed to return to the continent at once.

This offhand treatment of the island people angered Formosan-Chinese leaders, who complained bitterly that they had
been foresaken by the Emperor and deserted by the imperial
government. They refused to accept the situation quietly, vow-
ing to resist the Japanese if they should appear. For reasons of
continental politics having nothing to do with an interest in the
Formosans, the Chinese governor at Taipei proposed to evade
the Shimonoseki Treaty by various crude stratagems. While he
protested his undying loyalty to the Throne at Peking and to
the dynasty, he sent off telegrams offering the island of Formosa first to England and then to France, without success.
Concurrently he was persuaded to declare that Formosa had
become a "republic" with himself as "president."

Formosans, led by a Hakka scholar, rallied a defense force
with which they proposed to block the Japanese; the idea of a
Formosan republic provided an excuse to break away from the
continent. Here was another Great Rebellion in a new guise.
The governor-turned-president realized that he would be
brushed aside soon enough. Furthermore, he was disobeying
Peking's explicit order to withdraw, and he had no stomach for
direct confrontation with the Japanese. Twelve days after proclaiming the "republic," he vanished, bribing his way out of
Taipei and slipping across the Strait to safety in Fukien. All
semblance of order vanished throughout the northern region
where tens of thousands of continental Chinese troops, deserted
by their officers, began to flee to the ports and junk anchorages,
looting, burning, and killing as they went, and above all being
eager to leave Formosa before the Japanese "dwarfs" arrived.

The first Japanese came ashore near Keelung on May 30,
and by June 9 the northern districts were quiet from Keelung
to Tamsui. On June 17 ceremonies at Taipei marked assumption of imperial Japanese authority in Formosa and the Pescadores. A British editor at Shanghai remarked editorially,
however, that it was one thing to acquire a cage of wild beasts
and quite another to tame them.

A mixed brigade of Japan's Imperial Household Guards,
under nominal command of an imperial prince, began to move
down through the Hsinchu hills into the western coastal lowlands. Disorganized Chinese troops moved on before them, re-

treating southward toward Tainan where a Chinese general known as "Black Flag Liu" promised to make a stand. He too pledged loyalty to Peking and at the same time sought Formosan support by proclaiming a second "republic." He then issued postage stamps and paper money while compelling the wealthy gentry and local merchants to contribute heavily to his war chest.

On coming into the western lowlands in June the Japanese began to meet fierce opposition wherever Formosans resorted to guerrilla warfare. Midsummer tropical storms, floods, terrible heat, and lack of experience in jungle warfare slowed the advancing column. After two months on the way some fourteen thousand Japanese troops had reached the town walls of Changhua, about 135 miles south of Keelung, but only half that number managed to reach Chia-yi, fifty miles farther along the road to Tainan. Malaria, cholera, typhus, and dysentery had taken a frightful toll, and near Tainan the imperial prince himself succumbed to tropical disease.

Naval transports moving south by way of the Pescadores began landing reenforcements at points near Tainan and Takao. On October 5 Black Flag General Liu deserted his "republic" and his troops, disguised himself as an old woman, and sailed off to Amoy across the Strait, taking the treasury with him as his own reward. With this, organized resistance ceased; on October 21, 1895, the Japanese flag flew over the gates of Tainan. The High Command declared that the pacification campaign was at an end.

This was premature, for a decade of bitter guerrilla warfare lay ahead. It was one thing to drive fifty thousand ill-led continental Chinese troops out of the island, but quite another to bring the Formosan Chinese under control in their own home territory. The two short-lived "republics" had been no more than confused demonstrations of the traditional Formosan desire to be left alone, to be free of tax-collectors and magistrates from overseas, and to be free to carry on clan and village quarrels without interference by an alien garrison force. The so-called Great Rebellions of 1714, 1787, and 1833, and the scores of serious uprisings during the intervening years of Chinese rule, had been shapeless and unsuccessful expressions of this search for autonomy. Now, among the Formosan-Chinese gentry, the idea of independence and of popular participation in island government had been introduced in terms not to be forgotten.

During the next fifty years this separatist tradition becomes more sharply defined as a Home Rule Movement, a search for political means to achieve the goal of Formosan participation in island government at all levels, within the overall Japanese empire frame of reference.

2. Japan Moves In

*P*OSSESSION of colonies was considered the *sine qua non* of a first class power in the late nineteenth century and Japan was determined to become one and be so recognized. Tokyo had exchanged the island of Sakhalin for the Kurile Islands by peaceful negotiation in 1875 and had annexed the Ryukyu Islands in 1879, but these actions did no more than define Japan's borders at the north and clarify an old relationship at the south. Annexation of Formosa was fundamentally different, something of a new order of magnitude in national ambition, and a true colonial venture. Unlike the Okinawans in the nearby Ryukyus, the Formosans were neither physical, cultural, nor linguistic cousins of the Japanese, and in area and potential wealth Formosa greatly surpassed both the foggy Kuriles and impoverished Okinawa.

It is not difficult to realize the position in which Tokyo's leaders found themselves in 1895. Japan was no larger than California and much less well endowed in natural resources. The Japanese felt surrounded and threatened; imperial Russia held Sakhalin directly to the north and was pushing hard to obtain a foothold in Manchuria. The Maritime Provinces bordering on the Sea of Japan were Russian territory, and the Trans-Siberian Railroad, then under construction, would soon make it possible for the Czar to move troops swiftly from Europe to the port of Vladivostok nearby. In China Great Britain's representatives—Alcock, Parkes, Wade, and their successors—made no effort to conceal a desire to curb development of Japan's economic interests. Spain's sluggish rule in the Philippines posed no threat at the south, but less than forty years had passed since Commodore Perry of the United States Navy had brought his Black Ships to Japan and had proposed that the United States develop strong American positions in the nearby Bonin Islands, Okinawa, and Formosa. In 1895 American jingoists were loudly preaching "Manifest Destiny," urging construction of a great naval base at Pearl Harbor in Hawaii, and the American Secretary of State (Richard Olney) proclaimed the need for a permanent display of American military might in the Pacific. Naval Captain Alfred Thayer Mahan's War College lectures, published in 1890 and entitled *The Influence of Sea Power on History*, had become the bible of expansionists and the source of the German Kaiser's ranting nonsense concerning a "Yellow Peril."

Japan took its place as a colonial power against this international background. As Formosa was the only prize salvaged from the humiliating confrontation with Russia, France, and Germany in 1895, the assumption of sovereignty took place in an atmosphere charged with emotion. Tokyo knew that China would be happy to see this prize, too, snatched away if pretexts could be found to induce further European intervention. Prominent Chinese were boasting that they would retake Formosa within five years. Questions of internal security therefore became an obsessive concern to admirals and generals sent to govern the island during the next half-century.

These circumstances cannot justify, but do help to explain, the harsh severity with which every slight manifestation of Formosan discontent and every hint of rebellion was dealt with from 1895 until the end of World War II. Questions of national pride or face modified all Japanese programs in Formosa, dictating an intense effort to show the world that a capacity to colonize and modernize was not a monopoly reserved to Caucasian Christian nations. Many proud Japanese resented the presence in Asia of hundreds of Caucasian missionaries and laymen preaching the God-given superiority of Western cultural, educational, and political institutions, the arrogant idea of the "White Man's Burden."

Japan had her own version of Manifest Destiny. Long ago the ancient idea of the Middle Kingdom and a tributary world had been borrowed from China and it was now, in the late nineteenth century, being recast as a modern myth that placed the divine Japanese Emperor at the center and summit of human affairs. All other Asian nations were conceived to be tributary, arranged around and below Japan. Among these inferior peoples the Japanese moved about as the Emperor's agents, proud missionaries proclaiming his greatness, goodness, and authority. It was conceived to be Japan's obligation to purge Asia of encroaching Western colonialism and to lead a Pan-Asian community through technological, social, and political reform. Admirals, generals, and civic leaders dedicated themselves to spreading the "Japanese Way of Life," first in Okinawa and Formosa, then in Korea, and at last throughout East Asia, the Indies, and the mid-Pacific islands.

A majority of leaders at Tokyo were agreed upon the ultimate goal—the preeminence of Japan in Asia—but the problems to be solved were questions of priority, direction, and timing. A "continental clique" advocated a thrust westward through Korea into Manchuria, North China, and Mongolia, and a "southern clique" insisted upon a drive southward along Asia's sea frontiers to reach the wealth of the tropics. The resources of sparsely settled Manchuria and Mongolia were still to be uncovered and developed, and an occupation of that vast hinterland would require an immense capital investment of time and money before the homeland, Japan proper, could anticipate a profitable return. The generals who dominated this continental clique, however, were less interested in economics than in checking Russian expansion and in creating a barrier between Russian Siberia and China proper. Advocates of the southern drive, on the other hand, noted that the food, manpower, and mineral resources of South China, Southeast Asia, and the Indies were already being developed under European management and could be speedily put to use in the imperial interest. Control of China's great seaports alone would mean virtual control of inland continental resources and of commerce flowing to the sea.

Although the Triple Intervention in April 1895 severely checked the ambitious continental clique, it merely increased a fierce determination to move in that direction. The cynical behavior of the three European powers stimulated a desire for revenge and an equally profound indifference, henceforth, to the Western "rules of the game" by which Japan's more moderate leaders desired to conduct international relations. To the Army leaders, the formalities of treaties, conventions, understandings, and gentlemanly promises might be employed if expediency dictated, but it had been made clear to the Japanese that Western diplomats held these things sacrosanct only so long as it served their own interests and they had the power to support them. Japanese admirals and generals would do the same.

The breakthrough to the south—the acquisition of Formosa—marked the first successful step toward realizing a grand imperial design, and the importance attached to Formosa was reflected in the quality and rank of men sent to govern the island throughout the next fifty years. A majority were of cabinet rank in the national government and one of them (Katsura) was thrice premier.

The Triple Intervention prompted Japan's Minister to China (Count Hayashi Tadasu) to confide to his diary that Japan must wait quietly for an opportunity to act in her own interest: "When that day arrives, she will be able to follow her own course, not only to put meddling powers in their place, but even, as necessity arises, meddling in the affairs of other powers." [1] Somewhat later the most distinguished Civil Administrator sent to Formosa (Baron Gotō Shimpei) was to write that ". . . our nation's history as a Colonial Power commences with the story of our administration of Formosa, and our failure or success there must exercise a marked influence on all our future undertakings." [2] Concurrently a distinguished Japanese historian and Diet member wrote that "Western nations have long believed that on their shoulders alone rested the responsibility of colonizing the yet unopened portions of the globe, and extending to their inhabitants the benefits of civilization; but now we Japanese, rising from the ocean in the extreme Orient, wish as a nation to take part in the great and glorious work." [3] In this attitude of emotional commitment, the Japanese carried forward the reorganization of Formosa, making it a colonial laboratory for policy and a testing ground for administrators destined one day to move on to larger fields in Asia.

SETTING UP THE NEW ADMINISTRATION

Within eighteen months after the first Japanese stepped ashore near Keelung, more than sixteen thousand Japanese civilians had come in. An area within the walls of Taipei was cleared and drained to make way for a "Japanese town" of offices, shops, and homes built to accommodate administrators, technicians, craftsmen, and merchants. Ramshackle accommodations for military camp followers sprang up wherever room could be found for them. The élite Household Guards Division that had suffered heavy casualties between June and October 1895, was replaced by a garrison of rough conscripts.* The jobbers who crowded into Taipei and the lesser garrison towns were a shifty lot of carpetbaggers holding dubious military supply contracts. Riffraff from the underworld of metropolitan Japan, including scores of pimps and prostitutes, made up a floating population of fortune-seekers attracted to the new colony. Even the least respectable persons among the new proprietors—the master race—shared some degree of privilege. In quarrels with the native Formosan Chinese, a Japanese was usually assumed to be right.

Enormous practical problems had to be solved as speedily as possible. It was necessary to police and manage a population of some three million disgruntled new subjects in a territory largely unexplored and unsurveyed. Although the Emperor Meiji benignly declared that Formosans were to be treated as equals under Japan's new Constitution and as brothers within the Japanese nation-family, it was not within the samurai character or tradition to admit equality or brotherhood with a subordinate people of a different race and language. To merit such

---

* On the overland march from Keelung to Tainan and Takao (Kaohsiung) the Guards had suffered 32,315 casualties. Only 164 died in action and only 515 were wounded in the field, but there had been 4,642 deaths from disease, and nearly 27,000 men had been hospitalized or sent home as unfit for further duty in the new colony. Among the victims was His Imperial Highness Prince Kitashirakawa, who died of malaria and dysentery at Tainan. Ten years later the Russo-Japanese War casualty record reflected the lessons learned in Formosa, for 58,357 Japanese died of enemy action, and 21,802 died of disease, but of these only 5,877 were the victims of typhoid and dysentery.

consideration the island people must first be made over into "true Japanese," speaking the national language and behaving and thinking as proper Japanese subjects.

At Tokyo, technical arrangements for managing the new colony were worked out by trial and error. Agencies and factions pushed and tugged to secure shares in the administration. In June 1895, a "Special Bureau of Formosan Affairs" was established in the Cabinet, with the Prime Minister as President, assisted by the Chief Cabinet Secretary, the Chief Secretary of the Cabinet's Legislative Bureau, and the Vice-Ministers for Army, Navy, Foreign Affairs, and Finance. A junior member named Hara Kei unsuccessfully advocated the appointment of civilian governors-general. It was apparent at once that this cumbersome Bureau involved too many overlapping and conflicting agencies. It was canceled in April 1896 when a new Ministry of Colonial Development was established. But this was premature; Formosa was the only colony and did not require a full-fledged Ministry. It, too, was abolished in October 1898. Such frequent changes at Tokyo generated confusion and uncertainty at Taipei.

The idea of representative government in any form was new and untried in Japan. The National Diet—an elected body—was a device permitting the Emperor and his ministers to "hear the people," but it was not taken very seriously by the military establishment nor by the entrenched administrative bureaucracy. The Constitution itself had been carefully designed to shield both bureaucratic and military interests from meddling interference by elected bodies. Thus the Army and the Navy were held responsible to the Emperor in his role as supreme commander in chief, although he acted only upon the advice of the Army and Navy ministers, the Premier and the Privy Council. The civil bureaucracy was dominated throughout by graduates of the Law Department of Tokyo Imperial University.

The generals and admirals considered Formosa a war prize and were determined to have it remain a preserve of special military interest, a forward base to be prepared for later military adventures. As an island under military control it could be made unusually secure, and as a "stone aimed at the south" its military importance took precedence over all other considerations in the military mind. Japanese civil interests in mining, agriculture, forestry, industry, and commerce would be allowed to develop within the overall military frame of reference but must give way at any point of conflict. Formosan interests—the interests of the subordinate local inhabitants—would be policed to suit these overriding Japanese requirements.

Thus Formosa was destined to be governed by admirals and generals from 1895 until 1919, and again from 1936 until 1945. The nine civilians who served as governors between 1919 and 1935 were tough bureaucrats, experienced in police administration at the prefectural and national levels. Each was nominated from the highest civil ranks and enjoyed the protocol privileges of the Prime Minister, Chief Justice and Cabinet ministers, but in every case the appointments were subject to concurrent approval by the military at the Cabinet and Privy Council level. This ultimate weight of the military in all administrative affairs in Formosa must be kept in mind.

It is noteworthy that Governors, Civil Administrators, and their senior subordinates assigned to duty at Taipei between 1894 and 1924 were without exception men born in pre-Restoration Japan, and the younger men were all reared in the authoritarian "command-and-obey" tradition of the samurai class. The new island government nevertheless was essentially a "young" administration, attracting recent university graduates and ambitious young men just returned from study overseas, in the United States and Europe, and each seemed filled with new ideas and eager to test the latest theories and techniques in his field. This they could do as long as they worked in harmony with the armed services. The Formosans had little to say one way or another; they lacked leadership and were seldom consulted on questions of general policy.

From the beginning the new administration lacked technical facilities for efficient work; the Chinese Governor Liu Ming-ch'üan's post and telegraph systems, introduced between 1885 and 1890, had fallen into total disrepair and disorder by midyear 1895. The short Keelung-Hsinchu railway had to be totally reconstructed, and the dilapidated rolling stock replaced. There were few roads and no bridges to facilitate police control and economic development, and the ports had been neglected

after 1891. The first great problem, therefore, was the improvement of the harbors and development of overland communications. This would "open Formosa's doors."

Admiral Kabayama Sukenori, the first Governor-General,
was preoccupied with military problems such as the repatria-
tion of the Imperial Household Guards Division, shattered by
disease, the introduction of a permanent garrison force, and development of communications adequate for military purposes.*
Regular army units, a special gendarmerie force of thirty-five
hundred men, and a civil police force of about the same
strength were brought down from Japan to impose order. Lines
of authority were ill defined, command responsibilities overlap-
ped, and supplies were scarce—producing local interservice rivalry and generating serious administrative disputes at Tokyo.
On July 2, 1896, Kabayama was recalled and replaced by General Viscount Katsura Tarō, who held the Taipei office for
three months only.†

Formosa's third Japanese governor was Lieutenant General
Count Nogi Maresuke who had driven the last Chinese troops
from South Formosa and taken the surrender of Tainan in October 1895. One year later, on October 14, he inherited all the
confusions generated by continuing uncertainty at Tokyo.‡

---

* Admiral Count Kabayama (1837–1922) came of a notable Kyushu family
that had for centuries been responsible for management of Satsuma's interests
and defense on Japan's southern frontier. An ancestor, Kabayama Hisataka,
had led the Japanese invasion of Okinawa in 1609. Posing as a merchant,
Kabayama had surveyed Formosa in 1873. Transferring from Army to Navy
in 1884, he later served as Navy Minister (1890–1892), and as Chief of Naval
Staff during the Sino-Japanese War. After governing Formosa briefly
(1895–1896) he became in turn Home Minister and Minister of Education,
serving thereafter as Privy Councillor from 1904 until his death in 1922.

† General Katsura (1847–1913) was a Yamaguchi samurai who had spent
three years in Germany as a military student, served as Military Attaché at
Berlin, and as Commander of the Third Army Division during the Sino-
Japanese War. He was subsequently War Minister, Grand Chamberlain, and
Keeper of the Privy Seal. During his first Prime Ministership he concluded
the important Anglo-Japanese Alliance, and in the second, completed annexation of Korea and revision of Japan's unequal foreign treaties. He became
Prime Minister a third time in 1912. For services to the State he was made
successively Count, Marquis, and Prince.

‡ General Nogi (1849–1912) of Yamaguchi had distinguished himself in the
Kyushu Rebellions (1873–1877) and the Sino-Japanese War (1894–1895). He
was to become a national hero in the Russo-Japanese War (1904–1905) and
President of the Peers' School (1907). On the death of the Emperor Meiji

Under great handicaps Nogi made considerable progress, re-stricting civil police forces to the towns, sending regular army units into the hills in pursuit of outlaws, and employing the gendarmes as a mobile force to aid one or the other regular units when necessary. Management of the telegraph and postal services was transferred at last from the army to the civil au-thority, the Bank of Japan opened a branch at Taipei, and the first of the great economic combines—the Mitsui Company—sent down representatives to assess business prospects. Slum clearance and housing projects went forward rapidly at the cap-ital, making it possible for Japanese of every class to bring in their families. This made for a more stable administration, and Taipei began to take on the character of a substantial Japanese town set down within the walls of a Chinese city.

A Bureau of Industry (embracing agriculture and forestry), was set up to inaugurate long-range economic planning. The first Director was a young man, thirty-four years of age, whose life throughout reflected the best qualities of dynamic leader-ship in the New Japan.

Dr. Nitobe Inazō came from a cadet branch of the Nambu Clan, feudal lords of Morioka in northern Japan. In his youth he was known by an adoptive name, Ota Ienosuke, and under that name attended a foreign language school and then the newly established Sapporo Agricultural College in the Hok-kaido, a frontier developmental project. There, under the influ-ence of a noted American missionary-teacher (Dr. William Clark), he became a Christian convert. Soon after this a death in the family caused him to assume the name Nitobe Inazō under which he was to earn a worldwide and well-deserved reputation.

From Sapporo the young scholar went to the Johns Hop-kins University in Baltimore, Maryland, where he was an asso-ciate of Woodrow Wilson and John Dewey in graduate semi-nars. After taking a degree (and meeting Mary Elkington, who was to become his wife), he went on to Halle University in Germany for an additional degree in philosophy. Turning homeward again, he paused in Philadelphia for his wedding with Miss Elkington, daughter of a prominent Quaker family.

(1912), Nogi and his wife committed suicide, thereupon becoming heroes in the public esteem, and "Guardian Spirits of the Empire."

By then Nitobe had published important papers in the Japanese, English, and German languages and, upon returning to Japan, at once joined the faculty at Sapporo and became concurrently an advisor to the Governor of Hokkaido. There, on that cold, sparsely settled northern frontier, he gained his first practical experience in preparing long-range agricultural development programs. These brought him to the attention of the Central Government. He was called down to Tokyo in 1896 and from there was sent on to survey and to manage the complex problems of subtropical agriculture, forestry, and industry in the new colony.

Formosa's potential was obviously great; the soil was rich, splendid forests covered two-thirds of the island, and the climate permitted year-round production in the fields. The colonial subjects were an intensely industrious people. The lowlands, however, were crowded with Formosan-Chinese farmers and townsmen who resented Japan's presence; there were no accurate land-surveys, no census records of value, and only the most primitive forms of transport and communication. The unexplored high mountains were inhabited by an unknown number of untamed aboriginal tribes.

Nitobe needed information in great detail, the raw data with which to work in the Bureau's Taipei offices. Every other branch and agency of the new government also required a similar fund of basic facts and figures, indispensable to an orderly and efficient administration. It was at this level and in these fact-gathering operations that "modern Japan" met "traditional Formosa" in every town, village, hamlet, and farmhouse. No household escaped the ultimate consequences of the fact-finding field surveys.

The technicians, hired in Japan for temporary duty to meet Nitobe's requirements, encountered formidable obstacles as they moved out into the Formosan countryside under police or military escort. The first of these was the inability to communicate directly and clearly. Simple private and personal misunderstandings such as haggling over the price of eggs or the hire of rickshaws could flash into a public quarrel erupting into local riot. When these were put down with harsh action, as they often were, the work of the fact-finding agencies became more difficult. Interpreter-translators were the first great need of the day.

The Japanese found about two thousand small private Chinese-language schools still in existence, with a total enrollment somewhere above thirty thousand. Each school was an independent unit maintained at village expense or by private philanthropic subsidy. All were devoted to rote memorization of Chinese characters and the Classics, scanning ancient commentaries, and practicing calligraphy. The projected modernization program, however, needed more than skilled young calligraphers and classical essayists. Within two weeks after flag-raising ceremonies at Taipei (June 1895) the government had established a Temporary Bureau of Education to plan the training of translators, interpreters, and clerks. Within a month a small school opened in a temple topping a hill near Shih-lin, north of Taipei, and there several Japanese teachers proposed to instruct sons of leading Formosan-Chinese families. A Normal School was established to enroll sixty Japanese who were to study Formosan dialects, and thirty Formosans were recruited to study Japanese. A Compilation Office began to produce textbooks in quantity and soon hundreds of Formosans were enrolled in language courses in makeshift schoolrooms and meeting halls. It was a good beginning, but only hundreds of interpreter-translators were in training when Dr. Nitobe reached Formosa, and thousands were needed.

The administration required accurate information, wanted it at once, and was frustrated by Formosan reluctance to cooperate in projects of which they had little or no understanding. The Japanese complained that they were too often victims of willful misinterpretation and deliberate falsehood. As soldiers, gendarmes, and police moved through the countryside with too few interpreters, or none, giving sharp orders and demanding prompt action, the Formosans used every deception to evade compliance. Commenting upon the "Republican Tiger" that had appeared so boldly in May 1895, and had vanished so ingloriously in October, a British editor had written:

There is metal [sic] in the islanders which Japan has not encountered at any time during the war, and if we mistake not, we shall see some fighting on Formosa. . . . In addition to being somewhat trained, they are actuated and bound together by the nearest approach to patriotism and unity of interest to be found in China, and therefore possess the valuable adjunct for a successful warfare in which their confreres on the mainland lacked.[4]

This elementary "patriotism" had nothing to do with love of country or love of China; *the Formosans merely wanted to be left alone*. Traditional aversion to mandarin rule imposed from the continent was promptly transferred to the government brought in by the Japanese strangers, the "dwarfs" from the north, but if any Formosan thought the Japanese would be content with the old haphazard administration, confined principally to garrisoned towns and suburbs, he was quickly disillusioned. The newcomers proposed to explore and patrol every path and road, to survey, record, and tax every cultivated acre, and to count and register every individual in the colony.

In the larger towns, where friction was eased by a greater supply of interpreter-translators, Formosans soon discovered that cooperation with the Japanese could bring substantial material benefit. The government was spending lavishly for local goods and labor as it created public services benefiting all. In the countryside however, the changes demanded in support of Dr. Nitobe's elaborate plans constituted a broad attack upon the entire traditional structure of Formosan community life. The prime difficulties arose when surveyors, sanitation officers, tax assessors, teachers, agricultural specialists, and foresters began to move out under military escort to bring about this controlled revolution in the distant countryside.

GUERRILLA WARFARE, 1895–1898

Things went badly in the rural districts. The Formosan defense units (*t'uan-lien*) organized in 1895 by the landholding gentry were soon disbanded when many of the gentry class and the local literati recognized the personal material advantage of cooperation with the Japanese, or at least the wisdom of silent neutrality. Scattered partisan forces presented a different problem. They had first been loosely organized by local communities and led by popular local figures, but as they scattered before the oncoming Japanese, they were driven farther and farther from home base. Cut off from home supply in strange communities, they tended to become outlaws, scavengers, and bandits, gathering in large bands under leadership of the more aggressive members.

Hakka villagers in the far south had attempted to drive the incoming Japanese from their territory in October 1895, using arms abandoned by fleeing Chinese soldiers. Two months of hard marching and countermarching were required to impose an uneasy truce upon the region south of Takao. The approach of the New Year (1896) brought a major attempt to rebel in the north. As the Japanese prepared to celebrate in Taipei, they saw unusual signal fires blazing on the hills nearby. Dawn on New Year's Day revealed large bands of armed men moving in toward the city. Sixty Japanese soldiers were killed and many wounded before the rebels were driven off, but as they retreated, 128 Japanese were killed in outlying villages. Among them were the teachers at the isolated temple-school beyond Shih-lin.* Davidson wrote that "in some instances the Japanese were tortured to death, burned at the stake, and in almost every case where the Japanese had been captured, such of the bodies as were recovered were found to be frightfully mutilated." [5]

A campaign of bloody reprisals thereafter continued for six weeks. Father José Álvarez, then living in Formosa, wrote that the Japanese action in the Gilam area was particularly brutal and that scores of Hakka villagers, guilty and innocent alike, were flogged without mercy, that many were tortured and beheaded, and that families, friends, and neighbors were com-. pelled to witness revolting postmortem abuse of the dead.

Six months later—in June 1896—a massive disturbance in the Tau-lok (Toroku) district in Tainan was led by a Hakka villager who believed that Russia, Germany, and England would soon force Tokyo to give up the island. Japanese living nearby took refuge within·the walls of Changhua while the troops moved out with orders to kill every living thing within a radius of five miles around Tau-lok. Thirty villages were razed. According to a local missionary (Father Francisco Giner) and a visiting scientist (Dr. Albrecht Wirth), the horrors of Gilam

* This temple became a Shintō shrine, and the spirits of the murdered teachers were considered patrons of all teachers and all educational projects on Formosa thereafter.

were repeated, and the stillness of death lay over the countryside. These foreigners attempted to intercede, but the Japanese were angered by their protests.

This time the military had gone too far. Members of the Japanese civil administration at Taipei protested, the Tokyo press spread the story throughout Japan, and the Imperial Household lamely sought to administer an oblique rebuke to the Army by granting a token sum of money in aid of the ravaged district. Such mild and ineffective reproofs and gestures of "imperial charity" became familiar in later years and were not taken seriously by the Formosans. In Japanese eyes the token grant of a few yen from the immensely rich Imperial Household was multiplied in value to an incalculable degree because of the imperial association; the Formosans, who never succumbed to the mystique of the "Divine Emperor" tradition, considered such token grants a mockery.

Civilian protests at Tokyo were never effective to a significant degree. Many leaders took the position that the Formosans were now imperial subjects and must be made over into loyal and useful citizens, but the military authorities who in fact controlled Formosa continued to view it as essentially alien territory secured for military use.

Two major uprisings kept a large military force in the field throughout the autumn and winter months of 1896, and on May 8, 1897, Taipei itself was again threatened by some 2,000 rebels who sacked large establishments along the waterfront before being driven off to the hills. They left more than 200 of their men lying dead along the way. Foreign residents noted that savage military reprisals seemed only to stiffen the will to resist. Remembering that the Imperial Guards Division had lost only 154 men in action while driving 50,000 continental Chinese troops from the island in 1895, they now read with chilling frequency the casualty notices published at Taipei—"forty-eight Japanese killed, 500 rebels shot"; "128 Japanese killed, more than 600 rebels destroyed," and other figures in like ratio.

Disgruntled townsmen slipped away to join guerrilla bands in the hills. Many country people gave the outlaws support from admiration mixed with fear. Some rebel leaders professed a duty to protect the common people from oppressive rulers, a traditional Chinese Robin Hood theory and the theme of innumerable plays and stories, but it was apparent that others merely exploited popular discontent to serve selfish ends under pretense of "resisting the Japanese dwarfs." Under the circumstances it was easy for unscrupulous bandits to make false "collaboration" charges to justify robbery and murder for private gain.

In this general state of restless disorder the Buhong or Muho District in Taichung proved an exception, for there the great landholder Lin Ch'iao-tang (Rin Shōdō) kept his lands and the adjacent villages at peace, cooperating with the Japanese by using his estate guards, a private army, as an auxiliary policing force between 1895 and 1897. Elsewhere generally there had developed what might be called a nineteenth-century Vietcong situation. Wherever the Japanese were determined to impose order, the Formosan communities were equally determined to sabotage the effort.

The newcomers complained that they were ever the victims of unscrupulous interpreters and could trust no one. "The difficulty was, not to overcome them [the bandits] but to find them." Every member of a village community might know the identity of a wanted man and know his hiding place, but not a word would be said to betray him. "Sometimes our men would lodge at the village chief's house," wrote one official, "and would talk freely of all their plans for attacking the brigands, to find afterwards that their host was himself a brigand." [6] A farmer who had been seen in the morning quietly following his water buffalo and plow, under cover of night might be discovered slipping along country paths, well armed, to join night raids upon government supply dumps, telegraph lines, or outlying Japanese camps.

Many Japanese civilians regretted the severity of punishments imposed upon the rebels, for many men of goodwill had come to Formosa convinced that they were missionaries of the New Japan and that they had much of value to offer the Formosans. But having been reared in the samurai's command-and-obey tradition, they rarely thought it necessary to explain the ultimate purpose of the radical changes required in the modernization program. To them the values were self-evident, and the privilege of becoming one of His Imperial Majesty's subjects, now open to the Formosans, was quite beyond question.

From the outset a number of important Formosans collaborated willingly and were handsomely rewarded. The great majority, however, attempted to maintain a noncommittal neutrality, yielding as little as possible to Japanese demands. They complied with new rules and regulations if it was necessary to avoid penalty, but had always to consider the risk of reprisals at the hands of active rebels. All who took to the hills, determined to maintain independence, were invariably condemned by the government as "brigands."

The first thirty months of the Japanese occupation demonstrated the futility of the military or "rifle and truncheon" approach, the futility of brute force. When General Baron Kodama Gentarō replaced General Nogi on February 26, 1898, Tokyo announced that his Director of Civil Administration would be Dr. Gotō Shimpei, then Chief of the National Bureau of Hygiene. With these appointments the stage was set for the extension to Formosa of the controlled Meiji Revolution which even then was bringing Japan forward to a position of world power. Both men were exceptionally well prepared for the assignment.*

Kodama (aged 46), Gotō (aged 41), and Nitobe (aged 36) were members of that extraordinarily talented generation of young leaders who carried Japan forward from feudal isolation to a recognized place in world affairs within the lifetime of the

---

* General Kodama Gentarō (1852–1906), a Yamaguchi samurai, took part in Restoration battles (1868) and the Kyushu Rebellions (1873–1877). After serving on the General Staff and as President of the Military Staff College, Kodama toured Europe before becoming Army Vice-Minister and Director of the Military Affairs Bureau. While commanding the First Division during the Sino-Japanese War he was made a baron. During his tenure as Formosa's Governor-General (1898–1906) Kodama served also in three Ministries (Army, Home Affairs, and Education), was Vice-Chief of General Staff, and Chief of Staff to Field Marshal Prince Ōyama Iwao, Commander in Chief during the Russo-Japanese War. With such manifold responsibilities he was obliged to rely upon his Civil Administrator, Gotō, to an exceptional degree.

Gotō Shimpei, M.D. (1857–1929) had been born in Iwate Prefecture, a doctor's son. At the age of twenty he became an instructor at the Aichi Medical School, subsequently going on to take a medical degree in Berlin, Germany (1890–1892). On returning to Japan he served as Director of the Aichi Military Hospital, Chief Inspector of Military Hygiene (1894–1895) and Director of the Bureau of National Hygiene in the Home Ministry. At one time he was under arrest, charged with complicity in a political murder, but was released for want of evidence.

Meiji emperor (1852–1912). Such ardent reformers were inescapably restricted by conservative tradition and entrenched economic interests in Japan proper; in Formosa they enjoyed a free hand and could move forcefully in all fields. They were unhampered by consideration of Formosan interests or sensibilities and need make no concessions. Each knew that success would depend upon long-range planning, continuous, well-coordinated research, and the total regimentation of men and materials.

Before taking up the Taipei appointment in February 1898, General Kodama had been Army Vice-Minister and Chief of the Special Bureau of Formosan Affairs at Tokyo, hence he was well aware of the most secret plans of his ambitious military colleagues. Throughout his years in the Formosan service he remained preoccupied with military affairs at the national level.

As Kodama's chief executive officer Dr. Gotō was charged with day-to-day administrative chores. He was above all else a policeman, for it was his duty to discipline an unruly island people and to impose order upon communities determined to resist Japanese intrusion. On the other hand he worked closely with Nitobe in developing long-range economic and social reform programs. A German university training had sharpened Gotō's appreciation of the need to accumulate vast bodies of basic working data and to carry on fundamental research in support of modern agriculture and forestry. Experience as a military hospital administrator and wartime Inspector General of Military Hygiene brought him to the attention of senior military men in the national administration. He had learned to perform successfully within complicated civil and military bureaucracies—a civilian tolerable to the military who dominated the government.

Gotō's medical background was his prime qualification. The disastrous experience of the Imperial Household Guards Division in Formosa in 1895 had dramatized public health problems. If a Japanese administration were to survive there, revolutionary changes in general living conditions would have to be made. Vastly increased communication between Japan and Formosa meant that quarantine services were of utmost importance. Gotō, tough, ruthless, and brilliant, was preemi-

33

nently qualified to serve as the Governor-General's deputy and Civil Administrator.

After nearly a decade of confusion following Governor Liu Ming-ch'üan's retirement, the corrupt and inefficient administrations of his successors Shao and T'ang, the uproar of the "republics" and the years of Japanese campaigning to establish a grip upon the island, the foreign community at Taipei, and Formosan leaders everywhere, awaited the advent of Kodama and Gotō with keenest interest.

Tayal (Atayal) tribesman of
northern Formosa.
[Reprinted from James W.
Davidson, *The Island of Formosa, Past and Present* (New
York and London, 1903),
p. 563]

Tayal girl of northern Formosa, after attending a Japanese school for girls.
[Ca. 1938; photographer unknown]

Pepohuan (mixed-blood) bordermen, late nineteenth century. [Reprinted from George Mackay, *From Far Formosa* (New York, 1896), p. 234]

Bunun tribesman of northcentral Formosa. [Photographer and date unknown]

Viceroy Li Hung-chang (1823–1901), who signed the Shimonoseki Treaty ceding Formosa to Japan "in perpetuity," in 1895. [Source unidentified]

General Viscount Kodama Gentarō (1852–1906), Governor-General of Formosa from 26 February 1898 to 11 April 1906; posthumously created Count Kodama. [Reprinted from Takekoshi Yosaburō, *Japanese Rule in Formosa* (New York, 1907) frontispiece]

Nitobe Inazō, Ph.D., LL.D. (1862–1933), educator, economist, author, member of the House of Peers, Vice Director, General Affairs Bureau, League of Nations, etc. [Photo courtesy of Dr. James T. Watkins IV, Stanford University]

Gotō Shimpei, M.D. (1857–1929), Formosa's Civil Administrator from 2 March 1898 to 13 November 1906, and later President of the South Manchuria Railway Company, Count Gotō, Foreign Minister, Home Minister, Chairman of the Metropolitan Tokyo Reconstruction Commission (1923). [Reprinted from Takekoshi Yosaburō, *Japanese Rule in Formosa* (New York, 1907), p. 11]

A Formosan-Chinese farmer's son, of Fukienese descent, who was self-educated beyond the higher primary school, spoke two Fukienese dialects, Mandarin Chinese, Japanese, and English. [1937; author's collection]

Formosan-Chinese (Hakka) farming couple. [Reprinted from *Nihon Chiri Taikei* XI (Tokyo, 1931), p. 320]

A Formosan-Chinese girl of
the urban middle class.
[Author's collection]

Student leaders at the Taihoku Medical School, about 1925. [Reprinted from
J.-M. Álvarez, *Formosa: Geográfica e Históricamente Considerada*, vol. 2
(Barcelona, 1930), p. 405]

A young matron from a land-holding family. [Author's collection]

Formosan student at the Taihoku Preparatory School (Kōtō Gakkō), 1939. [Author's collection]

Lin Hsien-t'ang (Rin Kendo) (1881–1956), landholder, banker, philanthropist, and lifelong advocate of Formosan Home Rule. [Courtesy of Dr. Ong Yok-tek]

Lieutenant General Chen Yi (1883–1950), Nationalist Chinese "Chairman" of Fukien Province (1934–1941) and Governor-General of Formosa (1945–1947). As a reward for his ruthless suppression of the Formosan uprising in 1947, Chen was made Governor of Chekiang Province in 1948, but when in 1949 he was discovered to be negotiating with the oncoming Communists, he was arrested. His execution on the Taipei Racetrack on 18 June 1950 was represented to the Formosan people as "punishment" for his misdeeds in 1947. [Author's collection]

3. A Stone Aimed
at the South

FORMOSA'S FOREIGN COMMUNITY UNDER THE
NEW ADMINISTRATION

*I*N JUNE 1895, the Imperial Maritime Customs offices were closed and the foreign marines and gunboats sailed away. European merchants, missionaries, and consuls were confident that under the new administration Formosa's coasts at last would be lighted and patrolled, and that order would be maintained at the ports and inland towns. The British and German consuls were joined in 1897 by a Spanish colleague sent up from Manila to keep watch on developments in this restive new colony next door. Luzon itself was torn by insurrections; the recent execution of the young independence leader, José Rizal, had inflamed public feeling, and Spain was losing its grip upon the Philippines.

For a time the foreign community at Taipei showed modest growth and considerable diversity. The import-export business, so long stultified by mandarin conservatism and official chicanery, was expected now to pick up handsomely. Four new foreign firms came in at once. The government's elaborate plans for developing the economy would require machinery, machine parts, petroleum products, and miscellaneous technical equipment that Japan's own industries were not yet prepared to supply in quantity, if at all. Tokyo proposed major port developments, new railroads, telegraph and telephone systems, new power plants, vast irrigation works, and new industries. There should be a share in this for every well-established import-export firm in the Twatutia subdivision of Taipei.*

The total number of foreign nationals registered in 1898 was 9,126, including 8,973 Chinese who had opted at once to register as Chinese subjects under terms of the Shimonoseki Treaty. There were 135 Caucasians, of whom 70 were British subjects (including Canadians).

Living conditions improved rapidly between 1895 and 1900. By the end of the century the capital had artesian wells, an ice factory, electricity and gas for domestic use, and a fair telephone service available to government offices and officers. Some of these benefits were shared by the foreign community.

This was an era of crisis in China and of drastic change everywhere in the Pacific island-world. Every scrap of outside news was savored at Taipei; the arrival of a mail pouch was an event, bringing English-language papers from Yokohama and Kobe, Shanghai, Canton, and Hongkong. Antiforeign incidents throughout China led to the bloody Boxer Uprising at Peking in 1900. In the mid-Pacific, the American missionaries and their cousins in the business community at last managed the downfall of the Hawaiian monarchy, the creation of a "Republic" (1894–1898), and ultimate annexation of the Hawaiian Islands by the United States. The American war with Spain brought the American flag and American military interests to the Philippines next door and set in train a series of events of fatal interest to future Japanese-American relations.

A British resident (H.W.S. Edmunds) attempted to found an English-language newspaper (*The Formosan*), but the Taipei community was too small to support it. Every word published abroad concerning Formosa was eagerly welcomed on the island and so, too, were occasional Japanese reports and survey summaries issued by the new administration in the English, French, or German languages.†

---

* Other nations represented included: Spain, 2; Norway, 19; Korea, 18; U.S.A., 13; Germany, 4; the Netherlands, 4; Portugal, 3; Austria, 1; Russia, 1. Members of three small Indian Parsee firms (camphor exporters in South Formosa) were included in the British total.

† A spate of specialized articles and autobiographical memoirs by foreign residents appeared in the decade 1895–1905 in books published in Japan, Ger-

For some nine years the most prominent member of the foreign community was James Davidson who had "saved" the northern settlement in June 1895. On the arduous march southward with the Imperial Household Guards the young journalist had been deeply impressed by Formosa's physical grandeur and by the magnitude of the social and economic revolution the Japanese proposed to bring about. Davidson, who had accompanied Peary across the wastes of arctic Greenland, now settled down in subtropical Formosa to prepare a comprehensive history of this turbulent frontier island. As a well-to-do young bachelor he was a popular member of the Twatutia social life and he was popular, too, among Formosan Chinese who appreciated his interest in the island's past. His prestige among the Japanese was high, for members of the administration knew of him as a military school graduate, an explorer, and a man of demonstrated courage under fire. The imperial decoration conferred upon him by the Emperor Meiji in 1895—the Order of the Rising Sun—automatically gave him prestige within the Japanese establishment.

Many of the Japanese scientists and civil officers were less than a decade older than Davidson. His manifest interest in the new developmental projects won many friends. For example, Gotō and Nitobe, the two most important figures in the civil administration, called upon him for advice and information, and in return made available to him and his private research staff many important documents and investigative reports. Ino Kashinori—archivist, historian, and Japan's most distinguished authority on Formosan history—formed a close association with Davidson, providing him with essential materials for his book, published in 1903, *The Island of Formosa, Past and Present*.

Not all foreigners at Taipei shared Davidson's enthusiasm for the Japanese or the New Order. Many privileges once assumed to be the "foreigner's right" under the Chinese regime were now curtailed or abolished. Missionaries could no longer "table the passport" with veiled threats of intervention, and the tea and camphor merchant could no longer demand an instant

---

many, France, Canada, England, the United States, and even so far afield as Buenos Aires, the Argentine. At least forty serious essays appeared in Western periodicals.

audience with the highest authorities. Foreign gunboats no longer swung at anchor in the river. Bribes had become more difficult to arrange and Chinese compradores serving foreign firms could no longer buy their way so easily through official red tape.

It required many months to reduce a chaos of Chinese methods and records to the more exacting and orderly routine established under new Japanese laws and regulations, and the confusion irritated impatient foreign businessmen. Soon the most profitable commerce began to pass into Japanese hands. The opium and camphor concessions were taken over by the new Monopoly Bureau, and foreign traders were obliged thereafter to buy and sell only at the Bureau.

One disgruntled British businessman persuaded several of his local associates to appeal to the powerful British Chamber of Commerce in Shanghai, which in turn urged the British Government to protest the changes taking place in Formosa—the loss of preeminence in the camphor trade, the substitution of Japanese for British shipping in the scheduled island services, and the growing Japanese monopoly of the sugar market. The Shanghai body accused the Japanese Civil Administrator (Gotō) of "antiforeign tactics," and the charges were published in the *China Mail* (Shanghai) in May and June 1901, with strong editorial support.

But British missionaries long resident in the island felt that this was unfair. In a published counterblast, William Campbell warned that any attempt to bring pressure upon the Japanese would fail and would merely rouse Japanese indignation and antipathy, harmful to all foreign interests. Dr. Anderson and Dr. Barclay joined him, saying that in their view general social conditions throughout the island were rapidly improving under the new administration.

This was a fair judgment and it was significant, for Campbell and Barclay had each lived in Formosa for twenty-six years, and Dr. Anderson, the medical missionary, had been there for twenty-three. Nevertheless, the China-based missionaries who had *not* lived in Formosa, continued to complain bitterly for at least fifteen years after sovereignty had passed to Japan. They could not then nor thereafter forgive the Japanese for inflicting humiliating defeat on their beloved China, nor for demonstrating that modernization and social reform could take place on a revolutionary scale without massive missionary help. The Reverend Donald Ferguson, writing of the "Formosan Chinese" in *The China Recorder and Missionary Journal* (Shanghai, v. 40, 1909), noted rather spitefully that Formosan-Chinese converts who found Presbyterian church discipline too rigorous, usually "found a haven in the Roman Catholic church" and then went on to say of Formosa under the Japanese that ". . . opium smoking undoubtedly seems on the wane; but as opium smoking decreases, it almost seems that drinking, cigarette smoking, brothels, dishonesty, *etc.*, proportionately increase."

Thus the Old China Hands in trade and the China missions did not easily relinquish assumptions of innate racial superiority and of condescending patronage, but across the world in London a change was taking place. British antagonism toward an emergent Japan was melting away. The Chinese government was disintegrating and Chinese leaders, galled by defeat in 1895, were beginning to turn to Russia. This compelled England to look to Japan with increasing favor as a potential counterbalance in Asia, and led to the Anglo-Japanese Alliance of 1902. It suited London that troublesome Formosa, so long an irritant under Chinese misrule, had passed into the hands of a firm government. Conditions in the sea-lanes along the China coast were improved, and the Americans who had so recently taken the Philippines, would not now be tempted to "solve the Formosa problem" by a move to the north.

AN AMERICAN CONSULATE FOR TAIPEI

Curtailment of old privileges at Taipei appeared to be more than offset by prospects of a vast new market for machinery and related industrial supply. As the British and German consuls and businessmen began to compete eagerly for orders, American representation was conspicuously absent.

In 1895 General Delaware Kemper, the aging American Consul at Amoy, had tried unsuccessfully to draw Washington's attention to the political and military significance of the change in sovereignty, but there was no sign that anyone in the State Department had looked at a map or considered reports touching on new markets as well as new military frontiers. Formosa remained as it had been, an unrewarding and insignificant subdivision of the Amoy Consular District, until a Republican administration took office at Washington on March 4, 1897. This was William McKinley's "Manifest Destiny" administration, and in the distribution of election-year patronage, the Secretary of the Colorado State Republican party received appointment as United States Consul for Amoy, China. On April 12, therefore, Burlingame Johnson took the oath of office at Grand Junction, Colorado. It occurred to no one at Washington to notify General Kemper that he had lost his job.

Johnson reached Amoy on June 16, briskly turned the old man out, and moved into the consular offices and residence, obliging General Kemper to leave Amoy with what grace he could. The new Consul discovered at once the truth of his predecessor's complaints of inattention; he found the State Department a faceless bureaucracy, indifferent, and far away. Despite the fact that Amoy's old tea and silk trade was languishing, and the best prospects for future business lay in Formosa, all consular business relating to the island still had to be done at Amoy under terms of Sino-American treaties no longer applicable to Formosa. Fortunately the new consul's complaints reached Washington during that brief flurry of "reform" which every new administration is obliged to create; he secured permission to revive the United States Consular Agency on Formosa and asked James Davidson to accept the post.

The young correspondent was now two years along in his researches concerning Formosan history and was happy to assume the new responsibility. He agreed with Johnson that a more realistic policy was required to improve the American position in the rapidly changing colony, and put the case to his father. This wealthy and influential midwestern banker carried the argument to appropriate offices at Washington at about the time Admiral George Dewey sailed into Manila Bay to begin the American conquest of the Philippines. By taking up the White Man's Burden, the McKinley administration drew American attention to the Western Pacific as never before. In a burst of activity, the State Department removed Formosa altogether from the Amoy consul's jurisdiction, created a new "Formosa Consular District" and made the Ryukyu Islands a subdivision thereof. The new district itself became part of the

American consular establishment in Japan. Davidson, now twenty-seven years of age, became the first American Consul in Formosa, with an interpreter and a translator-clerk to assist him. The office opened for business on July 22, 1898.

Having made these sensible changes the State Department promptly lapsed into its old state of indifference.

Although Johnson at Amoy was thereafter relieved of direct responsibility in Formosa he could not remain indifferent to growing pressure along the coast of China, exerted from Taipei. Following precedents set by LeGendre and Kemper— and with no more effect—he presumed to report upon the military and political significance of Formosa-based activities. The Japanese, he said, were using Taipei as a headquarters from which to develop special interests in Fukien and were clearly determined to replace the Western powers in Chinese coastal commerce. Amoy was restless under this growing pressure. Formosans were coming into Fukien in large numbers, creating serious problems. Some who had found the Japanese administration intolerable made this the first line of retreat; those who considered themselves altogether Chinese turned their backs upon the island of their birth and cut all ties with it. Some set themselves up in business in Fukien but kept alive the ties of clan and family across the Strait. Many exploited the advantages of dual citizenship. Peking considered all Chinese inalienable subjects of the Middle Kingdom because of race, language, and culture, but those who had opted for Japanese citizenship after May 1895, could also claim official Japanese protection in China if they maintained registration on Formosa and carried proper papers when abroad. Among these "dual citizens" were criminal elements who had been rounded up on Formosa and given a choice between prison there or service in China as subsidized agents, working as narcotics peddlers, as spies, or as disruptive troublemakers creating "incidents" leading to Japanese "protests," demands, and interventions.

Johnson also reported that Tokyo was subsidizing a "Formosan Residents' Association" in Fukien in an effort to gain political influence in the Amoy region. From his own pocket (he said), he had contributed substantially to the new Anglo-American College recently founded as a goodwill gesture in

Amoy. The Japanese government, on the other hand, had given $10,000 to the Formosan Residents' Association in support of a rival institution.

Washington received all this without comment, sought no further information, and demonstrated a total lack of interest. London, on the other hand, closely watched these Japanese activities, clearly inimical to all Western commercial interests. On the pretense that Japan must have a base in Fukien from which to prevent arms smuggling *into* Formosa, Tokyo asked China for a concession or lease of territory at Foochow in May 1897, and on April 26, 1898, the British Minister at Peking cabled London that "the Chinese Government has granted a demand made by Japan that no territory in the Province of Fukien shall be alienated to any nation but Japan." [1] This was followed on May 30 by a terse cable stating that "a separate settlement at Foochow has been demanded by the Japanese Government."

FORMOSA AND THE AMERICAN CONQUEST
OF THE PHILIPPINES

Japan's first tempting opportunity to use Formosa for a thrust southward came prematurely. Filipino insurrectionists appealed for help in an attempt to overthrow the Spanish administration, and Spanish reprisals had filled Luzon prisons with young rebels; the execution of young José Rizal had created a martyr. Emilio Aguinaldo (then twenty-seven years of age) assumed command of the movement as hundreds of young men fled to the hills or left the Philippines. By terms of an uneasy truce, Aguinaldo, too, left Luzon for a time, and at Hongkong helped establish a "Revolutionary Committee-in-Exile" that sought foreign support for the rebellion and material help for colleagues who were playing cat and mouse with Spanish forces in the Luzon hills.

Governor-General Katsura at Taipei was well informed of the crisis at Manila. Returning to Tokyo in October 1896, he urged preparations for a Japanese strike southward when Spain would be too weak to offer significant resistance.

He was overruled; his colleagues at Tokyo assumed that war with Russia was inevitable and must be given priority in national planning. The Trans-Siberian Railway would soon be finished, and on the day that Russia could move armies to the

Pacific coast by rail, Japan's military problems would be multiplied. Russia had bribed Li Hung-chang to negotiate an anti-Japanese treaty (June 1896), to create a Russo-Chinese Bank, and to permit construction of an additional rail line across northern Manchuria in order to strengthen Vladivostok. Russia had also leased the Liaotung Peninsula, so recently retaken from Japan, and had secured permission to build the South Manchuria Railway leading to it. In Japanese eyes the Russian threat was very real.

Japan's continental clique found Formosa an embarrassment, absorbing money, men, and matériel far beyond expectation. General Nogi's costly campaigns to suppress rebels had been unsuccessful, for the Formosans (unlike the Chinese encountered in 1895) stubbornly refused to give up guerrilla operations—nor were their leaders so easily bought with "silver bullets." Here and there at Tokyo it was suggested that Formosa should be sold—to England, perhaps—so that Japan could be relieved of a costly burden while the nation prepared for the Russian war.

Word of this prompted a group of wealthy Formosan exiles in China to propose raising a huge sum that would enable Peking to buy back the island. Lin Wei-yüan, for example, promised to contribute four million taels, but the plan came to nothing.

The southern clique led by General Katsura managed to prevent any reduction in appropriations for the new colony, confident that proper long-range planning and technological development would make it a strong, self-sustaining military base guarding the southern frontier. There would be time enough to use Formosa after the Russian problem had been solved. Each aggressive European move in China strengthened such arguments, reenforced by the American conquest of the Philippines. By 1898 Germany, France, and England had each established new "spheres of interest" and had acquired harbors on China's coast from which unfriendly fleets might move against Japan.

Tokyo watched the United States move into the Philippines with great concern. An American occupation would close off one of the roads to the south which the southern clique proposed to use some day. The American advance to the Philippines was only part of a larger pattern of expansion. From the Japanese point of view "European imperialism in Asia" was being matched by American imperialism in the Pacific, for in 1898 Washington had taken the Hawaiian Islands, Guam, half of Samoa, and now the Philippines, including the Bashi Channel islands lying between Luzon and Formosa's South Cape. In Hawaii and on Luzon local insurrections and independence movements were being exploited to provide excuse for American interference, and Tokyo was determined that no rebellion on Formosa would encourage American intervention there.

When Admiral George Dewey entered Manila Bay on May 1, 1898, to strike Cavite, the exultant Filipinos thought he had come to help them throw off Spanish rule. On June 12 insurrection leaders enthusiastically declared themselves independent after 350 years of Spanish rule, and the Filipino Declaration of Independence was modeled on the American Declaration of 1776.

On August 13—the day on which the American Congress formally annexed the Republic of Hawaii—American forces occupied Manila. Luzon was in great disorder, prompting Admiral Dewey to invite young Aguinaldo to assist him in creating a new administration. For a few brief weeks the Filipinos imagined they were free and on September 9 announced formation of a "provisional republic." A revolutionary congress convened at Malolos, north of Manila, and agents began to go abroad to prepare for recognition among the Powers.

Across the world, however, Washington decided that the "little brown brothers" were not yet ready for self-government. When on December 10 Spain ceded the Philippines to the United States in the Treaty of Paris, the angry Filipinos discovered their claims for recognition had been brushed aside. Disillusioned leaders promptly proclaimed a constitution of their own making and took to arms. They were not prepared to exchange one set of alien rulers for another and were determined to prevent a successful American occupation. The situation was made to order for a Japanese intrigue in which Formosa would play a part.

On February 6, 1899, Spanish-American treaty ratifications were exchanged; on February 7 Brigadier General Arthur MacArthur's troops moved out from Manila to crush the rebel-

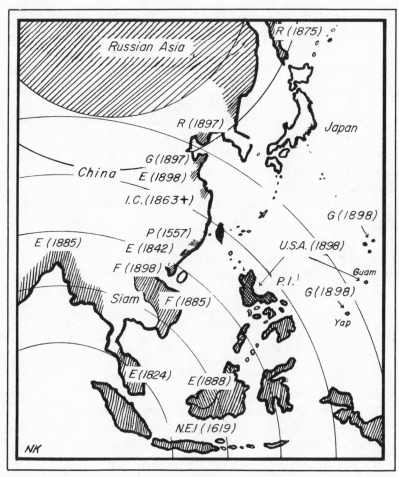

FIGURE 1. *Western pressures in East Asia and the Pacific in the nineteenth century.* *Russia* in Sakhalin (1875) and Liaotung (1897); *Germany* in the Marshall Islands (1885), in Chiao-chou (1897), in the Carolines and Marianas (1898); *England* in Singapore (1824), Canton and Hongkong (1842), Shanghai International Concession (1863), Burma (1885), Borneo (1888), Wei-hai-wei (1898); *France* in Indo-China (1885), Kwang-chou-wan (1898); *U.S.A.* in Hawaii, Guam and the Philippines (1898); *Portugal* in Macao from 1557 onward; the *Netherlands* in the East Indies from 1619.

lion, precipitating bitter guerrilla warfare destined to continue for three years. Washington assured an uneasy American public that this unfortunate colonial war was necessary to make the Philippines safe for democracy, and President McKinley assured the world that American rule was "designed not for our own satisfaction, or for the expression of our theoretical views, but for the happiness, peace, and prosperity of the Philippine Islands." The Filipinos saw it quite differently.

Japan and the United States now had a common frontier in open water below South Cape. From Taipei the new Governor-General, Kodama Gentarō, watched the Philippines insurrection with close attention. He could appreciate General Mac-Arthur's problems, so like his own in Formosa, but he saw an attractive opportunity to embarrass the United States and perhaps even to prevent a successful American occupation of the neighboring islands.

As Washington made clear its determination to crush the infant Philippine Republic, the Filipino Revolutionary Committee-in-Exile at Hongkong sent Mariano Ponce to Tokyo to appeal for help. The Foreign Office opposed any move to aid the Filipinos at this time; the confrontation with Russia must come first, and Japan could not risk antagonizing the United States until the Russian problem was solved. But the influential southern clique could not forego such a tempting opportunity; despite strong Foreign Office objections the Army General Staff authorized munitions sales to the insurgent Filipinos through the agency of the Ōkura Trading Company, working with a German firm. Delivery was to take place secretly through Formosa to Luzon across the Bashi Channel. The sea run was short, and Luzon had a thousand unwatched beaches at which contraband could be put ashore. On July 9, 1899, the *Nunobiki-maru* sailed from Kyushu carrying ten thousand rifles, six million rounds of ammunition, and other war materials destined for Aguinaldo's rebels.

At this moment Prime Minister Itō intervened, convinced that the risks of discovery were too great. One version of subsequent events says that the *Nunobiki-maru* sank in a storm near Shanghai—a perfect excuse for nondelivery of promised weapons—and another says that this "hot" cargo was off-loaded secretly at a junk anchorage on Formosa's western coast before the ship conveniently disappeared.

SUN YAT-SEN AND FORMOSA

Ponce, the disappointed Filipino agent at Tokyo, appealed to the exiled Chinese Sun Yat-sen for help. On learning of the secret arms shipment withheld from the Filipinos, Sun determined to get hold of it for his own use. He was planning a major uprising in South China at Waichow, some distance east of Canton, and ten thousand rifles would be most welcome. From the viewpoint of Katsura and Kodama this project was far more important than the Luzon operation, for a general rebellion in China would topple the Manchu government, precipitate chaos throughout the country, and possibly sweep the Europeans out of China. At the least it would weaken Russian arrangements in Manchuria and cause a serious diversion of Russian interest. A long period of painful national reconstruction in China would offer many opportunities for Japan to establish her own spheres of influence in the railroads, mines, and mills presently in European hands.

Katsura, now Army Minister at Tokyo, was quite prepared to use Sun Yat-sen to hasten the breakup of China. General Kodama was ordered to develop plans for a movement of troops from Formosa to Amoy, and Kodama in turn directed his Civil Administrator (Gotō) to assist the fiery Dr. Sun. Sun was ready to accept help from any source if it would further the Chinese revolution. He was convinced that he was using the Japanese rather than the reverse, and was blind to the manner in which Katsura and Kodama proposed to use him. Back and forth he traveled between Japan and Formosa, and at Taipei worked with Japanese agents assigned by Gotō to help him stage the so-called Waichow Rebellion, projected for late 1900. "I stayed in Formosa," wrote Sun, "and there I employed many Japanese military experts." [2]

To prepare the way, Dr. Gotō paid a visit to Fukien in April 1900, and at Foochow he addressed a large audience. The full text of his speech, later circulated throughout the province as a "proclamation" to provincial leaders, stressed the need for Sino-Japanese cooperation based on a unity of interests vis-à-vis the West and on ties of blood and culture. It was an odd performance, and may have been a little confusing to his Chinese audience, for he reviewed the history of European growth and expansion since Roman times, leading up to a special warning that Russia, France, and Germany were "diligently at work on China's borders." He bid for Sino-Japanese cooperation, especially in Fukien, urged the Fukien people to rid themselves of the old regime and advanced the specious argument that, to modernize, it would be cheaper for China to send students to Japan in large numbers. Tokyo, he said, had already sent men throughout the world, men who could now—in Japan—pass on the new technology to the Chinese, sparing them the cost and trouble of long sojourns in the West.

All went forward well enough with the Katsura-Kodama Plan in Fukien until June 1900, when the great Boxer Uprising in North China forced the foreign powers—Japan among them—to seize the Taku Forts and begin a march to relieve the foreign legations at Peking. The old Empress Dowager fled into the interior, disguised as a peasant, and total disintegration of the Manchu government seemed imminent. On August 10 General Kodama received orders at Taipei to prepare Formosa for troop movements into Fukien and South China, and an "incident" was arranged at Amoy—the burning of an unoccupied Japanese temple—to give an excuse for local intervention.

On August 27 General Katsura signaled Kodama to proceed with the cross-channel operation. Then, within twelve hours came telegraphic orders to "hold"; the British had anticipated Japan's move and had themselves moved into Amoy. Itō (now President of the Privy Council) refused to sanction Katsura's plan at the risk of a serious clash with England. Russia was still the prime enemy, and England's neutrality, if not her friendly support, was essential in the forthcoming conflict.

General Kodama at Taipei angrily asked permission to resign his governorship, but was refused; the factional conflict at Tokyo nevertheless forced a change of government, and on October 19 Itō once more became Prime Minister. Again he refused to sanction use of Formosa as a base for provocative action, and Dr. Gotō, the Civil Administrator, was ordered to expel Sun Yat-sen and to withdraw all support from the projected Waichow Rebellion. Katsura stepped down from the War Ministry, but to conciliate the southern movement faction, General Kodama took his place, serving concurrently as nominal Governor-General of Formosa, with Dr. Gotō carrying the chief burdens of the office.

KODAMA'S PLANS FOR A STRIKE INTO SOUTHEAST ASIA

While Itō sought to improve Japan's special position in Korea, and maneuvered skillfully to bring about the Anglo-Japanese Alliance of January 1902, Katsura, Kodama, and their partisans considered opportunities in Southeast Asia. England was being embarrassed just then by the Boer War in South Africa, and Russia was moving ambitiously in central Asia and the Middle East. France moved to support Russia as the prospect of a Russo-Japanese war increased. A leading French journal at Paris published a sensational document, allegedly drawn up by General Kodama in 1901, setting forth a detailed plan to use Formosa as a springboard for a swift, overwhelming attack upon French possessions in Southeast Asia. This "Kodama Report" included carefully prepared data sheets and a military analysis of the French position, the probable French reaction to Japanese attacks upon Hanoi and Saigon, timetables, and the problems of moving French troops from north Africa through Suez to Asia. It spelled out measures required to prepare Formosa as a forward base to sustain a Japanese strike.

Tokyo of course denounced the French publication as a forgery devised to embarrass Japan. Some editorial comment in the European and American press dismissed it as a hoax, and some considered it an unrealistic appraisal of "little Japan's military potential." A copy found its way into the military intelligence files at Washington where it lay, unremarked, gathering dust until after Pearl Harbor. By then (1941), with one minor exception, every local military construction project outlined in the Kodama Report had long since been completed and Formosa was ready to support Japan's advance into Southeast Asia and the drive to evict the United States from the Philippines. The Paris publication had reflected Japan's basic long-range planning for the frontier colony, but Washington failed to heed the implications.

While the American consul in Amoy fruitlessly attempted to call Washington's attention to Japan's activities in Fukien, directed from Taipei, the consul at Taipei wrestled with problems created in the new consular establishment by State Department indifference. Only Davidson's keen interest in the developing Japanese program prevented early resignation through sheer frustration. For example, no less than five years after creating the Formosa Consular District the Department continued to send out official mail in the China pouches or in the pouches for Hongkong, compounding this absurdity by addressing the mail to Tamsui which had never at any time been the seat of an American consulate. The exasperated Davidson pointed out that no direct shipment of commercial goods had *ever* gone from Tamsui to the United States, that shipments were made from Keelung port, and that documents were made and dated at Taipei. The Department nevertheless insisted that he must date official communications from Tamsui on the ground that Tamsui had been specified as the "open port" in the treaties *with China* nearly half a century earlier.*

The Consul was harassed by problems of inadequate appropriations and outmoded supplies. The Department continued to send out misprinted stationery until 1904, and the cipher code book in 1905 was one sent to the Amoy Consulate in 1875 and quite useless under new conditions. A request for new supplies required for daily business was not met for four years. At the end of 1903 the Consul was still begging Washington to answer his 1899 request for instructions governing disposition of salvaged cargo from an American ship that had burned in Formosan waters; the Japanese had most helpfully arranged for proper storage, but storage costs were mounting and the Consulate had insufficient funds to meet the annual charges.

Davidson warned that the United States was not taking advantage of developing commercial opportunities on Formosa, nor capitalizing upon Japan's interest in American technology; many of the young administrators and scientists now at Taipei had traveled or studied in the United States and were ready to place large orders for equipment if suppliers could be found. The consulate also needed much more than commercial information to pass along; the new Japanese officers requested many technical reports, ranging in subject from public sanitation to the management of American Indian reservations. To all this

* Department records continued to use Tamsui as the consular address as late as 1912. The *Foreign Service Register for 1949* perpetuates the error in its biographical lists (viz. Joseph W. Ballantine's career).

the Department at Washington remained supremely indifferent.

The Consul found himself engrossed in business relating to America's new possession, the Philippines. Many restless Formosans, seeking to explore commercial opportunities on Luzon, secured proper Japanese passports and came to the Consulate for visas, but after a very long delay Washington ruled that the ban on Chinese migration to American territory—including the Philippines—was based on race rather than on nationality, and that therefore the Consul at Taipei could grant permits to Formosan Chinese only for temporary residence related to business or travel, after completing an immense amount of documentation in each case. In commenting upon this "race-culture-nationality" question Davidson noted that foreigners at Taipei were finding it increasingly difficult to distinguish between upper-class, well-bred Formosans, and the "modern" Japanese, for the Formosan males were cutting off their queues, adopting Western dress, and speaking fluent Japanese.

To meet this increased flow of business, Davidson secured permission to appoint an assistant, nominating a local British resident named John Lambert. He then obtained a leave of absence and sailed off to Shanghai. Almost immediately Acting Vice-Consul Lambert was called upon to manage affairs relating to shipwreck, pillage, and murder—the last true case of "wrecking" in Formosan waters. The American ship *Benjamin Sewell* with a crew of mixed nationalities had stranded on Botel Tobago and had been plundered by the Yami tribesmen in October 1903. Several of the ship's company were killed, but the captain, the captain's wife, and a number of the crew managed to get away in the small boat. Crossing to the South Cape they took shelter in a miserable hamlet, sent word to Takao and Taipei, and waited for some relief. Lambert acted on standing instructions to render assistance to distressed American citizens, drew on the consulate's contingent fund, and made it possible for the totally destitute castaways to reach Taipei. There they made depositions concerning the incident and waited again for arrangements to be made for their relief and onward passage.

Lambert notified Washington of his action. For his pains he received a severe rebuke. The Department of State pointed out that some of the survivors were not American citizens and that he should have assisted only the captain. He was brusquely ordered to restore the "unnecessary and unauthorized sums" he had spent. These totaled $58.61. It did no good to point out that the captain of the American ship could not leave his wife or his men to starve to death on the South Cape beaches. During the prolonged and embittered correspondence which followed, Lambert resigned, Washington refused to reimburse him for the sums he was compelled to return to the consular account, and only years later did Davidson succeed in persuading the ship's owners to make good a "debt of honor."

After leaving Formosa, Davidson lingered in China and Manchuria to observe the outcome of the Russo-Japanese War, and then crossed Siberia and Russia into western Europe. His massive volume relating to Formosa's history and describing its resources had been published in 1903 at Yokohama, Shanghai, Hongkong, and Singapore by Kelly & Walsh, Ld., and in London and New York by Macmillan & Co. Everywhere he went—in Russia, western Europe, England, and the United States—Davidson was called upon to speak, was made a member of distinguished learned societies, and was generally acclaimed as a remarkable young man. At London, where he lectured on Japan's colonial development program in Formosa, he became a Fellow of the Royal Geographic Society, and in New York he paused to arrange publication of his observations made while traveling along the new Trans-Siberian Railway. In his final reports at Washington he urged the Department of State to pay more attention to the rich island lying before the ports of China and pressing southward toward the Philippines. He then resigned from the Foreign Service.*

Davidson's successor at Taipei (Fred W. Fisher) took up

---

* Davidson, who was only thirty-three years of age when he left the Service, produced no more books concerning Formosa. He had served briefly as U. S. Commercial Attaché, Shanghai (April–July 1904), as Consul at Nanking (Aug.–Sept.), Acting Consul General, Shanghai (Oct.–Dec. 1904), and Acting Consul, Antung, Manchuria (Jan.–Feb. 1905). He married at San Francisco in 1906, and thereafter developed extensive commercial, industrial, and banking interests in the United States and Canada. He served at one time as a governor and vice-president of Rotary International, becoming a world traveler. He died in 1934.

the old complaint that Washington expected every consul to do his duty with wholly inadequate funds. By then America was taking one-half of Formosa's foreign exports—principally high grade teas—and island imports from the United States were rising rapidly in volume and in dollar value. He, too, noted that the local Japanese administrators were seeking technical help and he thought Washington had an excellent opportunity to establish an influential position of advantage to American interests. There was clearly a need, he said, to keep watch on Japan's local military program, for soon after taking charge at Taipei he discovered that a consular clerk was a Japanese military agent. He also noted that he had reason to believe certain Japanese trade missions seeking passport clearance for Manila were actually military men in mufti; Formosa's usefulness as a way-station for clandestine passage into the Philippines was obvious—or so he thought—and the frontier position of the Taipei consulate deserved careful consideration.

Fisher also noted that in this era of keen national rivalries for place and influence in Asia the Germans maintained a consular establishment on Formosa out of all proportion to Germany's share in the import-export business. The Imperial German Consulate was housed in a handsome building at Twatutia and was operating on a budget of nearly US$8,000 per year—a large sum at Taipei. The British owned their own elaborate establishment at Tamsui and also paid annual rental of US$1,500 for a substantial branch office at Taipei, operating on an annual budget in excess of US$8,500. But Washington, Fisher noted, expected the American Consulate to operate on a budget of US$2,766, and his own salary (US$1,500) was considerably less than one-half that of his German counterpart. The Japanese were calling upon him for a stream of information and advice, and the Consul found himself paying out of pocket for many items needed in the discharge of official business. He was quite without funds needed to meet the social obligations of his position.

The Department of State met his plea for adequate funds by increasing the annual appropriation for Taipei by $244.

Fisher left Formosa in 1907. Russia's defeat at the hands of "little Japan" had affected the position of all the local consular establishments. War production had stimulated the growth of

Japan's great industrial and commercial organizations, and now, turning to more diversified interests, they were prepared to manage Formosa's foreign trade by way of their own headquarters in Japan proper through Japanese agencies in the colony. Foreign firms on Formosa continued to ship out tea and camphor in quantity but their share in the import trade diminished rapidly, lost to Japanese rivals. The decline in direct foreign trade meant a sharp decline in consular business, matched by a decline in the personal and social importance of the consuls. Spectacular victory over a Western power—the destruction of the Russian fleet near Tsushima—had enormously increased Japan's self-confidence and her determination to be rid of the last vestiges of the unequal treaty system. In the hands of Kodama, Gotō, and Nitobe, Formosa would become a showplace in Asia, proving beyond dispute that any Asian territory falling under Japanese control or accepting Japan's imperial leadership could anticipate prosperity and rising living standards. The consuls Davidson and Fisher were at Taipei during pivotal years when the island ceased to be an ill-managed Chinese dependency, exposed to the possibility of a foreign (Western) occupation, and became Japan's own "Treasure Island."

Sun Yat-sen, Liang Ch'i-chiao, and other leaders of the Chinese Revolution visited Formosa repeatedly during the first two decades of the century, noting the dramatic social and economic changes taking place, and dreaming of similar transformations in chaotic China, dreams not to be realized until after 1949.

The cost of modernization was high in terms of Formosan self-respect and individual freedom—a price the Japanese seemed never to understand. Given the traditional spirit of frontier independence and of resistance to authority, we are not surprised to discover that one of Dr. Gotō's first projects was to construct a large penitentiary at Taipei. Suitable smaller prisons were erected at the outlying provincial capitals. All were filled to capacity and overcrowded throughout the Kodama-Gotō era.

4. Regimentation and the Whip Hand

POLICING AGENCIES AND CONTROLS

IN ACHIEVING this twentieth-century revolution, Dr. Gotō drew on ancient authoritarian principles to justify regimentation policies. These were a natural expression of the samurai's command-and-obey tradition, severely reinforced by an ever-present expectation of war with Russia. Kodama and Gotō were determined that when the crisis came, the restive new colony would be under firm control.

Meiji leaders were well versed in the Chinese classical literature. The ancient *Book of Lord Shang* and its commentaries, for example, supplied classical justification for the harshest policies by saying that whatever the ruler desires is *right*, and whatever he does not desire is *wrong*. The Legalist philosophers held that opposition to the ruler's will is intolerable in the state; the common people exist only to produce food for the army, and ". . . the sole aim of the State is to maintain and if possible to expand its frontiers. . . . It is a misfortune for a prosperous country not to be at war." [1]

Elsewhere Gotō and Nitobe could find ample justification for a thorough regimentation of Formosan minds as well as bodies.

A Sage knows what is essential in administering a country, and so he induces the people to devote their attention to agriculture.

55

If their attention is devoted to agriculture, then they will be simple, and being simple, they may be made correct.[2]

The intelligent Prince, in improving the administration, strives for uniformity, removes those who are of no use, restrains volatile scholars and those of frivolous pursuits, and makes them all uniformly into farmers. . . .[3]

Gotō proposed to produce obedient Formosan farmers and semiskilled laborers trained for light industrial employment; there was to be compulsory education, so that every child in the island could read and write at an elementary level—enough to improve his economic productivity and no more. On completing primary school he should be able to read orders, patriotic slogans, and simple technical information—the directions on a bag of fertilizer, for example, or directions for simple technical operations, but he would not be encouraged to think for himself.

If study becomes popular, people will abandon agriculture and occupy themselves with debates, high-sounding words, and discussions on false premises; abandoning agriculture, they will live on others in idleness and seek to surpass one another with words. Then the people will become estranged from the Ruler and there will be crowds of disloyal subjects. . . .[4]

Dr. Gotō dreamed also of a university to cap the educational system in Formosa, of a first-class research institute devoted to tropical agriculture, tropical medicine, and forestry, and to studies of South China, Southeast Asia and the Indies, that is, research devoted to the interests of the State. By limiting opportunity for higher education, the Civil Administrator proposed to check the "volatile scholar" toying with independent ideas and dangerous thoughts; there must be order in the colony above all else.

On reaching Taipei in 1898 Gotō found the larger towns fairly quiet; the townspeople were beginning to discover economic benefit in the new order and were becoming reconciled to it. It had been said of the ancient Lord Shang that when his laws were enforced ". . . the people suffered from them, but after three years found them convenient," and so it proved to be on Formosa; after three years of Japanese rule a substantial number of thoughtful Formosan leaders appreciated the unprecedented degree of security maintained within the city walls, the growing security in the countryside, and the improved economic prospects. Tokyo was pouring money into construction projects everywhere, creating jobs and markets for local goods and services. Taxes were being collected with unprecedented rigor; nevertheless, it could be seen that they were being used to promote local growth and welfare. Traditional town gang warfare and clan quarrels were being suppressed with ruthless severity. Anyone who clashed with the police and escaped death or imprisonment had then to leave Formosa, accept the new order or take to the hills to join an outlaw band.

Country people everywhere were slow to accept the revolution. They saw little of the reconstruction at Taipei or of developments at the ports and along the rail lines; general economic benefits came last to the outlying hamlets. Farmers deeply resented the intrusion of Nitobe's surveyors, escorted by police or military units. Interpreters employed by the survey teams often took advantage of both sides when villagers were called upon to respond to questions probing into the private lives and fortunes of every clan and family.

General Nogi's effort to introduce the ordinary Japanese civil police system had failed, prompting Gotō to undertake a drastic reorganization by creating special forces to meet special problems. Army regulars—some twenty thousand men—were recalled to headquarters, given well-defined military duties and relieved of direct concern with police affairs. The large gendarmerie was reduced to mobile shock units ready for emergency use and speedy dispatch to any part of the island. Both the army regulars and the gendarmes were made answerable only to General Kodama acting in his military role, ready for action whenever the Civil Administrator applied to the Governor for help.

The civil police force, which answered directly to the Civil Administrator, was now enlarged, retrained, regrouped, and well armed. Five thousand men were assigned to permanent duty stations scattered through the countryside, and an additional three thousand were given special training for duty along the forest border and at key stations within the aborigines' territory.

The government had about one armed Japanese in service

for every one hundred Formosans, a formidable ratio. The system worked well enough when its founder (Gotō) was in effect acting Governor-General during Kodama's long absences, but in later years an intense rivalry sprang up between the gendarmes and the civil police, each striving to outdo the other in demonstrating superiority in detection and punishment of alleged subversion, but often using different criteria by which to test Formosan "loyalty to Japan."

The language barrier impeded growth of mutual tolerance and understanding; too much was demanded of a subject people in too short a time, and too little effort was made to explain the need for change. Japan's command-and-obey tradition allowed little compromise. The Japanese policeman knew that he was universally detested. For years officers stationed at isolated posts had to be perpetually on guard, knowing that villagers around him would gladly burn his house over his head or murder him on his rounds through the fields. The reaction to this knowledge was an occasional resort to acts of barbarous cruelty, committed in the belief that no village should forget that terrible reprisals would follow any violent defiance of police or civil authority.

"MUTUAL RESPONSIBILITY" AS A COMMUNITY STRAITJACKET

Japan's family registry system, adapted to Formosan conditions, provided a basic community control. Each Japanese family was obliged to keep up to date a record of births, deaths, marriages, and adoptions. These records were maintained at city, town, or county offices, to be consulted in legal affairs— matters of property, conscription, and the like. On Formosa the police maintained much more elaborate records on individuals and families who came to attention for any reason, favorable or unfavorable. Thus dossiers were built up on representatives of wealthy or prominent families willing to cooperate with the administration, and on uncooperative individuals, beggars, criminals, and the mentally deranged. In time, in every village, the police officer could at a glance determine the economic and social position of a subject by referring to notes on his family property, if any, his marriage connections, education, employment and usual haunts, and—most important—upon his "attitude" and the attitude of his family toward the Japanese government and people. Notes were made of all commendations, prizes, and awards for collaboration as well as of all conflicts with authority. Participation in organized activities of any kind—farmers' associations, recreational clubs, clan societies, and the like—gradually became matters of careful record as the system was elaborated through the years.

It is evident that Dr. Gotō took carefully to heart a passage from the *Book of Lord Shang* which said: "Generally speaking, in administering a country, the trouble is when the people are scattered and when it is impossible to consolidate them. That is why a Sage tries to bring about uniformity and consolidation . . ." [5] Using the family records, the Civil Administrator began to develop community controls of staggering complexity. Chief among them was the *pao-chia* or *hokō* system, based upon traditional respect and concern for the ancestors and the elders of a clan and family.

The ancient Chinese pao-chia system is said to have been devised by Lord Shang himself in behalf of his master, the Duke of Hsiao. A commentary written in the second century B.C. says that

> Duke Hsiao . . . ordered the people to be organized into groups of fives and tens mutually to control one another and to share one another's punishments. Whoever did not denounce a culprit would be cut in two; whosoever denounced a culprit would receive the same reward as he who decapitated an enemy; whoever concealed a culprit would receive the same punishment as he who surrendered to the enemy. . . .[6]

The Formosans had long ago introduced the pao-chia system as a traditional Chinese instrument for local village convenience rather than as an effective central government agency. In 1895 Japan abolished it, seeking to reduce the dangers of organized local resistance to the incoming regime. Now, to serve its original purpose as a hostage system, Dr. Gotō revived the pao-chia or hokō on August 31, 1898, making it an agency of police administration, later modified (in 1909) to enlarge support for the local civil administration as well.

Participation was optional for the Japanese, but each Formosan household was required to put forward a representative (usually a senior member of the family), who met with similar representatives from nine other families. The ten formed a unit known as a *kō*. A representative (the *kōchō*) of this unit then met with nine of his peers to form a *ho*, or unit of one hundred households. The exact number of households in each unit was variable, determined by convenience of location. Each ho nominated a chief (the *hosei*) who held office usually for two years and could be reelected. All hokō appointments were subject to police approval and were reviewed and confirmed by the provincial governor. Administrative costs were met by monthly household contributions.

Through this pyramidal arrangement the police could bring great pressure to bear throughout the community. Members of the ho and kō were held responsible, individually and collectively, for peace and order and for the proper conduct of community affairs. Failure to comply with orders or requests, or the violation of any law or regulation, brought penalties ranging from mild reprimand or embarrassing public censure (loss of face) to heavy fines levied on individuals, families, or the ho and kō. Village elders who served as hosei or kōchō might be subjected to rough interrogation and if "criminal negligence" were alleged, the local police office might order a flogging or an imprisonment.

If a wanted man were not produced promptly on police demand, a senior member of the family, the ho, or the kō might be obliged to take his place. Since the accused were usually considered guilty until proved innocent and "third degree" interrogation was often employed to extract information, the policeman's box at the village corner and the police office at district headquarters were looked on as "tigers' dens" into which no Formosan ventured willingly.

This system cruelly exploited respect for elders, affection for brothers and cousins, and family responsibility for a larger community interest, but it also had great administrative value of less personal character. Announcements and police directives handed to a senior hokō member were transmitted promptly down the line, each representative at the next lower level acknowledging receipt until it became a matter of record that all concerned were properly informed. No one could plead ignorance of the government's wishes. Conversely, each individual and household was expected to volunteer information and to report to the police the overnight absence of a family member or the presence of visitors staying under the family roof. It was extremely difficult for a stranger to pass through the countryside unnoticed and unreported.

By 1903 Dr. Gotō's agents had registered nearly five hundred thousand households in the hokō system and, long before the Japanese era came to an end, virtually every family on Formosa had been caught up in this web of mutual obligation that was in effect a hostage system.*

As an important supplement, Gotō founded a Youth Corps (*Seinendan*) to bring young men under more direct police control. Every youth was expected to volunteer on reaching the age of sixteen; applicants were investigated and subject to police approval before enrollment could take place. Members were harangued upon the privileges of Youth Corps membership and encouraged to think of themselves as an élite group. Held strictly to account and called upon to explain any failure to attend meetings or to appear when called upon for "volunteer work," they soon formed a well-drilled but unarmed scouting unit and police auxiliary, providing unpaid support for many community projects inaugurated by the government. For example, Youth Corps members assisted in rat-catching campaigns, in fire fighting, and in the semiannual compulsory housecleaning drives. They helped the census takers, assisted Nitobe's men in gathering economic data, and were assigned to afforestation projects. They were called out to assist in keeping trails, roads, bridges, and river embankments in good repair, and most important, they were expected to report promptly any unusual activity in the community. It was their duty to assist in searching out wanted persons, and late in the Japanese era they were drilled and indoctrinated especially to assist in "antispy" campaigns.

By 1903 Dr. Gotō had brought the Youth Corps membership to fifty-five thousand, and it grew steadily thereafter

---

* It was gradually liberalized. In 1920 the police acted in 242 cases of "joint responsibility"; in 1930 there were only five reported, and in 1932, none, and thereafter only three (in 1935). In 1938 there were 53,694 kō and 5,648 ho chieftains registered. Each was responsible for the good behavior of every individual within his group if the police chose to make an issue of it.

through forty years. Membership gave the police one more means to cross-check the character, activities, and interests of the individual. Great care was taken here to ensure that the Youth Corps organization, like the hokō, remained fragmented and localized; there was no province-wide or island-wide organization to tempt ambitious Formosans seeking a power base vis-à-vis the Japanese administration.

Village associations (*buraku-kai*), patterned after those in Japan, were introduced. Technically they were "private" and membership was "voluntary"; nevertheless families of even the most modest circumstance were expected to be represented, and government orders, "suggestions," and requests had mandatory effect. Japanese living in the community (usually officials in one capacity or another) were members, and "guided association programs according to Japanese interest." If a government request entailed expenditures for materials or consumed many man-hours of hard labor, the associations met the charge, relieving the government budget annually of large total expenditure. Youth Corps members were often called out to assist in public works projects paid for by the village associations; the hokō could be held responsible for any laxity, failures, or sabotage on the projects.

As in the primary schools, membership in these two agencies tended to blur old lines of clan rivalry and blunted traditional antagonism among Hakka, Cantonese, and Fukienese subgroups, thus contributing to the slow development of a sense of island-wide Formosan identity. Countering this, the police encouraged mutual talebearing and spying by members who wished to curry favor. Gotō was not prepared to go so far as the Duke of Hsiao, who proposed to "cut in two" anyone who failed to inform against his neighbor, but a carefully calculated system of rewards and punishments encouraged unscrupulous informers and grudgebearers, and penalized loyalty to friends, family, and neighbors.

THE NETWORK OF OCCUPATIONAL ASSOCIATIONS

With thoroughness that would have satisfied even the ancient Duke of Hsiao Dr. Gotō brought about "uniformity and consolidation" in every department and at every level of Formosan life. In 1900 he established "farmers associations" designed to advance Dr. Nitobe's programs and to give the police an additional check upon farm households. These organizations were repeatedly revised to provide for division and subdivision according to specialized activities and needs.* During the next forty years the number of associations became so great and of such extraordinary diversity as to suggest a pathological bureaucratic obsession. Dr. Gotō had devised a very useful tool for social control, but his successors, less able than he, carried the "association" and "club" idea to absurd lengths, creating supplementary organizations based on recreational interests and hobbies to complete the network entangling every individual.

Farmers, villagers, and townsmen were all encouraged to become dues-paying members of organizations founded by government officials "acting in their private capacity," or by prominent Formosans prompted to follow "suggestions" that were thinly veiled orders. Plans originating in government offices were passed along indirectly to the associations to be adopted by them as community projects. The associations were in effect supplementary agencies of government. Three decades after Gotō left the island more than 3,800 rural organizations were registered and operating, with budgets totaling in excess of fifty million yen—at that time nearly seventeen million U.S. dollars. As dues-paying members of these organizations, the Formosans were in effect subsidizing government projects—an indirect, heavy taxation.

From a general economic point of view the associations served admirably to introduce improved materials and techniques and to set up and maintain desirable production standards. The cooperatives enabled farmers to share benefits well beyond individual reach, and the associations and recreational

* Only a full treatise on Formosan agriculture could attempt to list and discuss them all. There were, for example, associations for the purchase and distribution of improved seeds, associations organized to develop rice-seedling nurseries, to purchase improved tools, and to distribute chemical fertilizers. Poultry farmers, pig farmers, cattle breeders, and oyster farmers were organized for mutual aid projects. Vegetable farmers, citrus growers, and banana gardeners formed associations; truckers, warehouse owners, and produce shippers formed clubs, and associations were founded to develop water resources and improve irrigation systems. Local mutual-loan societies became of prime importance, and late in the Japanese era even the tenant farmers were permitted to organize locally as a measure of protection against unreasonable landlords.

clubs as a whole contributed to the slow growth of a sense of community interdependence, a new phenomenon on Formosa.

These benefits were offset by the ever-present sense of coercion; every membership was a matter of record in the police files and few meetings could be held without the presence of one or two policemen. But as the Japanese kept sharp watch on the Formosans, so the Formosans kept their eyes on the Japanese among them, relaying fact (and fiction) from one community to another with astonishing speed. This unwritten communication, known to foreigners as the "bamboo telegraph," clearly operated beyond government control. Police outposts were scattered and vulnerable, and the policeman took care to be well armed as he cycled from village to village, threading his way along the narrow trails and field embankments. These difficulties in rural communication for policing purposes stimulated the rapid extension of telephone and telegraph services.

Regimentation and policing in the towns were comparatively easy tasks; all townspeople—including the Japanese— were registered in neighborhood associations, and the greater diversity of urban occupations produced a corresponding diversity of clubs, societies, and associations. Thus, Japanization began in the cities and spread slowly into the countryside, as the urban Formosans learned to speak Japanese as a second language and found employment in public and private enterprise where a knowledge of Japanese was mandatory. It was difficult for lawless elements to flourish undetected in the towns. Keelung, Taipei, Hsinchu, Taichung, Chiayi, and Takao were small cities, and developed no real industrial slums; only the most skilled lawbreaker could elude the community registration network. In Gotō's day disgruntled and displaced Formosans could cross to the continent with comparative ease, and the Japanese were glad to see them go. Others merely left the cities to settle in obscure hamlets not yet well policed, and hundreds took to the hills. The prison population remained well above four thousand annually until 1905, when it was arranged to substitute floggings and fines for prison terms in minor criminal cases.

DR. GOTŌ SOLVES THE BANDIT PROBLEM

Unlike the latter-day Huks in the Philippines, or the Vietcong of Vietnam, Formosan guerrillas at the turn of the century had no political ideals, no support from overseas, and no overall leadership within the island. Peking was preoccupied with the Boxer crisis and outlaws in the Formosan hills had no desire to resume ties with mainland China; they wished only to revert to the state of lawless confusion that had prevailed before 1895.

We have already noted that some bandit chieftains considered themselves traditional Chinese *hsieh*, knights-errant, the "protectors of the people" so popular in the Chinese theater. Many were in fact merely rural gangsters untroubled by lofty Robin Hood ideals, and were quite prepared to kill one another or to place themselves in the pay of clans or landlords as they had done throughout the eighteenth and nineteenth centuries. The general unrest generated by sweeping change gave them splendid opportunities to trump up and exploit collaborationist charges—an excuse to plunder, kidnap, or kill anyone accused of working on behalf of the Japanese police. Some regions were comparatively free of marauding bands, but others were notorious for the number and size of brigand organizations, ranging from gangs of ten or twenty members to organizations of two and three thousand men.

Bandit chieftains had found it fairly easy to come to terms with the Chinese magistrates and mandarins, but in Dr. Gotō they met more than their match. Gotō began mildly enough in 1898 by attempting to replace General Nogi's blunt and unsuccessful military policy with a system of persuasive rewards. It was announced that any outlaw who agreed to surrender and swear allegiance would be given temporary economic support for a probationary period and a choice of employment. For a time this quite lenient offer seemed to be working well; scores of outlaws straggled in to resume normal family life, and several well-known chieftains persuaded hundreds of their followers to surrender en masse. We cannot take Dr. Gotō's own published figures at face value, but at least they represent a *minimum* record. In the period 1897 to 1901, he said, the bandits had killed or wounded 2,459 people and had held for ransom no fewer than 4,653. Consequently, the government forces had killed more than 3,475 lawless persons and had placed at least 8,000 under arrest or had arranged for them to return peaceably to their homes.

In 1900 a radical policy change took place after Dr. Gotō discovered that many "converted" bandits were continuing to give secret aid to unconverted colleagues in the hills while enjoying the rewards he had offered. He turned on them savagely, staining an otherwise distinguished record by adopting Lord Shang's ancient advice that "to do things which the enemy would be ashamed to do is the way to secure an advantage." Late in 1901, after military and police forces had been concentrated in a great drive through southern Formosa, Taipei announced that some three thousand bandits had been killed. Many moderate Japanese in the government were disturbed by rumors that much of this "success" represented indiscriminate slaughter in villages merely alleged to be harboring bandits.

By 1902 brigands in central Formosa found it difficult to maintain themselves in the hills, as military roads and trails were pushing deep into remote areas and policing organizations became increasingly effective. Secret support for the outlaws began to diminish as the Formosan choice had to be made between brutal reprisals—terrorism—and the economic benefits of cooperation with the Japanese.

Gotō let it be known that a massive drive would soon take place in the west-central region and that the local hokō and Youth Corps groups would be obliged to assist. This meant that special pressure would be used to compel families to reveal any member who was in secret alliance with wanted men in the hills, and every outlaw knew that if he refused to give up, his entire family would be endangered. The Civil Administrator now used the carrot as well as the stick, renewing the attractive amnesty offers of 1898. Hundreds surrendered, ready at last to abandon a comfortless and dangerous life.

In Taichung the authorities praised the incoming men and proposed a celebration, a banquet following a grand "allegiance ceremony," to take place in the Tau-lok assembly hall on May 25, 1902. Everyone who was prepared to abandon life in the hills nearby and to swear loyalty to the Japanese emperor was directed to wear a large white rosette, enabling his hosts to give him special attention at the banquet. When some three hundred sixty guests were assembled in the hall on that memorable day, the doors were suddenly closed and every man wearing a white rosette was killed.

Many of Dr. Gotō's colleagues were dismayed when the story reached the newspapers of Japan proper. At Tokyo, members of the political opposition harshly criticized the government for this faithless act, noting that it would destroy all Formosan trust in His Imperial Majesty's administration. Gotō had played into the hands of foreign critics as well, for residents in China and Japan publicly questioned Japan's readiness for treaty revisions so ardently desired, and challenged Japan's claim to be recognized as an equal among modern nations. Diet members severely censured the colonial government, charging that Gotō's police action had "disgraced the nation." *

The fact remained that Kodama and Gotō were beyond reach of the Diet, and it is possible that Dr. Gotō was tempted to quote from the commentaries on Lord Shang and the Duke of Hsiao: "When [the law] had been in force for ten years the people of Ch'in greatly rejoiced; things dropped on the road were not picked up; in the mountains there were no robbers; families were self-supporting, and people had plenty; they were brave in public warfare and timid in private quarrels, and great order prevailed throughout the countryside and in the towns." [7]

In 1903, when the government had some thirty thousand

* Gotō later felt it necessary to publish some justification for this brutal act. A prominent Diet member (the historian Takekoshi Yosaburō) was subsidized to prepare a laudatory volume, published in Japanese at Tokyo in 1905 and in an English version in 1907, entitled *Japanese Rule in Formosa*. This was for an international audience, and there, buried on page 100, the notorious Tau-lok affair is dismissed with this brief notice: "On 25th May, 1902, a meeting was held for the purpose of accepting [the bandits'] allegiance; but although they presented themselves, they all proved so unmanageable that they were all killed in the hall where the ceremony was held." Elsewhere he published an assertion that the 1902 campaigns were so successful that whereas 4,043 bandits had been executed in the year 1902, only *eighteen* were put to death in 1903.

armed men stationed among the population of three million, Dr. Gotō announced that the pacification of Formosa was complete. He had prepared for the oncoming crisis of war with Russia and he had constructed a framework within which he and his colleagues could press ahead with the local social and economic revolution.

5. A Licensed Revolution

SOME consideration of the nearby international situation helps to explain, if not to excuse, the severity with which Kodama and Gotō imposed their will upon the emperor's new subjects. The "authorized revolution" took place in that tense decade between China's defeat (1895) and Japan's victory in the struggle with Russia in 1905. These years saw the virtual dismemberment of continental China by the European powers and the occupation of the Philippines by the United States. Kodama and his associates were determined that no sign of discontent within Formosa should tempt the moralizing, meddling foreign powers to consider intervention. They were also determined to show other Asian peoples what benefits might accrue if they looked to Japan for leadership vis-à-vis the predatory West.

It should be remembered that when the United States government began to pour billions of dollars into Formosa after 1950, and to boast of spectacular progress in an "underdeveloped" island, the Formosan economy proved able to absorb such massive infusions of capital and to elaborate the industrial structure only because this so-called Sino-American Development Program had a firm base. This foundation had not been laid down by the frustrated Chinese reformers Shen, Ting, and Liu, as Chinese propaganda would have the world believe, but was primarily the work of Kodama, Gotō, and Nitobe. They found Governor Liu Ming-ch'üan's innovative program had been wrecked by his successor; the telegraph and postal systems had been abandoned, the modernized mines and the short railway system were inoperable. The Japanese were obliged to begin again.

The administrative ambiguities that had hampered Kabayama, Katsura, and Nogi were largely cleared away by an Imperial Ordinance of October 22, 1898, assigning management of Formosan affairs to the Home Ministry with a provision that the governor-general (a military man on the active list) must at all times enjoy overriding authority. The laws of the empire—the new Meiji Constitution—would apply to Formosa, with appropriate exceptions, but to meet special local conditions the governor was authorized to issue special rules and regulations (*ritsurei*) which had the force of law in the colony only, and were not applicable elsewhere.

JAPANIZATION: REORGANIZING TAIPEI AND THE PROVINCES

The new administrators enjoyed great advantages: distance from the continent ensured insulation from China's spreading chaos, and distance from Tokyo minimized interference by meddling bureaucrats and inquisitive Diet committees. If the Formosans were fortunate in having such able men at the summit at Taipei, the Japanese were equally fortunate in having a pragmatic and industrious people to work with, one usually willing to adopt new tools, new techniques, and new organizations if thereby substantial material benefit could be gained.

For a time the new Japanese population was quite unstable; thousands of newcomers found colonial life too rugged, too strangely Chinese, or too unsafe, and chose to sail home again after a few months on the island. In 1899, for example, no fewer than nineteen thousand Japanese entered Formosa, but eleven thousand returned to Japan proper. Gotō rid the administration and the island of many incompetent officeholders, carpetbaggers, and parasitic camp followers who had swarmed in after 1895. Hundreds were dismissed to make way for men more carefully recruited for colonial duty. High wages and many perquisites made "overseas hardship posts" attractive, although it was well advertised that Formosa was no place to look for sinecure appointments.

Many incoming Japanese were "Meiji idealists"—young

men immensely stirred by and justifiably proud of Japan's spectacular achievements after the Restoration of 1868. From their messianic point of view, what was good for Japan should also be good for Formosans and ultimately for all other Asian peoples. At heart was a genuine desire to achieve modern living standards while at the same time reducing foreign intrusion upon Asian affairs. Even Nogi, Kodama and Gotō may be said to have shared this deep conviction that surely all Asians would welcome Japan's leadership toward a new world free of Western exploitation. The Emperor Meiji reflected a degree of idealism when he observed publicly that the Formosans must be treated by the Japanese as "brothers."

To make its policies and views known, the government sponsored establishment of a publishing company at Taipei in 1898, making its subsidized daily, the *Taiwan Nichi Nichi*, the mouthpiece for official interests. Soon thereafter Formosan investors helped found the *Tainan Shimpō-sha* (1899) and the *Taiwan Shimpō-sha* (at Taichung, 1901) in order to represent Formosan interests as well. Although Formosans sat on the board of directors, they were obliged to accept Japanese management of operations. For some years even the government's *Nichi Nichi* carried some pages in Chinese for the benefit of the older generation, and for a short time even issued a special Chinese-language edition.

As well-educated men, the Japanese leaders respected Chinese scholarship and sought to establish good relations with well-educated Formosans, the local literati.* Of these there were more than five thousand who had passed the lower examinations, and some three hundred and fifty who held advanced degrees. Thousands of other literate Formosans had not yet applied for the exams or did not propose to do so. To appeal to this class and to the gentry at large, General Nogi made awards to distinguished scholars and revived the ancient "feast of elders" at Taipei. General Kodama and Dr. Gotō enlarged on this, lauding the Confucian ideal of filial piety, and convening great entertainments for the elders at Taipei, Changhua, Tainan, and Fengshan. In an unprecedented gesture, Gov-

* For the following paragraphs I have drawn particularly upon Harry J. Lamley's unpublished study, "The Taiwan Literati and Early Japanese Rule, 1895–1915" (University of Washington, 1964).

ernor-General Kodama himself attended each of these festive meetings, conversed with the elderly guests and won respect and admiration among the gentry.

The convocation of a new Culture Fostering Society (*Yōbun kai*) on March 15, 1900, may be taken as a landmark occasion and the high point in Japanese-Formosan relations at the turn of the century. Some seventy leading men in northern Formosa accepted the governor's invitation to spend the better part of a week at the capital. The sessions opened with fervent lectures by the Governor-General and the Civil Administrator, who urged the Formosan people to conserve the best in the East Asian tradition while adopting and adapting the most useful modern technology. The week was filled with visits to new installations, offices, and enterprises ranging from hospitals and prison-warden training institutes to hydroelectric generating plants, post offices, and railway works. Kodama and Gotō hoped to make these instructive meetings an annual affair but signally failed to do so. Some of the guests were indeed impressed by Japan's manifest achievements but others remained skeptical. It has been said that the gentry were put off because they were preached to; they wished to be consulted. It is also possible that Gotō's harsh police measures, so soon to follow, chilled public support.

Some well-placed Japanese who delighted in Chinese literature and poetry made special effort to cultivate the friendship of well-educated Formosans, sharing with them the pleasures of poetry and wine at festivals, garden parties, and parties arranged to watch the rising of the moon. Quite consciously they attempted to bridge the social gap between the new rulers and the ruled, and were outspoken advocates of total assimilation of the island people to the Japanese nation, at all levels. Their campaign was strengthened, inadvertently, when thousands of Formosan expatriates began to drift back to Formosa from China, men who had elected to leave the island during the grace period, 1895–1897, but had found it difficult or impossible to adjust to continental life. Some had been unable to establish unquestioned ties with clans and families in ancestral Fukien villages and so remained outsiders and strangers. Others were unable to compete economically in the impoverished coastal districts, and not a few realized that prospects for the future under a progressive Japanese government might be better than life under the failing Chinese imperial administration. As of June 4, 1900, a census in Formosa showed that 2,650,000 Formosan Chinese had opted to remain in Formosa (or to return to it) when they were given the choice.

A substantial number of the old Formosan gentry nevertheless declined to cooperate actively with the new administration. A few professed to be moved by the old "Ming loyalist" tradition, implanted by the refugee courtiers and scholars who had crossed to Formosa with Koxinga so long ago. One scholarly family, for example, boasted that through seven generations no member had sat for the official literary examinations under the Manchu dynasty, thus demonstrating their loyalty to the Ming. Many others, making no pretense of Ming loyalty, simply withdrew from public activity, adopting a wait-and-see attitude toward the new government. To cope with the loyalist issue, the Japanese revived the Koxinga tradition, stressing the facts that Koxinga's mother was a Japanese and that he himself had been born in Japan.

Prominent Formosans who came forward to work with the Japanese in the new era were well rewarded. For example, the young man from Lo-kang (Rokko) named Ku Hsien-yung, who had so boldly summoned the Japanese to the relief of Taipei in 1895, soon became wealthy and influential through cooperation with the government. He was himself a figure of great presence and ability. In 1899 the administration placed him in charge of the salt gabelle with authority to nominate local salt monopoly office managers throughout the island. By tradition in China the management of the salt levies had always been a source of great wealth and so it proved here. Another Formosan to profit enormously through cooperation was Yen Yün-nien (Gan Unnen) of Zuiho, near Keelung, whose modest mining interests grew steadily until he became the employer of some ten thousand workers and one of the wealthiest men in the island.

A number of old landholding families and merchants began to invest heavily in overseas trading companies and in banks. Ch'en Wen-yüan of Takao opened branch trading offices in Yokohama and Kobe in 1901, and in 1903 helped establish the Taiwan Farmers and Merchants Bank. On returning from China one member of the Muho Lin clan began to invest in a number of economic development projects, including banks, sugar companies and the like. His cousin, heir to the senior branch of the Muho Lin family, remained in Amoy for some years longer, but now acted as an agent of the Formosan family rather than as a disgruntled "exile" interested in maintaining ties with the Manchu government. The aging Lin Wei-yüan of the Pankyo Lin clan, living in self-imposed exile, arranged to meet with Gotō Shimpei in Fukien in 1900. Having a change of heart, he arranged the recovery of important family properties that had been confiscated in 1895, and soon returned to Formosa to direct clan cooperation with the Japanese.

Many of these leading Formosans now took the position that Peking had deserted Formosa by ceding it to Japan without consulting the Formosan interest and therefore that China had forfeited Formosan allegiance. Ku Hsien-yung, for example, publicly urged Formosans to accept Japanese rule and give full cooperation in every field. Others confined themselves to writing poems that reflected the bitterness generated by China's abrupt and unfeeling desertion of the Formosan people. All thoughtful men could see that although taxes had risen and were now rigorously collected, there were unquestionable benefits. Workers' wages had doubled, farmers were being paid twice as much as in the past, and every family benefited by the rising standard in public health. The decline in death rates and in the incidence of cholera, plague, smallpox, and malaria could not be denied.

By the close of the Kodama-Gotō era (1906), the Japanese community itself had developed a marked and permanent colonial character. A great majority of the newcomers had settled in or near Taipei, and like their counterparts in British Malaya, French Southeast Asia, and the American Philippines, they quickly developed a master-race complex. Even the least competent Japanese officer or government employee enjoyed special advantages as he went about his daily assignments. Local vested interests—Formosan interests—were brushed aside if they stood in the way of Japanese projects. For example, if a Japanese engineer wished to drive a road through a town he did so with little reference to Formosan rights, interests, or ownership; walls were torn down, houses razed, cemeteries moved, and land expropriated as the engineering plans required. There was little or no compensation offered in many cases, and there was no provision for redress.

Gotō proposed to convert shabby Taipei into a model colonial capital, a city to rival Western colonial outposts in Asia—Hongkong, Manila, Singapore, or Saigon. This would advertise in brick and stone, boulevards and parks, the advantages of modern Japanese leadership in Asia. The Civil Administrator dreamed of a viceregal headquarters, a base from which imperial authority would someday extend throughout the Pacific islands, Southeast Asia and the Indies. The great size and solidity of the administration buildings exceeded any local need and left no doubt that the Japanese had come to stay.

The Temporary City Improvement Committee established in 1898 soon became a permanent planning bureau.* The Committee was set up after a great midsummer typhoon caused the Tamsui River to rise twenty-two feet within a few hours, and winds and torrential rains caused immense distress. More than three thousand buildings were destroyed or heavily damaged. Rain-soaked mud-brick walls collapsed under the weight of tiled roofs, and hundreds of lighter buildings were blown or washed away as the river waters spread eastward through the town. Within the next four years no fewer than twenty-four disastrous typhoons struck Formosa. After each storm (and after serious earthquakes) the government took the opportunity to enforce new building codes and to clear the way for much solid new construction. Concurrently the Forestry Bureau, under Nitobe's direction, began an elaborate reforestation program in the hills, designed to check soil erosion and to restore the woodland cover stripped from the watershed in the eighteenth and nineteenth centuries.

A first master plan for Taipei provided for a population of 150,000. This was then revised to anticipate the needs of 600,000. Remembering the great boulevards of Paris and Berlin, Kodama, Gotō, and Nitobe tore down Liu Ming-ch'üan's heavy city walls, to create a great rectangle enclosing parks, an administrative district, an official residential area, and a section given over to private Japanese commercial interests. This area,

---

* This agency, housed in temporary quarters, continued to work intensively between August 15 and October 23, 1945, preparing blueprints for the reconstruction or rehabilitation of Formosa's war-damaged cities and towns.

the site of the old Chinese city, came to be known as the *jō-nai* ("within the castle enclosure"). The old city gates were preserved as decorative monuments and made the focal points for wide, radial tree-shaded boulevards and avenues leading out to the countryside. (See Figure 2)

The official residence for the Governor-General, a massive building set in spacious lawns and gardens, was designed in viceregal proportions to emphasize the importance of the Governor's person and office. A much more modest red-brick Victorian dwelling nearby provided an official residence for the Civil Administrators. These and the parks and plazas of the jō-nai were arranged to provide a setting for the towering Government-General Building, projected by Gotō but not completed until 1918.* The ponderous "Prussian mansard" style of many official buildings reflected Dr. Gotō's taste in Western architecture and his distant student days in Berlin.

Following ancient Sino-Japanese traditions a number of guardian shrines and temples were established in the northern suburbs. The Taiwan Grand Shrine was erected on a commanding site overlooking the Keelung and Tamsui rivers and the city. Here the government housed symbols of Shintō deities said to be special guardians of the colony, chief among them the spirit of Imperial Prince Kitashirakawa-no-Miya who had died of dysentery and malaria on the march to Tainan in 1895. On the banks of the Keelung River nearby stood one of Formosa's most revered temples, the Kiem-tan-ssu (Kentanji). Also in the northern quarter stood a beautiful new Zen temple, patronized unofficially by Governor-General Kodama, and an elaborate Confucian temple founded by leading Formosan

---

* Much of the building was gutted by fire in 1945. The Civil Administrator's residence and the massive Railway Hotel nearby were destroyed. On fleeing to Formosa in 1949 Generalissimo Chiang Kai-shek rehabilitated the Government-General Building and used the plaza fronting it to stage grand reviews before visiting dignitaries. Dr. Gotō would have smiled, perhaps, when it became the "Temporary Headquarters of the Government of the Republic of China," visited solemnly by the ambassadors and ministers of many barbarian nations. The "classical Roman" building erected in the jō-nai park in 1914 commemorated the Kodama-Gotō administration and quite appropriately housed collections of ethnographic materials and natural history specimens from Southeast Asia and the Indies.

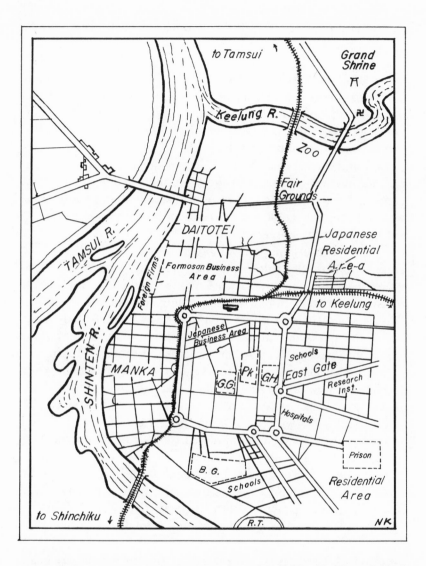

FIGURE 2. *General plan of Taihoku (Taipei) before World War II.* The principal
Government-General buildings (G.G.), Government-General Hospital (G.H.),
other administrative offices, residences, parks (Pk), and the Japanese business
district lay within a rectangle of tree-lined boulevards marking the site of the old
Chinese city walls. Wide plazas, parks, botanical gardens (B.G.), and gardens
around official and private residences, hospitals, schools, shrines, and temples
gave Taipei a spacious air when the population was only 300,000 in a city
planned for 600,000 residents. After 1945 the incoming Chinese used the
riverside race track (R.T.) as an execution ground.

gentry and paid for largely by Ko Kenei (Ku Hsien-yung).

Gradually these northern suburbs became a recreational area as well, marked by playgrounds, a ballpark, athletic fields, and a zoological garden. The suburbs beyond the East Gate (Tō-mon), became a district of schools, research institutes and hospitals, and of the principal Japanese residential settlement. The southern suburbs, between the jō-nai and the Shintiem River, were soon filled with large official residences, clubs, tea-houses, and a racetrack. Not far distant, in the slums of Banka, lay the licensed quarter. To the west, between jō-nai and the Tamsui, lay the principal Formosan residential and commercial area and the enclave of foreign residences, warehouses, offices, and the Twatutia Foreign Club.*

When the urban renewal program was well advanced at Taipei the Planning Bureau began to redevelop other cities and towns, beginning in 1906 with Chia-yi (Kagi). One by one the provincial centers took on something of the character of Taipei—the grid and radial street patterns, the shaded boulevards, the parks and monumental fountains, and everywhere the heavy Prussian mansard architecture of official buildings.

We need not follow in detail the trial-and-error changes in developing administrative divisions and subdivisions until the final pattern was settled. There were five large provinces (shū) in the populated western and northern regions, and two less highly organized and less populated divisions (chō) on the eastern coast. The Pescadores, now known as Bōko-tō, formed a unit, a chō, which remained throughout the Japanese period essentially a naval preserve dominated by the Makung Naval Base. These five provinces and three districts were subdivided into fifty-five counties (gun) embracing a total of 273 town and

---

* We may anticipate here to note that under Japanese restraint, the violent traditional feuding between the old villages of Twatutia and Banka simmered down, becoming little more than "chamber of commerce" rivalry, juvenile gang conflicts, and teenage schoolground quarrels. The two suburbs were absorbed administratively by Taipei City in 1921. The American consular offices and residence were removed to small rented quarters on the boulevard leading out to the Grand Shrine. A number of large nineteenth-century foreign residences became tenements, among them the old German Consulate, which in 1938 housed one Formosan extended family said to number some two hundred members.

village units. Each province (shū and chō) had a principal town for administrative headquarters and each county had a focal point—a village or market town—to serve as the local police headquarters and economic base for the territorial subdivision. Great effort was made to draw the administrative boundary lines along ridge crests or other topographical features enclosing stream drainage basins, thus forming "natural" economic and policing units.

Dr. Gotō gave close attention to problems of administration in the high forest country. Many Japanese shared the Chinese view that the headhunters were beyond reach of civilization and could not be made over into law-abiding imperial subjects. They urged the Civil Administrator to create a permanent reservation in which the aborigines could be confined until at last they slowly died away. Gotō disagreed. He asked the American consuls to keep him supplied with all official American publications concerning the American Indians. Senior police officials were sent off to visit American Indian reservations in the United States and the Bureau of Indian Affairs at Washington, D.C. Leading Japanese anthropologists were summoned to study the problem. After five prolonged and perilous field trips the eminent Dr. Torii Ryūzō and his associates published illustrated notes (in French and in Japanese) describing the languages, physical characteristics, and customs of nine major tribal divisions, with many subgroups.

On the basis of these studies Gotō projected a long-range program in which he proposed to restrict "raw" or untamed aborigines to a temporary reservation and to begin a program of civilizing education for young aboriginal leaders in the rising generation. He drew a line encircling the interior high country—some 7,407 square miles, or more than one-half Formosa's total area. To this he assigned a special police force and established a permit system controlling passage into and out of the reservation. He proposed to reduce this special area by gradually shortening the boundary as border aborigines became civilized enough to be admitted to unrestricted association with Formosa's low-country inhabitants. He wanted to keep interference with the hill people at a minimum until they could be considered ordinary subjects of the Emperor. The census of 1905 showed a total aborigine population of 113,163, living in 723 villages, each ranging from three to more than three hundred household units.

All land within the unsurveyed interior—the Special Aborigine District—was declared to be State property. Gotō believed, correctly, that the lowlands must be brought under full control before much could be done for the mountain people. He founded five schools along the East Coast and projected forty more to be set up, one by one, when it became practicable to do so at appropriate locations. The eight thousand Ami tribesmen along the southeastern coast (the Taitung area) were easily persuaded to cooperate with the new administration. They were not headhunters but sedentary farmers who retained traces of seventeenth-century Dutch influence and of fairly close relationship with the southern Ryukyu Islands. The Chinese had not ventured into the Taitung region until the 1870s, and the Japanese found only some twelve hundred settled among the Ami people in 1895. Soon a Japanese administrative headquarters, a governing staff of thirty members, a garrison of three hundred soldiers, and a settlement of about four hundred fifty Japanese (including teachers) had come in. Ami chieftains of seventy-four villages nearby agreed to maintain order and keep the peace in return for payment of a monthly fee. Coming to an understanding with the wilder mountain people—especially the Atayal and Bunun tribes of the central and northern high ranges—proved far more difficult. James Davidson had joined the exploring party (sent off to Botel Tobago in 1896) whose reports subsequently persuaded Gotō to leave the primitive Yami tribesmen undisturbed until more progress had been made in developing the controls on Formosa proper.

PROBLEMS OF PUBLIC HEALTH AND HYGIENE

The fearful military casualty lists of 1895 lent special importance to Dr. Gotō's program for port quarantine controls, public health measures, and the organization of sanitation and medical services. If the Japanese were to hold on in Formosa and demonstrate a capacity to lead in Asia, there had to be spectacular change in all aspects of public health administration and public hygiene. Since Dr. Gotō's long-range program

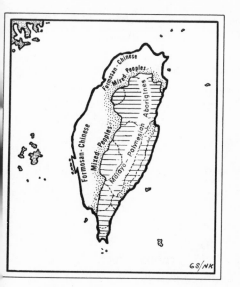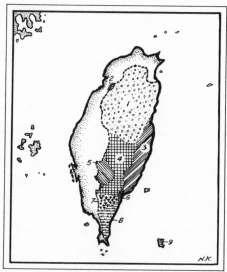

FIGURE 3. *Formosa's ethnic frontiers in the late nineteenth century. Left,* Aboriginal and Chinese settlement areas. *Right,* Principal tribal divisions among the aborigines: *1,* Tayal (Atayal); *2,* Saiset; *3,* Ami; *4,* Bunun; *5,* Tsuou; *6,* Pyuma; *7,* Tsalisen; *8,* Paiwan; *9,* Yami. (From Torii Ryūzō's "The Ethnological Map of Formosa" in *Report on the Control of the Aborigines,* 1911.)

formed the pattern for most major developments throughout the Japanese half-century, we will find it useful here to anticipate and to summarize the record down to the eve of the Pacific War.

Gotō began by shifting responsibility for public health and hygiene from Army Headquarters to a new Sanitation Office established within the Bureau of Police Affairs. This was reasonable enough under the circumstances prevailing in 1899, for the Formosans en masse had yet to be convinced of the value and importance of even the most elementary public health measures. There was no choice but total compliance with regulations if bubonic plague, cholera, and smallpox were to be brought under control.

The enforcement of unprecedented rules therefore meant police intrusion upon private property and an irritating disruption of many traditional Formosan-Chinese customs. A stream of orders poured forth from police stations in every town and village. The cumulative effect was soon apparent, and Gotō's successors had statistical evidence that Formosa had ceased to be a notorious "pesthole of the East" and was moving to second place in Asia—after Japan proper—in matters of general health and hygiene. Bubonic plague ceased to be a problem, cholera became rare, and smallpox was drastically reduced by house-to-house inoculation campaigns. Dysentery and malaria remained stubborn enemies long after Dr. Gotō left the island, nevertheless under his administration a beginning was made in curbing them.*

A prime difficulty lay in the Japanese failure to explain clearly the purpose of many irritating directives; often the ordinary policeman himself did not understand the long-range purpose of orders he was called upon to enforce. The government engaged in a massive campaign against rats, contaminated water supplies, and unsanitary household arrangements. Special problems included the ancient Chinese custom of keeping encoffined bodies in the principal room of the house—sometimes for long periods—until soothsayers appointed an appropriate day and place for burial.

The ordinary policeman often mistook a state of cleanliness for a condition of sanitation and was satisfied with appearances. Nevertheless the cumulative effect of Gotō's intensive clean-up program was soon reflected in the annual statistical reports. Compulsory semiannual housecleaning under police supervision took place in every town and village—vastly irritating and inconvenient to the Formosan householder. Community organizations, under police supervision, were compelled to maintain a reasonable state of cleanliness near community water sources—wells and springs—and there was an annual increase in the number of artesian wells in public service. On the eve of the China War (1936) no fewer than 129 towns and villages had municipal water systems, and the majority of small hamlets had

* Bubonic plague, rare by 1911, had disappeared by 1917, not to return as a public menace until 1946, after the advent of the Nationalist Chinese. A cholera epidemic took 4,300 lives in 1919–1920 but then did not reappear until a mild outbreak took six lives in 1932, when traffic with Shanghai greatly increased during the Japanese attack on that city. A few cases appeared among troops returning from China during the Second Sino-Japanese War (1937–1941) but no public threat occurred until an epidemic in 1946 took 1,400 lives. For the political consequences, see Kerr, *Formosa Betrayed*, pp. 174–183, "The Break-up of Public Health and Welfare Services."

at least conduits and public taps delivering water conveniently from protected sources. The larger cities established sewage treatment plants and all cities and towns were serviced by regular night-soil and garbage-collecting agencies maintained at the public expense. That nothing comparable could be found in Fukien (or in any other province of China) was a fact well known in Formosa.

Dr. Gotō inaugurated the public hospital and medical services in 1898 by constructing a large Government-General Hospital within the jō-nai and a Medical College and Red Cross Hospital nearby, just outside the East Gate. Soon similar but smaller hospitals were established at the provincial capitals and, with a very small token grant of Imperial Household funds in 1899, he founded the first of a series of charity hospitals. Several of the major government bureaus built hospitals for the use of their own personnel—the Railway Bureau Hospital, for example—and by the end of the Japanese era the Government-General was supporting fifteen hospitals in and near Taipei, including institutions for mental patients, the victims of leprosy, tuberculosis, and other major infectious diseases.

One by one private institutions began to appear, and be fitted into Dr. Gotō's overall program for Formosan medical services. The majority were small, poorly equipped, and soon technically obsolete. Doctors long resident on Formosa, far from the mainstreams of medical development, found it difficult to keep abreast of professional colleagues in Japan proper, and had only the most indirect access to the technical developments in medicine and surgery taking place in the United States, Canada, and Europe. Some official establishments, paralyzed by an ultraconservative bureaucracy, changed very little after the dynamic Dr. Gotō left the scene.* Nevertheless, from his later posts in Government, Gotō watched the expansion of medical services on Formosa with justifiable pride, and in 1936, seven years after his death and on the eve of the China War, the Formosan people were served by no fewer than 270 hospitals and clinics, large and small.

* In 1937 I noted that nurses attached to the Taihoku Penitentiary (founded by Gotō in 1899) were continuing to wear high-button shoes, mutton-chop sleeves, and "Salvation Army" bonnets introduced as the regulation costume in Gotō's day.

The Civil Administrator proposed to train doctors, medical technicians, and pharmacists for local service, and in time, to promote research.

The *Medical College Journal*, published continuously from 1898 until 1945, reflects growing Japanese concern with the medical and health problems of tropical Southeast Asia. Physicians and surgeons graduated from the full course established in the Faculty of Medicine in 1934 (or from recognized schools in Japan and abroad) were licensed to practice in Formosa as "Class A" doctors. Men who completed a special medical short course were certified as "Class B" doctors, subject to periodic reexamination and refresher courses. Formosans who wished to practice traditional Chinese medicine—the application of herbs, needles, cautery, and plasters—were licensed as "Class C" professionals. It was Gotō's idea that in due course Classes B and C would be replaced everywhere by fully qualified Class A men.

The Medical College never lacked applicants; doctors in all classes enjoyed high prestige and an assured high income. They preferred, too often, to settle in or near large towns. To counter this the Government devised a scholarship program for students who would agree to accept, upon graduation, a subsidized assignment to an outlying community for a specified period. There the young doctor was at liberty to carry on a private practice but under obligation to assist the local police in developing public hygiene projects and to attend the needs of public charity clinics if called upon to do so.

LANGUAGE PROBLEMS AND LAND REFORM

The Civil Administration desperately needed translators and interpreters—a practical matter of having instructions understood—and many Japanese were convinced that Formosans could not be made over into "true Japanese" until all spoke the national language. The substitution of one language for another in a population of 2,650,000 was a formidable task.

By 1902 the language-training program was being pushed vigorously at three normal schools, four language institutes, and one hundred thirty primary schools. Gotō prepared to open middle schools, higher technical schools, commercial schools, and a university designed to absorb the Medical College and to provide a research center for colonial administrative problems far beyond Formosan shores. The majority of these higher schools were not established before he left the island, but he saw them all set up before his death in Tokyo, in 1929.

The educational pabulum was meager in the primary schools—a little reading, writing, and arithmetic, a smattering of history and geography, and a great emphasis upon "ethics," or how to behave as a loyal and obedient Japanese subject and as a filial child. But even this slight content was enough to make young Formosans aware of a world beyond the island and beyond China and Japan. Of greater importance, common schooling gradually created a sense of *Formosan* identity or common interest. That is to say, children of Amoy, Cantonese, and Hakka descent, speaking separate dialects at home, and living hitherto in separate community groups, now mingled in classrooms and playgrounds, and were subjected to a common routine and discipline. Local dialect barriers and narrow village and clan loyalties began to give way. Children heard parents complain bitterly of Japanese police pressure and severe economic regimentation, but they also heard parents and grandparents tell of the chaotic economic and social conditions they had known under nineteenth-century Chinese administration.

Textbooks used in Formosa were modified versions of texts used throughout Japan proper, providing a fund of myth, folklore, and fact shared henceforth by the Formosan child with his peers throughout the empire. Since many parents expected children also to learn to speak and read Chinese, a bilingual élite began to develop within the Formosan-Chinese population. It was soon discovered that even a superficial knowledge of Japanese words and phrases won preferential treatment by the new administration. It ensured employment, for the demand for interpreters was overwhelming; for example, Dr. Gotō brought eight hundred surveyors from Japan proper to work on topographic mapping projects and sent seven thousand agents into the field to collect census data. Nitobe's many economic research surveys involved scores of field teams, and every Japanese police officer, doctor, and public health technician needed an interpreter in the course of his work. By 1905, when the first great mapping projects were complete and the first full census ready, there were sixty thousand Japanese civil-

85

ians on Formosa, but few had acquired a precise knowledge of Chinese, and comparatively few had bothered to pick up even a useful smattering of the local dialects. It was a Formosan obligation to learn Japanese.

Gotō and Nitobe launched these grand investigative projects from the summit of authority, expected accurate returns, and tolerated no refusal to cooperate; nevertheless, the survey teams met hostility, evasion, and deception at every turn, for the Formosan merchant, farmer, and landholder knew that when his name and his properties had been registered, he would be at the mercy of the new administration, and especially of the tax-collector.

The inaccuracies of nineteenth-century Chinese official records were now revealed in their true dimensions. According to the Chinese land registers surrendered to the Japanese, a total of 867,000 acres were yielding revenue, whereas Gotō's men discovered that the figure should have been 1,866,000 acres. This meant that when the new records were complete, tens of thousands of Formosan landholders were compelled to pay taxes on land never before taxed. This was a source of angry discontent.

After five years of labor and an expenditure of three million yen, it was established that there were more than thirty-nine thousand landed proprietors receiving rents in cash or in kind. Gotō proposed to compel them to accept government bonds in exchange for hereditary rents wherever this could be arranged, and in 1905 the administration began distributing bonds to a value of nearly four million yen. Many families reinvested this new capital in small businesses, banks, and light industries; but many others, selling prematurely, or investing unwisely, soon found themselves impoverished. The total effect was beneficial, however, for there was considerable stimulation of the economy as old economic confusions gave way to a more rational management and use of capital.

A Commission for the Investigation of Laws was set up to explore the legal jungle, the vast confusion of traditional codes and practices that must be brought into conformity with the modern Japanese legal system.* Many nineteenth-century laws

* This legal survey was directed by Dr. Okamatsu Santarō, then twenty-nine years of age, but already Professor of Law in Kyoto Imperial University.

had been based on China's imperial codes, issued at Peking and applied throughout the empire, and many more were local customary laws of Fukien and Kwangtung, brought into Formosa by émigrés. There were, in addition, local codes and usages peculiar to the island; for example, many farmers in the Tainan region held land titles granted in the Dutch and Koxingan periods, and others held later grants and titles. Thousands were cultivating fields cleared and settled beyond the old official limits of Chinese law and registry, and thousands held ill-defined areas of farmland and forest secured through private negotiation with the aborigines. The Chinese magistrates' courts had treated each category of land tenure according to the personal interests, understanding and probity of the mandarin called upon to consider individual cases.

The Land Commission faced an enormous task. Land registry problems were complicated by joint tenures of great variety. Some tracts were held in common by clans having only vague definition, or were controlled by schools, temples, or unregistered brotherhoods with private and secret arrangements for distributing produce and income. Many claimants enjoyed only fractional or residual rights to income from land registered in the name of the family, clan, or village. Untangling and defining precise claims stirred petty local controversies to white heat and revived long-dormant feuds.

At last the Japanese grew impatient and set terminal dates for complicated litigation. If a claimant were unable to produce satisfactory proof of ownership within a prescribed time, confiscation followed and the disputed land was put up for sale. Such Draconian measures meant that some farmers lost lands cleared and first cultivated by seventeenth- and eighteenth-century ancestors. Many found themselves with too little land to sustain a large patriarchal household. They were compelled therefore to lease or sell these insufficient plots to more fortunate neighbors, to rich landholders, or to the Japanese corporations just then beginning to form large sugar estates. Thousands of farmers were compelled to become tenants or to become hired hands in a floating labor market. No single issue inflamed Formosan antagonism toward the new administration

---

Like Nitobe and Gotō, Okamatsu represented the extraordinarily talented "young revolutionists" of the Meiji era.

as did these problems of land registration and reform, an irritation felt in every district, and only gradually offset somewhat by the slowly rising general standard of living.

A REVOLUTION IN PUBLIC SERVICES

Kodama needed a developed communications network to serve military needs, Gotō required transport and telecommunications to support police administration, and Nitobe needed roads and railroads to speed the flow of produce to ports and markets. As in Japan proper, railroads came first, beginning with a light push-car system known as the *daisha* ("Tai [wan] car"), developed for military use and adapted to general transport. Soon a network of feeder lines converged on the main railroad, and over the daisha tracks farmers, foresters, and miners were soon moving vegetables, fruits, grains, coal, charcoal, and firewood to market in unprecedented quantities and with unprecedented speed, and bringing back into the hinterland and foothills cheap manufactured goods and foodstuffs hitherto rare or unobtainable in distant hamlets.

By 1905 Liu Ming-ch'üan's meandering railway had been realigned, rebuilt, and extended; the sixty miles of track had been extended to three hundred, and work was moving forward rapidly on an additional seven hundred, completed soon after Gotō's departure. Although the National Treasury (Tokyo) subsidized construction of the main line and supplied equipment, a considerable burden fell upon Formosans living along the right-of-way, who were compelled to yield land for nominal sums or for no more than a useless medal or an inscribed cup honoring the "loyal subject" making a "gift" to the Emperor. Men between the ages of eighteen and forty-eight were conscripted for local labor as the lines advanced, section by section, and village organizations along the way were called upon for general maintenance work when the lines were finished. These "volunteer" contributions in the aggregate cut construction costs to a significant degree. Compulsory sacrifice of land, labor, and matériel provoked resentment, nevertheless the public soon began to appreciate the new opportunity to move freely about the island and the ease with which crops and handicrafts could be moved safely to larger, better markets.

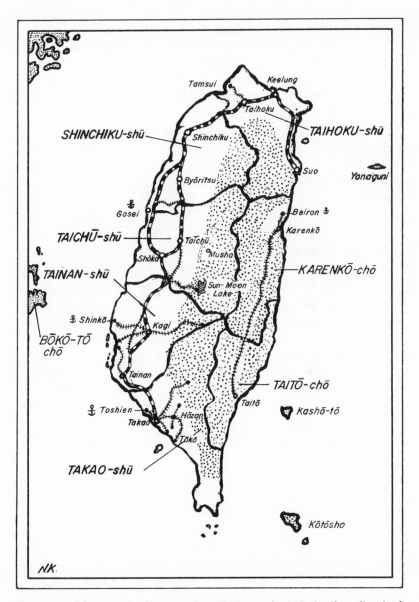

FIGURE 4. *Administrative divisions (-shu and -chō), and principal railway lines in the Japanese Era.*

—————————— Administrative boundaries
– – – – – – – Main lines
╫╫╫╫╫╫╫╫ Principal feeder lines

Exports now went to Japan or were shipped directly to Western markets. Japanese shipping companies developed round-the-island as well as round-the-world services. Except in the tea business, the foreign middleman rapidly became an obsolete institution. One by one all but the largest foreign firms closed down their Formosan offices. Those who remained— Britain's Jardine Matheson Company always the leader among them—handled export-import shipping, but now only a modest share of the total traffic.

The introduction of a stabilized, standard monetary system was a major advance in the general economic revolution, creating for the first time a reliable framework for the island economy as a whole. The Bank of Taiwan, founded in 1899, undertook the task of bringing order out of the nineteenth-century chaos. Under the Chinese administration all transactions not made on a barter basis had had to be carried on with strings of pierced copper coins of great diversity and unstable value, with Mexican or South American silver dollars, or with the Spanish dollars of Charles IV. The Japanese found that these heavy coins were often shaved and were sometimes beaten smooth to enable local shopkeepers to imprint private seals or shop marks on individual pieces. By the end of the first decade of Japanese rule (1905) the Government-General had succeeded fairly well in introducing the Japanese decimal coinage and paper currency throughout Formosa and in making its use obligatory.

New opportunities for employment presented themselves everywhere; for example, the new Central Meteorological Observatory at Taipei promptly set about solving that nagging nineteenth-century international problem of coastal lighting by increasing the number of lights and beacons from a total of six (in 1895) to thirty-two, adding ten branch observatories and one hundred forty-seven outlying reporting stations. From 1898 until 1941 the records of the Taipei Central Observatory were distributed regularly to other observatories throughout the world.

Taipei City led in all things during this era of headlong change. Modern services were designed first to satisfy Japanese interest and convenience, but as the new technology spread beyond the capital—the concentrated Japanese community—

Formosans, too, became dependent upon the public services and came to expect them as of right.

In 1903 the first large hydroelectric generators went into service in the hills east of the city, at the headwaters of the Shintiem River, marking a giant step forward into the twentieth century. With this new source of power small light industries began to develop in and near Taipei—a glass factory, for example, and a paper mill—and it became possible to add heavy-duty, electrically operated equipment and new machine shops to the Keelung Harbor development complex. By 1905 some fourteen hundred miles of telegraph wire were in use and more than one hundred post offices had been opened for public business.

DR. NITOBE'S LONG-RANGE ECONOMIC
DEVELOPMENT PROGRAM

Behind all this driving activity lay Dr. Nitobe's long-range program for the development of agriculture and forestry, water resources, and power, a program requiring total regimentation. He saw rice as the essential "Formosan crop" (produced principally in the wet northern region), and sugar as the great "profit crop"—the Japanese crop—produced in the warmer, drier southwest. As Japan's own living standards rose steadily, the demand for sugar would increase, and by pushing production in the colony Tokyo could meet the nation's total sugar requirement, thus saving foreign exchange.

Nitobe's agricultural plans required an elaborate organization of laboratories, field stations, and experimental farms concerned with rice and sugar; with the development of improved breeds of poultry, pigs, and cattle; with tea, vegetables, vegetable fibers, and fruits; and with tests of fertilizers and irrigation techniques as well. A farm agent system was established to ensure that every farmer in every district would understand instructions and would be encouraged (or compelled) to push for ever higher production levels.

The results were spectacular, and to achieve them the government brought unremitting pressure to bear upon the individual. There was often stubborn resistance, and from time to time there were violent protests. To provide a frame of reference for these protests—noted in subsequent chapters—we must here anticipate and summarize the ultimate gains in the overall economy.

Eighteen years after Nitobe left Formosa he was gratified to learn that his research stations had developed a new strain of rice and that total production was rising at an astonishing rate. On the eve of the second war with China the island was producing some fifty million bushels of grain, or more than twice the quantity required to feed the Formosan population of that day at a high consumption level. The annual per capita consumption of meats (principally pork), vegetables, and fruit placed Formosa beyond comparison with any provincial area in China, and well ahead of the poorer northern prefectures of Japan proper. Farmers appreciated the value of the new *hōrai* type rice and learned the utility of chemical fertilizers that made such high yields possible. The farm household preferred to plant rice, a crop harvested twice annually, for the grain could be eaten at home, sold for cash, or stored against a rise in market prices.

Sugarcane, by contrast, was difficult to grow profitably on small plots of land, required fifteen to eighteen months to mature, and then had to be cut and milled at once. It could not be stored nor consumed at home, and the cane farmer was obliged to sell to the nearest mill at prices set by businessmen far away in Osaka and Tokyo. In 1896 the total sugar yield was estimated to be about forty thousand tons per year, produced by an inferior cane and by extraction methods little changed since the days of the seventeenth-century Dutch administration. The first "sugar plan" was ready in 1897, and one modern mill began operations in 1902, but because of great unrest in the countryside it was necessary to build the factory within high walls, surrounded by gates, gunports, and a permanent guard. Blockhouses and stockades were maintained here and there in the nearby fields, and farmers who ventured to collaborate with the Japanese at the mill were liable to rough reprisals at the hands of dissenting neighbors.

But within three years conditions became more settled and the general economy improved. As the utility of modern techniques was demonstrated, and high profits began to be advertised widely in Japan proper, corporations with great political influence at Tokyo and Taipei began to influence and distort the Nitobe program. Beginning about 1905—the year after Dr. Nitobe left the island—the local civil administration became in large measure an ill-disguised agency of the great metropolitan sugar interests. Annual production figures, rising through four decades from forty thousand to one million four hundred thousand tons, reflect the magnitude and success of Nitobe's work. His program was modified from time to time after his departure, but even today (1974) the sugar industry owes much to Nitobe's vision and comprehension of Formosa's total agricultural potential.

Such economic growth could be achieved only through total mobilization of the agricultural population. The chief agencies for this were an elaborate irrigation system and an organization of "agricultural associations," both state controlled. By constructing and manipulating a vast irrigation network in the Chia-yi (Kagi) and Tainan areas—known as the Kanan system—the government controlled the water supply upon which more than three hundred thousand farm families were obliged to depend. The associations to which the farmer was required to belong guided and coerced him not only in the Kanan Irrigation District but elsewhere throughout the island. By "adjusting" the water supply over vast areas, Taipei secured the quantitative balance and rotation of crops it thought desirable, and by controlling the associations, it controlled the distribution of essential supplies of fertilizer, manipulated credit sources open to the farmer, and influenced marketing. The Formosan farmer ceased to be a free agent, becoming instead a small cog in a vast machine, obliged to turn at the speed and in the direction dictated by the government.

Kodama, Gotō, and Nitobe undoubtedly set Formosa on the road to an unprecedented prosperity. Although it was obvious from the beginning that a disproportionate share of the profit went off to Japan proper, every Formosan shared to some degree in the rising living standards: roads, railroads, telegraph lines, post offices, schools, hospitals, public welfare agencies, banks, credit and savings institutions were all part of the new fabric of twentieth-century Formosan life.*

* After leaving the Bureau of Industry in 1904, Nitobe returned often to Formosa, maintaining a lifelong interest in it. He became, in turn, Professor of Economics at the Kyoto Imperial University, President of the prestigious

First Higher School (Tokyo), professor at Tokyo Imperial University, Member of the House of Peers, and from 1920 to 1927 Vice Director of the General Affairs Bureau of the League of Nations, where he was said to have been sometimes called "the conscience of Geneva." In 1920 he visited the United States with Gotō Shimpei. He died at Vancouver, B.C., in 1933, where a memorial park has been established in his honor.

6. General Sakuma's Decade
(1906-1915)

$\mathcal{I}$N APRIL 1905 (two months after publication of the alleged Kodama Report in Paris) Franco-Japanese relations were again irritated when France permitted Russia's Baltic Fleet to refuel at Camranh Bay (now Danang, Vietnam). Paris shrugged off Tokyo's strong diplomatic protest of this "unfriendly act," and the Czar's fleet proceeded on its way toward Japan. One month later it lay at the bottom of the sea. The Tsushima Strait victory and the defeat of Russia's armies at Mukden meant that Japan had settled one-third—the Russian third—of an old score. Recovery of the Liaotung Peninsula (taken from Japan by the Triple Intervention) was now made possible. Russia's Manchurian railways passed into Japanese hands as well, and the way was cleared for the final annexation of Korea. Japan had a new frontier, and for the next thirty years the "continental expansionists" were occupied with military and political adventure in northeastern Asia.

As if to signal this new direction of prime national interest, General Kodama was relieved of his Taipei appointment on April 11, 1906, created a Viscount, and made Chief of General Staff at Tokyo. On November 13 Dr. Gotō, too, was recalled, made a Baron, and appointed first president of the newly established South Manchuria Railway Company.* This was the

* Viscount Kodama died within the year and was promoted, posthumously, to the rank of Count. Baron Gotō later became Minister of Home Af-

95

Army's powerful "front" organization, founded to develop a great military-industrial complex in Manchuria. The continental expansionists had won the day at Tokyo and called upon the talented, experienced, and ruthless Gotō to direct an economic revolution in the new territory. Henceforth, from a military point of view, the occupation of Formosa was a holding operation for two decades, an area of economic rather than of military interest.

To replace Kodama Tokyo sent down an aging general, Sakuma Samata, rewarding him after forty years of army service.* He was essentially a military policeman, experienced in putting down rebels at home, governing occupied territory in China and policing the national capital during the recent war with Russia. He was ill prepared to administer this complex new island economy.

Sakuma's senior associates, newcomers at Taipei, soon demonstrated that they still considered Formosa an alien war prize. Immense new industrial fortunes had been generated by the Russo-Japanese war boom, and Japan was moving into a postwar era of exceptional political and administrative corruption. Money poured into political party organizations to buy favors for the zaibatsu (the great industrial combines) and into the private accounts of bureaucrats well placed to give or withhold favors. General Sakuma's relations with the senior professional bureaucracy, the political parties and the zaibatsu represented such administrative corruption at its worst.

Long-range engineering projects initiated by Gotō and Nitobe were carried forward steadily, although not always with the same end in view. Formosa was no longer thought of as a "model for Asia" but as a special preserve offering generals, politicians, and industrialists a splendid opportunity to become very rich. War production in 1894–1895 had greatly enhanced

fairs, Foreign Minister, and Director of the Tokyo Rehabilitation and Reconstruction Commission after the great earthquake of 1923. Before his death (in 1929) he became Count Gotō.

* General Count Sakuma Samata (1844–1915), a Yamaguchi clansman, had helped Imperial Restoration forces put down rebels in northern Japan (1868), in Saga (1873), and in Kagoshima (1877). He had accompanied General Saigō Tsugumichi to Formosa in 1874 and had served as Military Governor of Occupied Areas in China (1895). During the Russo-Japanese War he commanded the Tokyo garrison.

the prestige of industrial leaders in Japan, and they had become indispensable in 1904–1905. With victory achieved, they were ready to diversify investments, including heavy investments in Formosan sugar, timber, and mines. Gotō's highly organized system of community controls offered a splendid instrument through which to exploit disciplined labor; and Sakuma's Civil Administrator, working through the Police Bureau and the research institutes, could manipulate the total economic program to the advantage of a few great industrial organizations.

Soon after Kodama and Gotō left the island the major research and planning agencies at Taipei were brought together in one Central Research Institute (*Chūō Kenkyū-jo*), of which the civil administrator became director. Under prevailing circumstances this meant that government laboratories and research agencies became instruments of influential private interests. All branches of the civil administration began to feel the pressure of private influence in and near Governor Sakuma's office.*

Formosa entered the second decade of Japanese rule fairly quietly and in good order. Gotō's large capital investments in transport and communications and in the research agencies were beginning to yield substantial returns. These, reinvested locally, relieved the National Treasury of a heavy annual charge and smothered criticism at Tokyo. Henceforth the national government advanced funds only for major capital developments such as harbor works, railways, and power plants. Local revenues plus unpaid local "volunteer" labor provided more than enough to meet ordinary administrative costs. To dramatize this (and to take to himself credit for Gotō's spectacular achievements) Governor Sakuma in 1906 ostentatiously presented a half million yen to the Imperial House as a "gift from loyal island subjects" and the Sakuma administration. To no

---

* The Chūō Kenkyū-jō, established in 1907 and modified substantially in 1921 and thereafter, embraced these departments and subdivisions: I. Agriculture (seedlings, horticulture, agricultural chemistry, botanical pathology, stockbreeding, and "applied zoology"); II. Technical Industries (organic chemistry, inorganic chemistry, electrochemical industries, and related problems); III. Forestry (all aspects of development, conservation, extraction, processing, and use of forest products); IV. Hygienics (including drugs and pharmaceutical research); V. General Affairs (overall planning and administration of the island economy).

one's great surprise, the Governor was soon thereafter granted new honors and made a Count in the Court hierarchy.

Blind, unorganized Formosan resistance to the Japanese presence was slowly giving way to a grudging acknowledgment of material improvements under Japanese administration. Nevertheless, the Japanese everywhere found themselves an unloved minority, for an appreciation of material benefits did not offset public resentment generated by police regimentation. The gentry especially resented assumptions of superiority that marked the usual Japanese attitude toward colonial second-class subjects.

To the illiterate common people, many natural calamities suffered in Formosa after 1895 were blamed upon the Japanese who had interfered with traditional religious ceremonies and disturbed the *feng-shui* ("wind and water") geomantic patterns with their roads and railroads, dams and ditches, and by relocating tombs and tearing down ancient shrines and temples if they stood in the path of the economic development program. For some years after the Boxer Uprising on the continent, Formosa was troubled by a proliferation of secret cults introduced by displaced Chinese who offered the ignorant countryfolk a mixture of debased Taoist and Buddhist magical practices suffused with strong anti-Japanese sentiment. Many village temples scattered over the Formosan countryside and foothills were the customary gathering places for community elders who had relinquished management of family affairs and were content to spend their days in gossip carried on over pipes and teacups. Under pleasant arbors in these temple courtyards they exchanged bitter comment on the new era, the enforced changes, and official Japanese intrusion upon traditional folkways.

A series of regulations issued in 1907 were designed to curb excessive expenditures associated with birth, death, and marriage rituals, and to suppress some of the grosser Chinese cult ceremonies, and festivals that consumed time, much money, and too many material offerings. Too many families were perpetually in debt, impoverished by an incessant struggle to maintain face in the community. In reducing the number of Chinese festival days, substituting Japanese national holidays in their stead, and introducing the modern (Western) workweek, the Japanese made a noteworthy advance; enforcement at first generated deep resentment, but as the years passed, the rising generation came to appreciate the economic benefit to every household. Taoist and Buddhist priests, magicians, and soothsayers who had thrived on the fees and food offerings associated with the old festivals and ceremonies naturally resented the curtailment, and tended to take the lead in secret cults preoccupied with anti-Japanese thoughts and the discussion of Formosan grievances. Temples and shrines therefore began to take the place of the old bandit headquarters as centers of popular discontent and subversive ideas.

Representatives of a modern evangelical Buddhism came down as missionaries from Japan proper, established private schools and chapels, and began to work among well-educated Formosans as well as among the colonial Japanese settlers. Weekly congregational services, Sunday schools, and enlightened pastoral work began slowly to bring about constructive changes at the larger Formosan-Chinese Buddhist temples and set a new standard for community responsibility among them.

The spread of literacy contributed to rapid social change. In 1910, for example, when the cruel Chinese practice of footbinding for girls was sternly prohibited, a great queue-cutting ceremony for men was held at Tainan to dramatize the break with the past in this most conservative old city. An effort to polish up Koxinga as an exemplary "loyalist" and to stress his half-Japanese ancestry, birth and training came to nothing, however.*

Taipei thought to hasten Japanization by settling agricultural immigrants from Japan proper in outlying districts. This was soon found to be impractical; even farmers who had survived in the most impoverished northern Japanese prefectures were unable to compete successfully with the industrious and skilled Formosan farmer. Cultural prejudice played a part in this failure, for the Japanese who had been at the bottom of the social and economic ladder in the homeland found himself

---

* Admiral Count Kabayama, revisiting Formosa on one occasion noticed the neglected Koxinga Shrine at Tainan, built on Commissioner Shen Paochen's recommendation (1875). He suggested that the Chinese shrine be refurbished, and that both Koxinga *and his Japanese mother* should be officially established in the local pantheon of Shintō guardian deities for the island. This was done.

automatically a privileged person in the colony, and was not easily reconciled to grubbing competition with the Formosans or civilized aborigines who were his neighbors. In the first agricultural resettlement program year (1909) about thirteen hundred persons (250 families) were brought down from northern Japan to settle at Yoshinō Village, newly established back of Hualien (Karenkō) on the eastern coast. The Government advanced money for land, houses, animals, seeds, and tools, asked for no interest on the loans, and demanded no taxes during the first four years of residence. Free medical service, schools, a shrine, a water supply, and a strong police force were provided at State expense, and for the impoverished Japanese immigrants the prospects seemed bright. Three years later a private company secured concessions to establish a similar immigrant plantation settlement not far from Yoshinō, calling it Oshikata-mura, but neither village project flourished.*

OPENING THE MOUNTAIN REGIONS

Governor Sakuma's men were first preoccupied with the profitable sugar industry: developing, adapting, and pushing forward Nitobe's long-range plans. Decisions made at corporation offices in Tokyo and Osaka were translated into policy directives at Taipei, favoring now one company and now another. Intense rivalry meant that, as bribery and collusion became common among senior bureaucrats and military officers charged with colonial administration, integrity of management was destroyed. The entire industry was shaken and public confidence undermined in 1907 when the president of the Taiwan Sugar Corporation—the largest—committed suicide on the eve of sensational disclosures of graft and influence peddling at Tokyo.

At Taipei, Sakuma's administrators continued to make Formosan land, water, and power resources available to friends and clients on a lavish scale, and with ruthless disregard for private Formosan interests—unless the Formosans were prepared to pay heavily for protection. At a word from the Civil

* The Government suspended the Yoshinō experiment in 1917, resuming it—again with little success—in the 1930s. At the onset of the second Sino-Japanese War (1937) there were no more than two thousand Japanese farm families registered throughout Formosa.

Administrator's office at Taipei, local policing agencies harassed small farmers showing reluctance to sell land or to sign contracts binding them to supply sugarcane only to certain mills at prices set by the mill owners.

When experiments in 1907 proved that concrete could be used to great advantage in constructing major irrigation works, the government inaugurated an eighteen-year building program for the central and southern regions, in due course completing a great system of dams and canals distributing water over 1,350,000 acres. Here some three hundred thousand farm families became dependent upon water supplied to them in quantities and at times determined by the needs of the great corporations. Concurrently they were obliged to become dues-paying members of local water-usage guilds and associations devised to recover costs of irrigation ditch construction and water administration. The big companies took the benefit.

By manipulating water supplies the Government imposed a three-crop planting cycle over a vast acreage: each field bore in succession sugarcane, grain, and vegetables, and then lay fallow for a season. Thus the Nitobe Plan in action raised the total output and improved quality, but it reduced the farmer in the sugar regions to a state of helpless dependence upon agencies operating beyond his control.

Good caneland suffered heavily when seasonal typhoons brought floods to the lowland. It was therefore necessary to enlarge Gotō's reforestation scheme and to develop techniques for strengthening riverside embankments. To supply power to the lowland mills, Taipei began to subsidize construction of small thermal generating units, beginning at Chia-yi in 1908. It was soon realized that the roaring mountain streams might be controlled in the high valleys and used to generate cheap power—a long, costly undertaking, but worth the investment. It was estimated that twenty years would be required to complete proper field surveys in the unexplored mountain country, to build dams, install generators, and construct power lines. It meant, too, the taming and training of headhunting tribesmen throughout the watershed area.

Men surrounding the aging General Sakuma were eager to have him abandon Gotō's conservative policies in the mountain territory. Some were impatient to exploit the vast timber reserves in the virgin forests Gotō had declared to be State property, others anticipated discovery of great mineral wealth in the high ranges. There were serious disagreements on policy when influential advisors became impatient to convert public lands to private use and were opposed by more conservative members of government, reluctant to modify or abandon the Gotō-Nitobe program. Powerful factions pulled and tugged behind the scenes and two civil administrators came and went before General Sakuma was joined by a tough, unscrupulous bureaucrat named Uchida Kakichi.

Uchida, then forty-six years of age, came to Taipei in 1911 after occupying key posts in the national administration of communications, shipping, and colonial affairs; he was above all else an expert in managing the exploitation of colonial resources for the benefit of private interests. He had at his command a police force of 3,240 Japanese, with 1,610 Formosan-Chinese assistants and the auxiliary Youth Corps numbering (in 1908) 129,022 officers and men.

Gotō's conservative mountain reservation policies were soon abandoned, State-owned lands were opened to private use, and troublesome considerations of public interest were brushed aside. The State foresters who had been concerned heretofore with erosion control and reforestation in the western foothills, were now called upon to follow military units into the interior in a merciless drive against the aborigines. Sakuma's chief forestry officer predicted that within three years the mountain people would be either civilized or exterminated, and Sakuma and Uchida left no doubt that they preferred extermination.

Uchida, the "colonization specialist," staged a Colonial Exposition in 1911 to celebrate fifteen years of Japanese rule in Formosa and to drum up popular support for the new policies. Important journalists, Diet members, and high government officials were brought down from Tokyo for indoctrination. The Exposition was held at Tainan, the old capital, conveniently near the richest untapped timber reserves. Soon thereafter the Sakuma administration subsidized construction of Asia's largest sawmill, at Chia-yi. From it a narrow-gauge rail line wound up through the mountain spurs to reach the Arisan Forest Station terminal at an elevation of 7,200 feet. This extraordinary line, forty-five miles in length, crossed sixty-five spectacular trestle bridges and passed through seventy-two tunnels. The whole was constructed by forced labor at great cost in human life, a private enterprise enjoying heavy government subsidy and drawing upon the police authority in the recruitment of Formosan Chinese and aboriginal workers.*

In due course the government opened two other great timber areas for private exploitation, each with its lowland sawmill and most modern equipment, its spectacular forest railway, and its well-patrolled cutting area.

A SUBJUGATION CAMPAIGN IN THE HILLS

Forest operations on this scale meant great intrusion upon the aboriginal hunting grounds and resumption of intense border warfare after some fifteen years of comparative peace. The mountain dwellers—principally the Bunun and Atayal people—struck back desperately along the narrow trails used by Japanese foresters, surveyors, engineers, and construction teams. Sakuma's men found it necessary to travel in well-armed groups, and many Japanese stragglers were ambushed along the way.

The Governor—a military policeman who found this defiance intolerable—prepared a five-year "subjugation plan," secured a special appropriation of fifteen million yen (then about seven million U.S. dollars), and sent his army regulars into the hills. From May until October 1911, some four thousand troops drove through the southwestern forests near Arisan. In 1912 these army units moved up through the central ranges, and in the following year began operations in the northeast, thus clear-

* Before 1945 the rail trip to the Arisan Station and the ascent of Mount Niitaka beyond (12,956 feet) had become one of the great tourist adventures in the Empire. Niitakayama ("New High Mountain") exceeds Mount Fuji in altitude by 561 feet. In the nineteenth century Europeans called it Mount Morrison. The Chinese call it Yü-shan, or Jade Mountain. The cryptomeria trees of the Arisan Forest resemble California's *Sequoia sempervirens.* One ancient specimen, 102 feet in circumference at the base, was protected and enshrined by the nature-loving Japanese as symbolic of them all. Arisan cryptomeria supplied the great logs used in construction of impressive Shintō gateways (*torii*) at the principal national shrines, thus providing a mystical link with the ancestral Yamato people who had formed the nation when these trees were saplings, some 2000 years ago, before Japan fell under the influence of continental Chinese culture.

ing the way for private timber interests to develop operations in prime forest areas.

The aborigines put up an extraordinary resistance. They took full advantage of the terrain they knew so well, preferring to strike from ambush in the narrow ravines and dense jungle rather than risk open battle. Sometimes they lured the Japanese into narrow passes and then sent down an avalanche of rocks and loose earth to block the exits, and sometimes they managed to surround isolated units with a ring of forest fire. The Japanese complained particularly of night raids upon sentry posts and small encampments.

Angered by such losses at the hands of tattooed savages who used only knives, bows, spears, and matchlocks, Sakuma permitted and encouraged his men to commit acts of revolting brutality, a campaign of terrorism in which there was no restraint and no pity. In an effort to deny food and shelter to the hidden enemy, his well-armed units burned villages and isolated huts indiscriminately and destroyed garden plots found in the forest clearings. In some areas every man, woman, and child encountered along the way was killed without consideration. Prisoners were treated like animals. In an effort to convince the aborigines that all resistance was hopeless and total submission the only way to survive, villagers were compelled to watch as these latter-day samurai tested their swords and swordsmanship upon trussed-up captives.*

For the "hunting season" of 1913–1914 General Sakuma sent twelve thousand army regulars into the field and, in the first military air action in Formosan history, an airplane was brought in to attempt bombing certain inaccessible villages of the Taruk (Taroko) tribesmen living back of Hualien. Naval vessels cruised offshore, lobbing shells into the high valleys, and it was here that the army tried unsuccessfully to prevent night raids upon Japanese encampments by surrounding them with barriers of wire charged with electricity. This brief and useless experiment gave rise in Japan to the legend that a highly charged "fence" was being constructed to surround the entire

---

* In a secondhand bookshop at Taipei, in 1938, I found a photo-album recording such scenes taken by a participant in a subjugation campaign. Three of the snapshots are reproduced on pages 94–95 of the *Civil Affairs Handbook for Taiwan (Formosa)*, OPNAV 50E-12.

aboriginal territory, and foreign correspondents, intrigued with the idea, soon spread word that Japan had developed an electric-fence barrier "hundreds of miles long." They confused the Hualien experiment with the modification and development of China's old guard-line, known hereafter as the *aiyu-sen*.* The Japanese created a new line by cutting wide swathes through the jungle, dividing critical forest areas into patrol zones and exposing important trails. Blockhouses were spaced along dominant ridges and along cross-country paths, and a code of drumbeats, beacon fires, and gunshot signals enabled government patrols to communicate across the territory of unsubmissive tribesmen.

Starvation and the loss of male leaders at last broke the spirit of resistance in the small mountain hamlets. By 1915, when Sakuma was recalled and Uchida left the island, 550 villages had submitted, but no fewer than 122 still held out, remaining long thereafter fairly secure in the most remote and highest central ranges. The 1915 census estimated the total number of aboriginal villages and house-clusters at 669, containing 22,811 dwellings and a total population of 132,894, of whom a majority were women. Sakuma's campaigns had left a legacy of smoldering hatred throughout the hills.

CONSPIRACIES AND REBELLIONS IN THE LOWLAND

During General Sakuma's term of office—the longest and most corrupt administration of the Japanese half-century— Taipei began to encounter a more sophisticated opposition among lowland Formosans. A new generation of bilingual community leaders had begun to appear among the scores of young men now passing back and forth between the colony and Japan proper. While at school in metropolitan Japan, the Formosans discovered that Sakuma's tough colonial administrators were by no means wholly representative of the Japanese people, and that many prominent Japanese regretted Sakuma's abusive policies. They saw, too, that the common people were also chafing

* On page 9 of her quaint book *Formosa Beachhead*, published in 1953, Geraldine Fitch says that the Japanese kept the aborigines behind 360 miles of barbed wire, some 230 miles of which were electrified. The author (or her informant) may have mistaken cross-country high-voltage transmission lines for "electrically charged barbed wire."

under an authoritarian rule scarcely less restrictive than the administration in Formosa.

Japanese newspapers and magazines were gaining readers in the colony. Young Formosans returning to the island discovered that many Japanese doctors, teachers, technicians, and minor civil servants were quietly critical of General Sakuma's policies and agents. It was in this Sakuma decade therefore that the old blind spirit of angry rebellion through guerrilla warfare began to be transformed into considered appeals to law, and the first thoughts of a local political movement began to take form.

Sakuma's men were openly contemptuous of public opinion and operated well beyond reach of "busybody" Diet members. Nevertheless, the Meiji Constitution provided certain guarantees of elementary rights for all subjects and prescribed remedies in the courts of law if these rights were violated. An incident known as the "Shima case" represents an early, ineffective attempt to appeal to the courts for protection.

On May 1, 1909, eight Formosan gamblers were arrested in a Hakka village southeast of Takao. During the subsequent police interrogations they fell into the hands of an officer named Shima, a sadist who flogged the men until three had died. Thoughtful Formosan leaders persuaded the angry villagers to hire an attorney and to lodge formal charges against Shima. After many months and considerable expense they managed to have him brought into the local court.

This Formosan attempt to challenge police authority in the courts was unprecedented; from Sakuma's point of view it was intolerable. The local judges were compelled to dismiss the case, holding that the "regrettable incident" had occurred while Shima was discharging official duties and that he was therefore not criminally responsible for the consequences.

This decision provoked a reversion to the old spontaneous direct-action traditions of the nineteenth century. Villagers mobbed the police station and the police retaliated with savage action. The campaign to terrorize the local district attracted wide attention in Japan proper, where the opposition press advertised the abusive character of Sakuma's administration and gave liberals at Tokyo a fresh issue with which to embarrass an authoritarian national government.

Soon after this a native of Hsinchu named Lo Fu-hsing (Ra

Fukusei) returned from travels abroad, deeply infected with "dangerous thoughts." * He was convinced that it would be possible to drive the Japanese out of Formosa and to associate Formosans with Sun Yat-sen's "glorious revolution" in China. The Manchu boy-emperor's abdication at Peking on February 12, 1912, spurred Lo to plot local rebellion on Formosa. Sakuma's troops were campaigning in the high mountains when Lo began to recruit a force with which he proposed to seize Taipei. It was a naïve undertaking, for he had no wide base or supporting organization and relied chiefly on disgruntled and turbulent Hakka communities in Hsinchu to carry out his design.

Sakuma's agents soon detected the plot and in December 1912, seized more than five hundred persons, gave them perfunctory trial, executed scores, and sentenced hundreds to imprisonment at hard labor. It was observed at British Singapore that hundreds of Formosan refugees were entering Malaya to escape vindictive police action.

The plot, the police action, and the mass executions were publicized throughout Japan, leading the opposition press again to attack the Government's Formosa policy. Stinging comment in the foreign-language press prompted important Japanese leaders to charge that the Sakuma administration had embarrassed the imperial government before the world. The savagery of police reprisals belied the picture of benevolent imperial leadership Tokyo was so eager to foster among restive Asians in Europe's Asiatic colonies and in the Philippines. Nevertheless, General Sakuma was merely "admonished" and not recalled, demonstrating once again that the Imperial Army was virtually untouchable, conceiving itself to be responsible only to the Emperor as Commander in Chief, admitting no error, and giving no slightest hint of retreat before public criticism of a general's actions in Formosa. Sakuma could not be removed by the civil authorities without concurrent approval by the Army Minister.

COUNT ITAGAKI AND THE "ASSIMILATION SOCIETY"

In the first four years of Japanese rule nine serious uprisings took place, but during the next fifteen years—from 1900

* His life overseas is obscure; some accounts say that he lived in British territory in Southeast Asia, others that he had been working on a sugar plantation in Hawaii.

until 1915—only ten major disturbances occurred. Manifest economic and social gains had moderated Formosan reaction to alien controls. Unorganized, scattered guerrilla activity proved useless; the Formosan outlaw was no match for the highly organized Japanese establishment. Slowly the Formosan gentry began to understand their problem in political terms. Had the Japanese administration met them at least halfway, Formosa could indeed have become a model colony and an advertisement for imperial rule.

But Japanese liberals who advocated generous policies and full assimilation found it rough going after Kodama, Gotō, and Nitobe left the island. Neither the entrenched bureaucracy at Taipei, the military who considered the island a special preserve, nor the privileged colonials who had settled in Formosa as-technicians and managers of mines, forest projects, and great plantations would approve of any move threatening the prerogatives of the "master race" or circumscribing its authority.

There now came into prominence a remarkable Formosan named Lin Hsien-t'ang (Rin Kendō) who throughout the next forty years would remain the most consistent and influential spokesman for the island interest. He had been born in 1881, the son of a great Taichung landholder (Lin Ch'iao-t'ang), and had been an impressionable fourteen years of age when Ch'iu Feng-chia attempted to win autonomy or independence for the island in the days of the short-lived "Republic." In 1902, when Lin was only twenty-one years of age, he had been appointed chief of the Muhong (Muho) District. Visiting Japan proper on one occasion (in 1907), he met the noted Chinese revolutionary Liang Chi-ch'iao, who advised young Lin that it would be useless for the Formosans to look to China in their unhappy confrontation with the Japanese at Taipei. Instead, he counseled, they should attempt to win the sympathetic interest and support of Japanese moderates and liberals. Four years later Liang visited Formosa, at Lin's invitation, and again cautioned moderation and nonviolence in seeking modification of Sakuma's harsh policies. Early in 1913 Lin went to Peking, where he again met Liang and other Chinese leaders and, in midsummer, went on to Tokyo, convinced now that it was useless to look to China for help. In Tokyo he sought out prominent Japanese known for their comparatively liberal views. On this occasion, for the first time, he met the aged Count Itagaki Taisuke, inviting him to visit Formosa for a firsthand look at the unhappy situation.

Itagaki, the founder of the Japanese Liberal Party (the *Jiyū-tō*), was known as an advocate of genuinely representative government and as a severe critic of Prince Itō's Constitution, designed to protect the military establishment by placing it beyond civilian control. Itagaki's egalitarian views, however, were not incompatible with fervent nationalism and a belief that all Asians could unite under Japan's leadership in resistance to Western encroachment.

Reports of the Lo Fu-hsing affair and its bloody aftermath had prompted the old statesman to remind Tokyo that the late Emperor Meiji had promised Formosans full equality under the law and "brotherhood" within the empire. With the support of two Japanese liberals named Nakanishi Ushirō and Satō Gempei, Lin asked Count Itagaki to become patron of a proposed "Assimilation Society" (*Dōka-kai*) and a supporting newspaper. Although in his seventy-seventh year, Itagaki went to Taipei in February 1914, to see for himself how matters stood in the colony.

Governor-General Sakuma considered him a meddling, eccentric old radical, but did not dare deny him permission to enter the colony. This brief visit was crowded with interviews with Formosans and local Japanese. He was assured that thoughtful Formosans appreciated the social and economic benefits of Japanese administration during the preceding nineteen years, and that they wished to become loyal and useful subjects. The Formosans insisted, however, that they must be relieved of unlimited economic exploitation and police pressure. The Governor-General and the Civil Administrator (Uchida) were bitterly criticized.

The old man was housed in a large foreign-style residence adjacent to the Twatutia Foreign Club, and all Formosans who wished to call on him for conversation and advice were made welcome. A young Formosan teacher named Ts'ai Pei-ho (Sai Baika) served as Itagaki's interpreter. Sakuma's police agents kept close watch on them all.

On this first visit the Count agreed to support the Formosan application to form an Assimilation Society, and was listed as honorary president. The permission was granted, and Itagaki promised to attend the founding ceremonies.

In December he returned to Taipei, receiving a tremendous popular welcome. The Governor-General, however, managed to avoid meeting him by arranging to be in Tokyo at that time; the Civil Administrator pointedly refrained from paying the courtesy call that protocol and common civility required, and saw to it that sharp watch was kept on the activities of the enthusiastic Formosans associating themselves with these activities.

On December 20 Count Itagaki addressed more than six hundred enthusiastic Formosans (and a few Japanese) who had assembled for the inaugural ceremonies of the Assimilation Society. He called for a joint Sino-Japanese effort to resist the encroachments of white imperialism and outlined his idea of a suitable program to hasten the assimilation of the Formosan people to Japan proper. Economic and social equality were the themes of the day. Two days later a similar meeting marked inauguration of a Taichung branch of the Dōka-kai, and on December 24 a Tainan branch was established, after which Itagaki left Formosa.

Within the first month the Society enrolled more than three thousand members, but of these only forty-four were Japanese. Sakuma and Uchida reacted vigorously to all this; any movement toward liberalization obviously threatened the Governor-General's sweeping authority, and the Japanese residents throughout the island became alarmed. They numbered only about one hundred twenty thousand, whereas the Formosans numbered above three millions. Political equality was out of the question.

On Itagaki's departure the government, through the newspapers, attacked all Japanese associated with the Assimilation Society, excepting only Count Itagaki. On January 23, 1915, the Governor-General charged the Society with "illegal acts," and on January 26 the police permits were withdrawn and the Society forced to disband. Young Formosan leaders were called in for intensive and threatening interrogation, Ts'ai Pei-ho (Itagaki's interpreter) was dismissed from his teaching post, Lin Hsien-t'ang and his brother were abused in the newspapers and in official speeches, and the two principal Japanese advocates were arrested, tried and convicted of "a fraudulent solicitation of funds." The sentences were heavy. At Tokyo an angry Count Itagaki succeeded in having the sentences suspended, but by then great damage had been done to the ideal of "assimilation."

Frustrated young Formosans were embittered by evidence that so many Japanese colonials supported the governor. Sakuma's bloody campaigns in the hills and the suppression of a new uprising in the lowlands added to the sense of disillusionment. The "assimilation" idea lost its appeal; it seemed no longer either possible nor desirable. What was needed now was recognition that Formosa must occupy a special place within the Empire, achieve Home Rule, and be represented in the national government by Formosans prepared to defend and advance Formosan interests. In this new movement, Lin Hsien-t'ang assumed the leadership.

THE LO CHUN UPRISING AND GENERAL SAKUMA'S RECALL

While Itagaki and Lin encouraged propertied and well-educated young men to promote assimilation with Japan proper, a Chinese fortune-teller and a minor Formosan Chinese village clerk were planning general rebellion in the Hsinchu District.

A Fukienese immigrant named Lo Chun had formed a secret cult and had persuaded many illiterate and superstitious peasants that he possessed magical powers. In time he became acquainted with a disgruntled Formosan who held a small position in the village administration but smarted under discrimination and police pressure. The two began to plot rebellion. Hundreds of Lo's followers were slowly drawn into the scheme, persuaded that at the proper moment the "Holy Man" would invoke a great wind that would sweep the Japanese "dwarfs" out of the island. He promised to supply them all with magical charms that would make them invincible in any conflict.

A small incident—a personal quarrel—roused the ignorant cultists prematurely in two villages southeast of Takao. Fifty-one Japanese were killed by mob action before the authorities reestablished control. Sakuma then sent in his men. Hundreds of Formosans were rounded up to witness the execution of fifty-one Formosan men, women, and children, taken at random from the crowd, and when this formality had been completed, the troops spread out through the countryside to seize and kill "conspirators." No time was lost in asking questions or checking evidence. Later estimates placed the number of Formosans killed at four thousand; men and women were tortured to secure evidence and confessions, the jails everywhere were overcrowded, and the trials were travesties of legal process. Of the 1,413 prisoners taken before the judges, 866 were condemned to death and 500 were sent to prison for long terms at hard labor.

Day after day, a few at a time, the victims were led out to execution. Sakuma was determined to make this an unforgettable lesson. In revulsion, many Japanese protested at Taipei and warned Tokyo that there was now danger of a general rebellion. The metropolitan press spread the story across the nation and opposition political leaders condemned the Government for condoning this barbarous affair.

Japan was just then celebrating the official enthronement of the Taishō emperor; this gave the Government a face-saving pretext for declaring an amnesty as a gesture of "imperial benevolence." Tokyo directed Sakuma to commute death warrants into sentences of life imprisonment, but for ninety-six Formosans the act of clemency came too late.

Sakuma, Uchida, and their colleagues at Taipei believed themselves cheated by such "soft" civilian policy, imposed upon them in the Emperor's name, and keenly felt this loss of face before their subject people. When the nationwide coronation ceremonies had ended, Sakuma's police resumed the search for conspirators, claiming discovery of fresh plots to justify scores of new arrests. Once again the metropolitan press reported a series of executions in the colony and charged that Sakuma and his men were challenging the authority of the Central Government and flouting the new Emperor's will. Put publicly in this light, Tokyo had to act.

The toll of executions in this second period had reached thirty-seven by May 1, 1915, making a grand total of one hundred and thirteen judicial murders in all when Governor-General Sakuma was recalled and the case officially closed.

7. The Home Rule Movement

*G*ENERAL Sakuma's departure in May ended a decade of exploitation such as Formosa was not to see again until after the Surrender in 1945. The Civil Administrator, Uchida, stayed on at Taipei until October 19 in order to supervise a second elaborate exposition. This celebration of Japan's twentieth year of sovereignty became an occasion to advertise island products and investment opportunities throughout Japan, and to convene a conference of leading scientists, industrialists, and economists. They were asked to review past achievements and to assist in modifying and enlarging the basic Gotō-Nitobe economic development program.

Tourists were invited to attend the exposition and see the island. With them came correspondents from the leading metropolitan newspapers. Elaborate exposition festivities could not conceal evidence of Formosan discontent and the correspondents were delighted to publish stories of corruption in the Sakuma administration, to expose police brutality in the lowlands, and the bloody nature of the subjugation campaigns in the hills. Sensational stories appeared in Japan proper throughout the autumn and winter of 1915–1916, intermingled with news of the Great War in Europe, of England's confrontation with disaffected Ireland (the Easter Rebellion), and of German attempts to subvert the Irish people. Japanese journalists were prompted to ask rhetorically if Formosa might not one day become Japan's "Ireland of the East."

A much more substantial question had been raised behind

the scenes at Tokyo at the outbreak of the European war. London and Berlin each sought to enlist Japan's support, the Imperial General Staff inclined to an alliance with Germany—or at least a declared neutrality—whereas civilian leaders urged alignment with England and France, whose parliamentary institutions appealed to them. The Anglo-Japanese Treaty of 1902 had also to be considered and the question was colored by memories of the Triple Intervention. Where lay Japan's maximum advantage?

In great secrecy London offered Tokyo a splendid bargain: if Japan's navy would patrol Britain's lifeline in the Pacific and Indian oceans and on through the Red Sea as far as Suez, Japan would receive in payment all German concessions in China and all German territory in the Pacific, north of the equator. Here at a stroke was opportunity to be avenged for Germany's part in the Triple Intervention while meeting treaty obligations to Great Britain. Possession of Germany's mid-Pacific islands— the Marshalls, the Carolines, and the Marianas—would be an important step toward the Kodama-Gotō goal of a great maritime empire. Tokyo accepted the British offer and sided with the Western Allies.

WOODROW WILSON AND THE HOME RULE MOVEMENT

A first unforeseen consequence of the decision was spectacular industrial growth, soon altering the political balance between the conservative Japanese countryside and the dissatisfied urban proletariat. New factories appeared in all the great cities, pouring out munitions for the Allies and producing immense quantities of cheap consumers' goods to fill worldwide markets no longer being supplied by western Europe. By war's end Japan's shipyards had produced a merchant fleet to operate throughout the world and Japanese salesmen had captured distant markets from which they had no desire to retreat when the armistice came. There were new accumulations of capital available for investment in colonial Formosa.

Within Japan itself there were extremes of wealth and poverty and new alignments of corporate interest meddling in an explosive political situation. New leaders demanded a larger share in the national administration. Thousands of young country people crowded into the great city slums, creating a restless, floating population whose discontent was a new political phenomenon. Politicians—liberal and radical alike—talked much of "human rights" and demanded wider suffrage for the Japanese electorate.

Hundreds of Formosan students in the major Japanese cities heard party leaders debating the suffrage question. They read innumerable Diet speeches condemning or extolling the British, French, and American parliamentary systems, and in this heady atmosphere attentive young men from the colony felt they had discovered sympathetic friends at the capital who could understand their quest for relief from economic exploitation and unchecked police rule.

Meanwhile the Army nominated elderly Andō Sadayoshi to succeed Sakuma without suggesting in any way that the choice had been influenced by public censure of the Governor-General or by criticism of military capacity to direct a civil administration. General Andō had served with distinction at the Battle of Mukden in 1905, but here again nothing in his military career had prepared him for the assignment to Formosa. A mild and indirect concession to public opinion was made in the appointment of a new Civil Administrator, however, for by prevailing standards Dr. Shimomura Hiroshi was a "liberal." He was only forty years of age, had studied abroad (in Belgium), and had served on three noted university faculties (Waseda, Chūo, and Hōsei, in Tokyo). In sending a legal specialist to the colony, Tokyo recognized the importance of growing conflict at Taipei between the policing agencies, responsible to the Ministry of Home Affairs through the Governor-General, and the courts of law, responsible directly to the Ministry of Justice at Tokyo. There were serious technical questions involved and these in turn were complicated by problems of prestige and privilege (face) between competing government agencies. Too often the individual Formosan found himself the victim of intense bureaucratic rivalries.

While Andō and Shimomura worked to repair damage done during Sakuma's prolonged administration, the American people far away were attempting to keep clear of the European conflict. The decision at last to enter the European war filled the Japanese press with news and comment. In sixty years Japan had come a long way from the days of bows and arrows, spears and matchlocks, used in the Meiji Restoration battles, to its present status as a partner of Italy, France, and Great Britain. Now, with the United States, it had become one of the "Big Five" world powers.

On the American declaration of war, President Woodrow Wilson at once moved to a preeminent place among world leaders. Every Wilsonian message, idea, and statement of principle received international notice and debate. This was most emphatically a development not anticipated by Tokyo or London when they struck the secret bargain concerning postwar disposition of Germany's concessions and possessions in Asia and the Pacific. Wilson knew nothing of that agreement.

Wilson's fervent allusions to "freedom," "democracy," and the "rights of man," and his promises of "self-determination" and "equal opportunity" for all made excellent slogans with which to win support among free peoples and to subvert minorities held under Austrian or German rule, but they were like sparks from a wind-swept fire, soon leaping across all national and territorial boundaries, kindling hopes in every restless Asian colony. The American President's words received worldwide publication. On January 8, 1918, for example, Wilson addressed the United States Congress in these terms:

> Free, open-minded and absolutely impartial adjustment of all colonial claims, based upon a strict observance of the principle that in determining all such questions of sovereignty, the interest of the populations concerned must have equal weight with the equitable claims of the Government whose title is to be determined.[1]

One month later the President said:

> People are not to be handed about from one sovereignty to another by an international conference or an understanding between rivals and antagonists. . . . National aspirations must be respected; people may now be dominated and governed only by their own consent. "Self-determination" is not a mere phrase. It is an imperative principle of action, which statesmen will henceforth ignore at their peril . . ."[2]

Against this background of international comment on "human rights," a number of Formosan students at Tokyo secured police permission to form a "Taiwan Youth Society"

(*Taiwan Seinen-kai*), and to publish a monthly journal devoted to Formosan history, poetry, essays, and folklore. It was proposed to include editorials and essays to engage the interest and support of Japanese leaders. The young men were particularly eager to win support of sympathetic spokesmen in the National Diet.

At that time all Formosan students in Japan proper were under police surveillance as a matter of course, but publication of the student journal violated no rules then in force. Nevertheless, the military authorities at Tokyo and Taipei were angered by this attempt to bring pressure to bear upon the Taipei administration through the Diet. These were "dangerous thoughts" that might lead to some curtailment of military privilege in the colony or subvert discipline at Taipei. The new journal was promptly banned in Formosa.

By midyear 1918, Japan's chief ministers saw that major political concessions were necessary in Japan proper if great crises were to be averted in the metropolitan areas, and none could tell what repercussions might occur in the colony. On June 6, therefore, the wartime Premier, General Count Terauchi, recalled General Andō from Taipei and sent a career military policeman to Formosa to replace him.

The new Governor-General, General Baron Akashi Motojirō, could be expected to keep a firm grip upon the Formosans, for he had served in rebellious Korea as Commander in Chief of Gendarmes, Army Chief of Staff, and Chief of the Department of Police Affairs. He was not a "second Sakuma" however; Akashi had served as Military Attaché in Japan's embassies at Paris, Berlin, and St. Petersburg, and with his comparatively wide knowledge of international affairs could be called upon to represent his Government with distinction if the "colonial question" became serious at conferences certain to follow a European armistice. ·

Premier Terauchi Masataka, a tough old samurai, found the Presbyterian college professor Woodrow Wilson a most disconcerting ally, and so, too, did the Prime Ministers of the other colonial powers. One month after the Akashi appointment, the American President shook the world order by setting forth in essence the Fourteen Points which were to become the basis for his armistice program and the subsequent peace negotiations. The occasion was America's Independence Day, July 4, 1918, and the setting was Mount Vernon, home of America's most distinguished colonial rebel and revolutionist, George Washington. Said President Wilson to a worldwide audience:

> The settlement of every question, whether of territory or sovereignty, of economic arrangement or of political relationship [must be] . . . upon the basis of the free acceptance of that settlement by the people immediately concerned, and not upon the material interest or advantage of any other nation or people which may desire a different settlement for the sake of its exterior influence or mastery. . . .
>
> What we seek is the reign of law, based on the consent of the governed and sustained by the organized opinion of mankind.[3]

To the military at Tokyo and Taipei and to all ultranationalists in the Empire these were subversive ideas; to young Formosans who read them in world press dispatches, and heard them quoted in public debate by Japanese liberals, they offered a splendid ideal. The American President seemed to be speaking in their behalf.

After the Dōka-kai incident in 1915 the government sought to counter youthful enthusiasm for alien Western ideas by encouraging conservative older people to organize, granting them rewards and privileges of a flattering nature. For example, new business opportunities were opened to the cooperative Ko Kenei and Gan Unnen who each now maintained large establishments in Tokyo and spent many months of the year at the national capital. They in turn contributed heavily toward the construction of an elaborate Confucian temple at Taipei and to a newly established "veneration society" dedicated to the worship of Confucius. A less dramatic but more effective measure in 1918 was the creation of local "advisory councils" throughout the island. Older men were appointed to membership, soothing their desire to be consulted in public affairs. In fact, it was representation without authority.

DANGEROUS THOUGHTS FOR COLONIAL SUBJECTS

In turning to Wilsonian idealism, the younger Formosans were not looking for foreign intervention nor for a return to China. After twenty years the movement toward *assimilation* had ended in failure; for the next twenty years they would demand Japanese recognition of a distinct Formosan identity within the Japanese empire and a representation of Formosan interests, per se, at the national level in Tokyo. Lin Hsien-t'ang, now thirty-seven years of age, engaged Ts'ai Pei-ho as an aide and secretary and became the principal patron and spokesman for the Formosan Home Rule Movement.

Students in all the world's colonies were becoming ardent political activists. Roxas in the Philippines, Nehru in India, and Ho Chi-minh in Vietnam were young men in their twenties; Sukarno was an ambitious boy of sixteen when Wilson stated the case for all colonial subjects in Asia. Students led the 1917 rebellion in Korea and the May Fourth Movement in China. While at school in London, Leiden, or Paris the Indians, Indonesians, and Vietnamese enjoyed comparative freedom of speech and association; but when at home in the colonies, they risked persecution, imprisonment, or exile if they agitated against the colonial administrations.

There were at that time some two thousand Formosan youths in Japan proper, members of this great informal international student fraternity seeking political recognition and social equality. They too discovered that freedoms enjoyed at the national capital were not to be enjoyed in the colony, but their reaction was singular; a majority were not seeking independence but acceptance and equality *within* the empire. They had their parents' testimony that ordinary living conditions had improved immeasurably under Japanese administration. Unlike the British, Dutch, or French colonial administrations, the government at Tokyo was driving hard to raise living standards in every village and to educate the masses. There was no prospect then that Japan would ever be compelled to give up the island and there was little inducement to look across the Strait to chaotic China.

Japan was the most advanced nation in Asia, a recognized world power associated with Britain, France, and the United States, the nations holding keys to the technological future. In this future the Formosan students were determined to share. Anglo-Saxon ideas of law and representative government seemed to hold answers to their problems, and the development of an elected island assembly at Taipei and of Formosan representation in the National Diet at Tokyo seemed not unreasonable objectives. The time seemed right to press for recognition.

Lin Hsien-t'ang and his young associates were encouraged in September, 1918, when General Count Terauchi was obliged to relinquish the premiership at Tokyo to make way for Hara Kei, a party leader and the first commoner to reach the premier's office in modern times. Liberals in Japan and abroad hailed the change as a major concession to popular demand for wider suffrage, and on the thirtieth anniversary of the Constitution (February 11, 1919) some three thousand Japanese university students demonstrated as they submitted petitions for broader representation. From the Formosan point of view there was added advantage in Japan's nationwide preoccupation with questions of racial equality. Tokyo's delegation to the Versailles Conference had been instructed to demand an "equality among races" clause in the Treaty text; failure to secure it caused intense disappointment, bitterness, and heated debate throughout Japan.

Seizing on this the Formosans took every opportunity to remind the Japanese public that consistency required a review of the situation in Formosa and an end there to racial, social, and political discrimination. Premier Hara's "liberal victory" proved more apparent than real; the diehard conservatives were pushed further to the Right and superpatriots developed an irrational mistrust of the masses. Hara's elevation was seen as a threat to age-old imperial institutions and traditional vested interests.

Bloody events at St. Petersburg, Moscow, and Ekaterinburg heightened Japan's century-old dread of Russia; the revolution brought communism to the very shores of the Japan Sea and to the common land frontier shared with Russia on Sakhalin Island. When the Bolshevik "dictatorship of the proletariat" announced its determination to foster world revolution, Japan's security agencies were driven to extremes. There was without doubt a proliferation of subversive organizations in Japan's great industrial slums, perhaps the largest in the world at that time. Now the Army, the Navy and the Home Ministry vied with one another in elaborating counterintelligence organizations and policing units, and in demonstrating how severely thorough each could be in defending imperial institutions. Every proposal for liberal reform was looked upon as a probable act of subversion. Detection and suppression of "dangerous thoughts" became a pathological obsession in many quarters.

Against this background the Formosan students began a campaign to win concessions in the colony. The idea of "assimilation" so briefly advanced at the time of Count Itagaki's visit was no longer attractive. It was now proposed to use political means to bring about reform in the Government-General, and to do so by educating the Japanese to the need and by rousing the Formosans to join in political action. In 1918, therefore, an "Enlightenment Society" (*Keihatsu-kai*) was founded at Tokyo. Members were asked to speak at liberal meetings and were encouraged to issue pamphlets describing the unsatisfactory state of affairs in the colony. Every opportunity was seized to ask for a Formosan voice in the National Diet. Prospects for administrative change seemed bright, but the young men soon discovered that freedom to debate colonial policy in Tokyo did not extend to the colony itself.

Governor-General Akashi refused to allow them to establish branch organizations in Formosa and forbade them to send in or circulate their "seditious" literature. Soon the War Ministry persuaded the Home Ministry to direct the Metropolitan Police Board to cancel organization and publication permits at Tokyo. General Akashi would make no concessions to a movement seeking special political or cultural status for a subdivision within the empire. Henceforth the lines were to be drawn sharply between Island people who desired to preserve a Formosan cultural identity and Japanese conservatives who were determined to "Japanize" Formosa.

THE STRUGGLE FOR RECOGNITION AND ADMINISTRATIVE REFORM

Dramatic events elsewhere once again had repercussions in the island. A series of anti-Japanese demonstrations in Korea beginning in March 1919, were suppressed with great brutality. It was generally conceded that "Wilsonian idealism" had added fuel to the fires of Korean nationalism. The bloody affair evoked international criticism and condemnation of Japanese colonial administration, the Emperor lost face, and Tokyo was obliged to review policies affecting the national and imperial prestige. Japan was now a member of the League of Nations, and had assumed control of Germany's former possessions in the Pacific under a League Mandate. If long-range goals of the expansionists were to be achieved, Japan's image as a champion of "exploited Asians" had to be refurbished.

For the first time in twenty-two years the administration at Taipei was altered significantly by an Imperial Ordinance, issued in August 1919, providing that the Governor-General henceforth need not necessarily be a man on the active military lists, and that civilians might be appointed to the office. If a civilian became Governor-General, he would apply to the Taiwan Garrison Commander for military help in time of crisis, and if he were a military officer, he would assume command of the Garrison himself. This technicality meant little to the Formosans, but it represented a major concession wrung from the High Command at Tokyo by Premier Hara.

After conferences at Tokyo relating to this modification in military policy, Governor-General Akashi set out again for Taipei, traveling by way of his native Fukuoka. There he suddenly fell ill and died. To the astonishment of the public in Japan and in Formosa, he had willed that his ashes were to be taken on to Formosa for burial. Hitherto all Japanese who could afford to do so had sent the ashes of the dead back to Japan proper, the "homeland," for burial. Now, with dramatic force, General Akashi had stated his belief that Formosa was an inalienable part of the empire and true "home territory." Year after year thereafter, the number of Japanese mortuary shrines and cemeteries in Formosa increased, and—more important from a legal point of view—Japanese families began to transfer the all-important basic family registers (*ko-seki*) to Formosa. Family elders went down to live with sons and daughters settled in the colony, and children born of Japanese parents began to consider themselves natives of Formosa. It was no longer thought necessary to send school-age children back to Japan proper for primary education.

General Akashi's death gave Premier Hara opportunity to break with the past and make a conciliatory gesture. On October 29, 1919, Baron Den Kōjirō, a civilian, became the eighth

Governor-General.* He had much administrative experience and his civilian status looked well in the public eye. As he took up his appointment the metropolitan press again and again raised the question of Formosan discontent, using materials supplied by Formosan students in documenting criticism of the government. In February 1920, a formal petition was laid before the House of Representatives asking for a colonial parliament or assembly at Taipei through which the island people could influence local budgets, taxation, and matters of general policy.

The Formosans were encouraged to know that the issues were beginning to be defined at the national level and to be brought before the Diet in proper form, and so the students at Tokyo decided to organize once more. Permission was granted, and in March 1920, a "New People's Society" (sometimes called the "Taiwan Culture Society") was established. Lin Hsien-t'ang and other wealthy Formosans supported it, and Lin himself subsequently became its president. In July a magazine entitled *Taiwan Youth* (*Taiwan Seinen*) began to appear, with Ts'ai Pei-ho as the editor.†

Over the objection of some members, the new Society and its spokesmen decried the old concept of full assimilation and proposed, instead, the preservation of a distinct Formosan-Chinese cultural identity, and the creation of an elective, local island parliament or assembly, with elective representation in the National Diet at Tokyo. The principal advocate of this view was Lin Ch'eng-lu (Rin Teiroku) who had taught in China for a time after graduating from Meiji University in Tokyo. On returning to Tokyo he became associated with the noted Dr. Yanaihara Tadao, a distinguished and scholarly critic of Japan's

---

* Baron Den Kojirō (1855–1930), bureaucrat and businessman, had served as Chief of Police in several prefectures before becoming Vice-Minister of Communications (1898). Leaving government service, he became an important businessman (with the Kansai Railway Company), entered politics, and served in the House of Peers before reentering the Government as Minister of Communications (1916). He had traveled widely in Europe and America.

† The magazine appeared in both the Japanese and Formosan-Chinese languages, and continued to be issued at Tokyo until 1932, when it was transferred to Taipei. In 1946 sons of the students who had been at Tokyo in the period 1915–1925 revived the magazine as the "Formosa Youth Magazine" at Taipei. See Kerr, *Formosa Betrayed*, Chapter 10, "The Search for Recognition."

colonial policies. It is noteworthy that Ch'eng and his associates (including Yang Chiao-chia [Yo Choka]) did *not* advocate "return to China," but called, instead, for a special island legislature. On the one hand, old China was unattractive, convulsed by warlord rivalries and notorious for abusive rule in Formosa before 1895. On the other, many provisions in the Japanese Constitution could not apply to traditional institutions and special conditions in Formosa.

When the new Society and its publication appeared in Tokyo, ultraconservative "patriots" protested and the nationalist newspaper *Yamato* denounced all Formosans as "degenerate, not worthy of the status of Japanese nationals!," citing the "un-Japanese" content of the *Taiwan Youth Magazine*. When the Society sought permission to form an affiliated group in Taipei, the Governor-General was compelled to refuse permission. On this, the students decided to act, each upon his own responsibility.

Returning to Formosa for the long holidays, they began to travel from town to town, speaking wherever they could bring an audience together. Wilson's principles, the Versailles Conference conflict concerning racial equality, and the harshness of "Law Number 63" with its brutal provisions for "bandit suppression" in Formosa were all cited in presenting the case for home rule. While the young men were attempting to arouse and educate the Formosan public on these issues, the Japanese press at Taipei was reporting major debates in domestic politics at the national level, including the debates concerning "equal rights" and suffrage at home, and Japan's demand for "racial equality" principles in international affairs.

A majority of Formosan student activists came from propertied and comparatively well-to-do families, or were intelligent young men who enjoyed scholarship support by village organizations. They had great prestige among their own people. If they remained silent, they could expect to profit by small concessions and privileges, available to all Formosans who diligently sought to learn the Japanese language and to conform to Japanese ways. Instead, they chose a rougher course, exposing themselves and their families to economic reprisals by the government bureaucracy and to physical danger at the hands of the police. Too often the well-educated advocate of home rule found himself pitted against the ill-educated village policeman, possessing too much authority and endowed with too little intelligence, who thought it his duty to harass the students at every opportunity by interfering with travel schedules, interrupting appointments, causing embarrassment, expense, and loss of time. Informal gatherings were disrupted and auditors intimidated by threatening language; houses were searched, and families and friends of student leaders were subjected to incessant interrogations.

GRUDGING JAPANESE CONCESSIONS

The important ordinance making civilians eligible to the governorship was followed in 1921 by other legal adjustments described officially as "gestures of imperial benevolence"—concessions from above—in order to discourage any thought that Tokyo was in fact yielding to Formosan pressure. Henceforth the island would be governed under the laws of Japan proper, although the Governor-General was authorized to suspend any law if he deemed it necessary, provincial governors were authorized to arbitrate civil cases, and district officers and police chiefs retained authority to judge minor criminal cases. The old "Penal Laws Against Bandits" were retained, a catchall category "intended to punish atrocious crimes," and defined in terms sufficiently vague to provide ready excuse for action against any person or group displeasing to the law enforcement agencies. A key provision stated, "Irrespective of purposes, those who join together in order to achieve the purpose in view by violence or threats of violence are regarded as bandits. They are not treated in the same way as common criminals. They are as a rule dealt with most severely." [4] The penalty was death if two or more Formosans were convicted of association in an "act or threat of violence." This act applied only in Formosa. Little change had taken place. Flogging was abolished and the prison population increased at once. The Governor still possessed unusual powers, and Formosans still lacked adequate means of appeal when subjected to illegal or unfair pressures. Only the boldest dared seek redress. Retaliation was certain if any Formosan protest caused a policeman or the police organization to lose face.

In token of the relative liberalism of Hara's administration, it was arranged for Crown Prince Hirohito to visit Europe. Following a brief pause in Okinawa, the prince landed at Keelung in March 1921. After watching well-regimented ducks paddle about on the Keelung River near the Grand Shrine, he was taken to spend the night at Kappan-zan in a quasi-Western house built especially for the occasion, at great expense. The Japanese in Formosa were suitably awed by the visit; the Formosans were not.

They continued to call for justice in the colony and reasonable representation at Tokyo. In this year they presented the second of a series of annual petitions to the Diet—fifteen in all. The authors protested their loyalty and expressed their belief that creation of a special legislature for the colony would enhance Formosan ties with Japan. The Japanese residents in Formosa, on the other hand, protested vigorously that any concession such as this would lead on to a demand for independence.*

To counter Formosan agitation and to mollify prominent critics in the National Diet, it was announced that His Imperial Majesty was now pleased to permit formation of an Advisory Council (*Hyōgi-kai*) at Taipei, to assist the Governor-General. Formosans "rich in scholarship and experience" would be among its members, and through the Council the Governor would hear the people. It was left to his discretion to pay attention to what they might say. In short, this was institutional window-dressing.

The Governor was Council Chairman, the Civil Administrator was Vice-Chairman, and ex officio membership included the Chief Justice of the High Court, the Director of the Internal Affairs Bureau, and the Director of the Police Bureau—all Japanese. A majority of the other members, too, were Japanese. The Formosan minority included several men who had indeed grown very rich, though not in scholarship, through collaboration with the Japanese in 1895 and thereafter. Great landholding clans were represented, and the appointment of Lin Hsien-t'ang was ostensibly because of his great wealth and position as a leading citizen of Taichung Province. It was assumed,

* See especially Edward I-te Chen's "Formosan Political Movements under Japanese Colonial Rule," in which he notes that in all, no fewer than 17,262 persons (not including students) signed these petitions over the years, and that by boldly doing so they exposed themselves to police retaliation.

however, that his role as cofounder and chief patron of the Home Rule associations had prompted the Japanese to believe that he would now become less critical of the administration.

For each such concession to "liberals" at Tokyo, the government exacted a quid pro quo. On July 11, 1921, Premier Hara was obliged to recall Dr. Shimomura to make way for the appointment of a new Civil Administrator, Kaku Sagatarō. Kaku had spent many years at Taipei, serving first as a minor Bureau secretary, and then rising under General Sakuma to become, in turn, Chief of the Civil Affairs Bureau and then Director of the Monopoly Bureau. Many of his Japanese colleagues considered him a shady tool of big business interests willing to pay well for influence and advantage.

Soon after Kaku took up his important new post at Taipei, Premier Hara was assassinated (November 4, 1921). The assassin was officially described as a "demented youth," but the passionate political atmosphere of the day obscured a true record of this first of a long series of post-war political assassinations perpetrated by ultranationalists, including "patriotic Young Officers" and their associates. Hara's death was a violent warning that extremists were determined to check the development of democratic and representative processes throughout the Empire. It meant that mild administrative concessions approved at Tokyo thereafter were usually offset on Formosa by harsh police actions. These left no doubt that the professional patriots and the military still considered the Island dangerously "un-Japanese" territory, irreconcilably alien to the "true Japanese" tradition, and therefore requiring an iron fist in government.

Twenty-six years had passed since annexation. The first Formosan generation born under the Japanese flag was beginning to send its own "second generation" children to primary school. School segregation could no longer be justified on linguistic grounds. With appropriately condescending phrases, therefore, Baron Den, the Governor-General, announced that as of April 2, 1922—the beginning of the next school year—the children who were linguistically qualified would be permitted to enroll at any primary school. It soon became evident that urban schools in which the Japanese formed a great majority were to be favored in the quality of buildings, equipment, and teaching staff. Nevertheless, the formal declaration that discrimination in the schools had ceased marked an important step along the painful road toward peaceful accommodation.

But after every gesture of conciliation there was counteraction and coercion. Governor-General Den caused all government employees associated with the League to be dismissed. Japanese firms were encouraged to discharge personnel known to support the League's activities. The licenses of sympathetic merchants were revoked, and the Bank of Taiwan began to recall loans from "politically undesirable" Formosans. Lin Hsien-t'ang received many threatening letters and was sharply criticized in the press. Summoned to the Governor-General's office at last, he was severely admonished and forced publicly to announce that he was withdrawing from all political activity. (Only later could he reveal that he had been threatened with huge financial losses.)

Active leadership passed into the hands of Ts'ai Pei-ho who, with forty associates, petitioned the Taipei police offices for permission to found a "League for the Establishment of a Formosan Parliament." It was of course denied. Ts'ai then went up to Tokyo, renewed his application, and there it was granted. The Governor-General lost face, and was furious.

Faction began to undermine solidarity of purpose. This curse of old clan and village rivalries—the inability to compromise differences among leaders—became now an inability to adjust differing views on the problems of resistance to police pressures and on programs designed to secure meaningful concessions. A majority of leaders had decisively rejected the "assimilation" ideas of the Dōka-kai of Itagaki's day. The young activists at Tokyo were forbidden to extend their League for Local Autonomy (the Home Rule Association) to the colony, and in consequence another group had been formed at Taipei under the leadership of Dr. Chiang Wei-shui (Sho I-so). This called itself the "Taiwan Culture Society" or *Taiwan Bunka Kai*, and by publicly disclaiming any political aim and calling for harmony in Japanese-Formosan relations, it managed to secure permits to carry on in Formosa. The Society advocated preservation and cultivation of the distinctive Formosan-Chinese heritage and promoted education and popular interest in a broad spectrum of subjects such as traditional handicrafts, Chinese literature and folklore, and Western studies. In practical effect it soon became a thinly disguised "front" for the Home Rule Association based in Tokyo, but inevitably, though indirectly, developed a political character of its own.

The Culture Society supported the annual petitions for Home Rule, but over the years these became little more than a ritual gesture; according to the leading authority on Formosan political movements in the Japanese era—Dr. Edward I-te Chen—on February 28, 1921, Governor-General Den himself had appeared before the National Diet Committee on Petitions to urge that it deny Formosans a formal hearing. Although the petitions continued to be submitted annually until 1934, they were always tabled in committee and never brought to the Diet floor for a formal public debate.

Under increasing police pressures, the more active students found it too frustrating to follow councils of moderation. Professor Chen notes that in the economic boom immediately following World War I, the number of factories in Formosa nearly trebled between 1919 and 1929, and the number of Formosan-Chinese laborers in the principal industries rose to some sixty-three thousand. Labor disputes increased proportionately and the young intellectual activists gave leading workers advice and direction. This was anathema to the colonial administration and suppressive measures began to generate bitter debate within the Formosan groups.

University students home for the long holiday in 1922 campaigned as usual on behalf of Home Rule. In a sudden wave of arrests, seventy-three youths were detained, subjected to rough handling, and accused of subversion. No evidence could be produced to support the charges and the courts ruled that the students must be released.

Leaving prison, they returned to Tokyo, and there, in February 1923, published a petition addressed to the police administration at Taipei, repeating Formosan complaints and demanding recognition that a request for an islandwide, representative Assembly at Taipei and a voice in the Diet at Tokyo was neither subversive nor secessionist.

It was a bold gesture, supported by Lin Hsien-t'ang who now helped launch a new journal at the capital, a revived *Formosan Magazine* in slightly different form. He agreed to serve for a time as President of the Taiwan Culture Society. No Japanese at Tokyo could seriously accuse Lin of pro-Communist sympathies; it was well known that he was encouraging formation of Formosan agricultural cooperatives as a means to offset the influence of leftist agitators becoming active in the colony. These were representatives of the Japan Communist party and its affiliates sent into Formosa to subvert the farmers' associations, the new light-industry cooperatives, and new labor unions.

Lin's unfaltering support of the Home Rule Movement infuriated the chauvinists at Taipei. Despite his membership on the Governor's Advisory Council he was detained from time to time, subjected to prolonged and unnecessary interrogations, and on one occasion had to endure a public slapping by a fanatic Japanese "patriot."

So matters stood when Japan suffered the Great Earthquake of September 1, 1923. There was an instant tightening of all police measures throughout the Empire; militant Rightists were convinced that the radical Left would use the crisis to overthrow the imperial government, and hundreds of men on the police blacklists were jailed or executed without trial. Koreans at Tokyo suffered particularly harsh abuse in detention, and incidents of torture and execution became the subject of public censure and international comment.

The National Government was promptly reorganized amidst the smoking ruins of Tokyo and Yokohama. Gotō Shimpei, now Home Minister, took over presidency of the National Capital Reconstruction Board. Governor-General Baron Den was summoned from Taipei to join the Cabinet. To the profound disappointment and distress of all thoughtful Formosans, Den's place at Taipei was taken by Uchida Kakichi, the unloved bureaucrat who had served as Civil Administrator in General Sakuma's notorious administration. With Uchida as Governor-General and Kaku as Civil Administrator, the stage was set for the most serious confrontation between the Home Rule leaders and the Japanese administration.

8. The Angry Decade

ATTEMPTS TO SUPPRESS THE HOME RULE MOVEMENT

*T*HE GOVERNMENT decided to counter the Home Rule Association and Lin Hsien-t'ang's leadership by promoting a pro-Japan organization led by Ku Hsien-yung (Ko Kenei). For a quarter century Ku had prospered in close cooperation with the Government and by now was one of the wealthiest members of the Governor's new Advisory Council. As a staunch advocate of full Formosan assimilation to Japan he founded a "Public Interest Society" (*Kō-eki kai*) in November 1923. In the eyes of some Home Rule leaders he was an object of bitter reproach, an arch-collaborator.

Through his new organization Ku criticized the Taiwan Culture Society saying that by its attempt to preserve traditional Formosan values and folkways it retarded Japanization and prolonged the evils of colonial administration. He defended his own position by arguing that the emperor of China himself had cast off the Formosans, betraying them in 1895, that he no longer owed allegiance to China or the Chinese, but on the contrary, as a Japanese subject, it was a Formosan's duty to be loyal to the government at Tokyo. The great material benefit was obvious, he said; the Formosans had only to compare their present situation to conditions in war-torn, backward China.

Henceforth, to the great advantage of the Japanese, disagreement and factional and personal rivalries weakened all Formosan attempts to confront the Japanese police administration effectively. Ku's new counterpropaganda organization itself had been launched at a most inauspicious moment in the weeks immediately following the Great Earthquake.

Formosan students hurrying home for the winter holidays in 1923 were eager to tell of their September earthquake experiences and had much to say to one another concerning the fate of Korean fellow students who had been swept up in the police net at Tokyo. During the long journey by train and ship they discussed their own plans for the usual holiday campaign on behalf of the Home Rule Movement.

Upon reaching Keelung on December 10, forty-nine of the young men were seized as they came ashore, hustled off to jail, and subjected to long questioning. Fourteen were then indicted on charges of "subversive activity." Copies of the forbidden *Formosan Magazine* had been found in their luggage. They were "agitators."

After *pro forma* trials they were sent to prison and with them went Lin Hsien-t'ang and Dr. Chiang Wei-shui (Sho I-so) who had given the students financial help and moral support in a degree unacceptable to the administration. The light sentences—only four months in jail—were intended to intimidate rather than to punish, for Governor Uchida's prosecutors realized the flimsy character of the subversion charges. By this arrangement the men would have served their prison terms and have established "criminal records" before much of an issue could be made of the incident in the metropolitan press.

By late spring 1924, the young men were back in Tokyo, happy to know that the annual February petition had been presented in the Diet by two eminent sponsors. Dr. Kiyose Ichirō, an authority on British, French, and German law, had presented it to the House of Representatives, and Dr. Yamawaki Gen, a former judge in the high courts of Korea and an authority on British jurisprudence, had presented it in the House of Peers.

As usual, the Diet took no action, but the issue of administrative reform at Taipei was very much alive. The recent arrests and trials had revived public discussion of "Japan's Irish Question." The Home Rule Association wooed support at the capital through wide distribution of the *Formosan Magazine*, and of pamphlets stating the Formosan position. The principal spokesmen were Lin Hsien-t'ang's private secretary Ts'ai Pei-ho (Sai Baika) and Lin Cheng-lu (Rin Teiroku). Public discussion reflected three points of view. Japan's intellectuals—the university community, journalists, and many liberal politicians—supported Formosan demands for full equality within the empire while preserving a Formosan cultural identity. The Government—the professional bureaucracy—was determined to *assimilate* the island people, granting them political and social equality only after they had been made over into "true Japanese"—thinking, speaking, and behaving like Japanese in every way. The third point of view was that of the chauvinists, the military, and the great corporate interests, who held that it was useless to make concessions, that the Formosans could never be made over into "true Japanese," and that they should be kept inarticulate, regimented, and dependent, a great reservoir of cheap labor.

To relieve tension, some concessions had to be made. These were always announced with great solemnity as "acts of imperial grace" and evidence of a benevolent administration. Too often they proved to be empty gestures. For example, in 1924 it was announced that henceforth, by imperial grace, Formosan youths could volunteer for military service, and that Formosans who were civil servants above a certain grade would be permitted to wear short dress-swords on ceremonial occasions. From a Japanese point of view these were important concessions, for the sword was a cherished symbol of status and authority—one *almost* became a samurai by wearing it.

The Formosan knew how many excuses could be found to turn away volunteers for military service and how deeply Japanese patriots resented this opening of the honor ranks to inferior subjects. Students at Tokyo hammered away at the inequality theme, citing raw discrimination in the courts of law, and press restrictions permitting only three heavily censored newspapers in the colony. They emphasized the issue of racial inequality, a subject on which the Japanese Government was then taking a strong position in conflict with the United States. The American Congress had passed the Exclusion Act, and the Japanese people were deeply offended. Home Rule advocates reminded Tokyo that Formosan men were forbidden by law to marry Japanese women without special permission, although any Japanese male, if he chose, could take a Formosan girl as wife or concubine, without question.

At Tokyo Formosan pamphleteers and speechmakers were

not taken very seriously. They were too few in number in a vast student population, and could not be considered a serious threat to the national interest and safety. If they conformed to the regulations, filed proper applications, and secured valid permits, they were allowed to publish and speak without undue pressure from the Metropolitan Police agencies. At Taipei, however, authority took quite a different view. The Japanese were a small minority living among millions of Formosans, and every thoughtful Japanese sensed an underlying hostility among the common people.*

Uchida and Kaku, who were determined to allow no slackening of controls and discipline, felt it essential to choke off the flow of criticism at the national capital. Soon each young Formosan in Japan proper who advocated Home Rule found that his family and his friends in Formosa were being harassed. The milder forms of intimidation meant no more than prolonged delay and censorship of mail, or petty interference with daily home routines. Fathers and brothers were called at inconvenient moments to appear for prolonged and pointless questioning at the local police box, for example. In more serious cases the police contrived to damage or seriously disrupt the normal economic life of the clan and family, interfering with family business at the banks or credit associations, withholding licenses and permits essential to daily operations, and by countless petty irritations creating hardship. Sometimes parents or grandparents were held under arrest on unspecified charges "pending investigation."

During the midyear holiday in 1924, a new wave of arrests took place and again the courts dismissed untenable charges of "conspiracy." No one knows how long Uchida would have continued this cat-and-mouse game, for in the midst of it both Governor and Civil Administrator were forced suddenly to re-

---

* In 1924 a total of 183,317 Japanese lived among 3,614,000 Formosan Chinese. Nearly 56,000 aborigines were considered "assimilated," but an estimated 134,000 "raw" or untamed aborigines lived in the hills. Some 30,000 continental Chinese and 192 other foreigners (including Caucasians) were registered. Officialdom looked on the Christian converts with suspicion and latent hostility. Of these there were some 5,730 Catholics, 30,000 Presbyterians, and 600 "others," including 529 Japanese Methodists and Episcopalians.

sign. A major scandal was about to break into print, involving Uchida, Kaku, and men of ministerial rank in Tokyo; the affairs of the Monopoly Bureau were about to be investigated.

Governor-General Uchida had been in office less than a year. Each of the major political parties strove to exploit the situation. In the event, the Formosans became the true victims of a savage rivalry. Politicians at Tokyo professed deep concern for the welfare of Formosa and the Formosans, talked dramatically of the distant island of which in truth they knew very little. Soon support for a "tough policy in Formosa" became a test of patriotism at Tokyo. Uchida and Kaku were identified with the ruling political party, the *Kensei-kai*. Prominent members of the opposition party, the *Seiyū-kai*, had found it useful to champion the Home Rule cause, not through genuine concern, but as a means to embarrass the party in office. Now the opposition—the Seiyū-kai—proposed to discredit the Kensei-kai by exploiting the Monopoly Bureau scandal involving the manufacture and distribution of narcotics.

To divert public attention and censure, the Kensei-kai members attempted to "prove" that the Home Rule Association was subversive, its friends tainted, and its sponsors—Seiyū-kai members—possibly open to charges of sedition. An influential Kensei-kai member, Izawa Takio, was appointed to succeed Uchida as Governor-General. He was known in Japan as a tough former Inspector-General of the Metropolitan Police Board, and known internationally as one of the authors of the notorious Twenty-one Demands made upon China in 1915. It was Izawa's responsibility to prove the allegedly seditious character of the Formosan Home Rule Movement in order to embarrass the Seiyū-kai.

The Seiyū-kai members irritated Izawa by arranging to have a large deputation of Formosan Home Rule advocates travel from Tokyo to Taipei aboard the trains and ships transporting the new Governor-General and his suite. This generated a flurry of provocative press releases at every major stop along the way. Izawa could do little to curb such unfavorable publicity while in Japan proper, but at Taipei he promptly invoked the autocratic powers of his office to reshuffle administrative appointments throughout the island, giving seasoned police officers key posts and moving compliant judges into selected courts. Within a short while he had set the stage for the liquidation of the Home Rule problem.

The Public Prosecutor was directed to reopen recent cases on the basis of "new evidence." Ten students were retried in October—one of them *in absentia*. Five were acquitted and five were sent to jail for three months. Lin Hsien-t'ang's secretary and Dr. Chiang Wei-shui were again arrested, tried, and jailed for a period of four months. Such light sentences for "sedition" again made it very clear that the Prosecutor could not expect his charges to be accepted or sustained in any higher court, and the men would be free before appeals could be prepared.

The affair attracted nationwide attention. Leading members of the legal profession condemned Izawa, saying that he challenged basic principles of constitutional law by intruding upon the courts themselves.

A CRISIS FOR THE HOME RULE LEADERS

At the height of the excitement generated by these trials— on November 20, 1924—Lin Hsien-t'ang addressed a bold memorandum to Governor Izawa clearly stating the basic issues.[1] He took care to have it published simultaneously at Tokyo. Here, under twelve headings, the wealthy landholder, banker, and leading Formosan conservative set forth fundamental issues, giving the Japanese public an opportunity to measure the breadth and depth of Formosan discontent. Lin called for action on these points:

1. Local administration must be revised to permit greater participation by qualified Formosans.
2. There must be wider dissemination of primary education and less discrimination in the schools.
3. The abusive police system must be reformed.
4. Economic and social discrimination must end.
5. The use of opium must be forbidden, the licensing system abolished, and opium smoking totally suppressed.
6. Freedom of speech and of the press must be guaranteed.
7. The oppressive mutual responsibility system—the hokō—must be abolished.
8. Industrial development policies must be revised to admit larger Formosan participation, and Formosan interests affected by industrial expansion must be taken into consideration.

9. Passports for travel to Japan must no longer be required.

10. Riparian improvement guilds must be encouraged to enable farmers to develop the land, the Formosans must be given a voice in making long-range plans for flood-control and irrigation works.

11. Agricultural association regulations must be modified to permit greater consideration of Formosan interests.

12. Harsh laws governing the arrest and punishment of so-called bandits must be modified, and must not be used to restrain all criticism of the administration.*

Had Governor Izawa acted upon these questions as Lin desired, many entrenched Japanese privileges would have been diminished or destroyed, to be sure, but nothing in the list could be construed as a threat to Japan's sovereignty or as an implied threat of violence if the reforms were not forthcoming. Izawa and his men refused to concede that reforms were necessary. At Tokyo three of Japan's most distinguished jurists—all members of the Diet—appealed to the Supreme Court on behalf of the men recently convicted of "subversion." The case was debated heatedly by members of the legal profession throughout Japan, for Izawa's actions clearly undermined the integrity of the courts, but the Governor won the day; the High Courts at Tokyo found that under existing ordinances they had no authority to review judicial procedures and actions in the colony.

This disappointing decision was made known on January 20, 1925. The annual Home Rule petition was laid before the Diet as usual, on February 26, and as usual neither the Diet nor the Cabinet took action. This time, however, the Association took care to have it published in the English-language press in Japan with some slight hope that the Government would react to foreign comment. At the moment discrimination—the American Exclusion Act—was a keen issue and the Japanese electorate was being quadrupled under new voting laws.† Leading Japanese papers gave the petition editorial attention and law-

* Compare this list of grievances with the Thirty-two Demands presented to the Nationalist Chinese Governor-General Chen Yi on March 7, 1947. (See Kerr, *Formosa Betrayed*, Appendix I, pp. 475–479.)

† Effective May 5, 1925, the number of eligible voters increased from 3.3 million to 14 million, but this popular gain was offset on May 12 by enactment of a new and harsh "peace preservation" law.

yers throughout Japan rebuked Izawa, the Taipei administration, and the major political parties, charging that a controlled press in the colony had misled the public through distorted reports of the recent affair.

THE PIVOTAL GOVERNMENT CONFERENCES OF 1925

Soon the Home Rule issues lost news value in Japan proper, and at Taipei the news media concentrated on reports of a third decennial review and planning conference. Nitobe's program for sugar and rice was yielding splendid returns to Japanese investors and to local farmers as well. It was now proposed to diversify production of fruits, vegetables, and livestock to meet growing demand in the metropolitan markets of Japan proper and in the large continental port cities nearby. The time had come to plan a decade of intensive light-industrial development related to Formosa's burgeoning agricultural economy and great timber resources.

The Taiwan Electric Power Corporation, formed in 1919 as a joint venture in public and private capital investment, was ready to move forward with major construction. Elaborate surveys made by the American J.G. White Engineering Corporation had demonstrated feasibility of high dams in the western foothills. On this basis a second American firm (J.P. Morgan and Company) agreed to float a U.S. $22,000,000 bond issue— the only large foreign investment ever allowed to penetrate the Formosan economy in the Japanese era.

The Taipei administration now asked participants in the Third Conference to contribute detailed planning, and the light-industry development program inaugurated here ultimately brought substantial change into every Formosan community. New jobs drew laborers from the most remote lowland farms, and new types of employment required specialization and new training.

After a new dam raised the level of Sun-Moon Lake in the western hills, a series of generating units began to provide power for harbor works and industries scattered along the entire western coast. This project required an elaboration of flood-control and forest-conservation programs on the high watersheds, and this in turn brought new pressures to bear upon the aborigines far back in the wilderness. Concurrently the government retreated from Sakuma's unlimited exploitation policies and set aside four million acres of timberland as "prime forest reserve."

In the lowlands a rapid development of light industry took place, related to Formosa's own agriculture, forestry, and mining. New factories were established to produce chemical fertilizers, pulp and paper products, industrial alcohol, carbon black, cement, and ceramic products.

To support this expanding economy, it was decided to develop technical and commercial education by creating specialized middle schools and colleges, and at last—in 1927—Gotō Shimpei's projected research university was established at Taipei as the Taihoku [Taipei] Imperial University (after 1945 renamed the National Taiwan University).

The elaborate Third Conference plans were publicized throughout Japan in an attempt to attract investors. Skeptical Formosans wondered what part they might be allowed to play in developing their home island. They had been denied a fair share in the profitable sugar industry, and they chafed under rules, regulations, and manifold restrictions designed to check Formosan competition with Japanese interests. There had been a proliferation of small Formosan banks and mutual credit associations before World War I, but in 1918 the government began to find pretexts for closing them, one by one. They were charged with "irregular practices," mismanagement, or failure to meet stringent banking regulations applied with ill-concealed discrimination.

Many of these charges were well founded, but it is noteworthy that in the effort to herd Formosan depositors and investors to Japanese banks, the number of Formosan financial institutions, large and small, had been driven down from more than fifty to only three.

Lin Hsien-t'ang believed that Formosans must participate in new industrial expansion programs to a significant degree if they were to achieve substantial influence at Taipei. To this end he founded the Taito Trust Company in 1926, with an initial capital of five million yen (then about U.S. $2,500,000). Through this new company and through his Changhua Bank, he undertook promotion of modest Formosan enterprises in segments of the economy not yet dominated by the great Japanese combines. He wanted Formosans to become something more than a common labor force, and by enlarging his patronage of promising young men—students in Japan and abroad—he was in effect cultivating future leadership for an emerging middle class.

FORMOSAN MODERATES AND RADICALS PART COMPANY

Lin and his moderate associates were encouraged at one moment when Prime Minister Wakatsuki Reijiro told the House of Representatives that Formosa must be given some measure of Home Rule as soon as possible, tempering this with the observation that a move in that direction could only take place when standards of living in the colony had been raised. As for a separate colonial parliament, that was out of the question; Japan could not have two legislative bodies within the Empire. Formosan Chinese must be prepared to find a place in the National Diet.

As if to offset this modicum of hope, a serious rift began to appear in the Formosan organizations calling for representation. The industrial expansion program led greedy opportunists in the Taipei administration to reward themselves and their corporate friends at the expense of the Formosan farmer. A large area of bamboo-producing land in central Formosa was confiscated on the pretext that the Formosan claimants could not prove clear title. Much of the land was then sold to the Mitsui interests, and the rest distributed among retiring government officials. This produced a bloody local conflict and brutal police action. It also prompted members of the Culture Association to campaign vigorously among the farmers, urging them to unite. By midyear 1926, scattered farmers' groups were merged into a Formosan Farmers Union (*Taiwan Nōmin Kumiai*), and this in turn produced a Leftist leadership receiving official support from the Japan Farmer-Labor Party. Within a few months the Union claimed a membership of some twenty-four thousand individuals.

At this time Lin Hsien-t'ang unquestionably enjoyed the highest degree of public confidence. Now, at the age of forty-five, his leadership met an unprecedented challenge. The founders of the original Assimilation Society and the later associations advocating Home Rule were growing older, and for some the idealism of university youth was giving way to cynicism. Lin's moderation and patience seemed ineffective. Prolonged debate and endless frustration strained old friendships as Governor-General Izawa increased the tempo and severity of attacks upon Home Rule leaders.

A crisis came on February 5, 1926. When the Home Rule advocates assembled once again to sign and send off the annual Diet petition, Izawa's police suddenly broke up the meeting, ordered the Formosans to disperse and, after an angry clash, marched fourteen men off to prison.

Through the next fortnight resentment swept the Island as everyone connected with the Home Rule Association hotly debated what course to take. Before any concerted action could be agreed upon, Izawa's police and the gendarmes struck again. At midnight on February 20, hundreds of homes were broken into during a house-to-house search for Association members and their known advocates. Many were treated with harsh abuse and scores were placed under arrest. Intermittent search continued for weeks as the interrogations opened new lines for investigation. Thousands of Formosans were called into the police stations for prolonged questioning and there followed the usual rigged trials, convictions, and sentences based upon trumped-up conspiracy charges. Izawa seemed determined to goad the Formosans into open rebellion, thus giving him a free hand to destroy Formosan leadership once for all.

Tokyo was compelled to intervene and on July 16 Governor-General Izawa was recalled. There was no hint that this was more than a routine reassignment but it was noteworthy that Izawa's successor represented the "other side" in this seesaw policy conflict between police and judiciary in the colony. The new Governor-General, Kamiyama Mannoshin, was a distinguished jurist of ministerial rank and an authority on Courts of Administrative Litigation—agencies established to resolve conflicts between government offices and to "hear the people" who wished to bring formal charges against the administration. Although Kamiyama placed some restraint upon the police and so eased tensions for a time, public confidence in the government had been irreparably damaged. The

Home Rule Movement organization, too, had suffered a heavy blow.

Dr. Chiang Wei-shui urged young people to leave Formosa and many did, disillusioned, cynical, and embittered. Members of the Association who were incurably political went over to China to plunge into the nationalist movements of the 1920s, electing to follow either Mao or Chiang after the Great Schism of 1927. Among those who aligned themselves with the Communists was Miss Hsieh Hsüeh-hung of Taichung, who went on to attend the Moscow Labor University in 1926–1927, the year in which Chiang Kai-shek's eldest son Ching-kuo began his long sojourn in the Soviet Union. Another Formosan named Ts'ai Chin joined the Communists and stayed with them for many years, making the Long March to the northwest in 1934. Hsieh on returning from Russia slipped back into Formosa to work as a secret Party agent but was arrested again and again by the vigilant Japanese police. After serving several short prison terms she was at last sent to the penitentiary.*

Some disaffected members of the Association remained in Formosa to form a Taiwan Proletarian Youth League (*Taiwan Musan Seinen-kai*), which was alleged to have enjoyed the support of the Japan Communist party. Left-wing organizations never became popular, they were generally ineffectual, and were continuously circumscribed and harassed by the police.

In all, about eight thousand Formosans living in continental China at this time took the trouble to register at the Japanese consulates in order to enjoy the benefits of dual citizenship in a country ruled by generals and torn by civil war. It is not known how many more gave up all claims to protection as Japanese subjects and faded into quiet anonymity as businessmen lost in the great cities. Scores of young men left Formosa in this decade to study abroad—in Japan proper, in China, and in the United States, Canada, or Europe, after which they returned to teach in China or to enter the Nationalist Chinese government

---

* After seven years Hsieh was released because of extreme ill health. She then lived quietly in Taichung, under close surveillance, until 1945. (On her unsuccessful bid to assume a role in the 1947 uprising, see Kerr, *Formosa Betrayed*, pp. 279–280.) Ts'ai Chin slipped back into Formosa after 1950, "repented," and, as Ts'ai Hsiao-cheng, became associated with Chiang Ching-kuo's policing agencies.

service.* A few returned to Formosa rather than to China, entering business or the teaching profession, always sympathetic to the Home Rule Movement but taking no prominent or active role in its affairs. Such, for example, was Lin Mou-sheng (Rin Mōsei) who returned to Formosa to teach after earning a doctorate at Columbia University in New York.

Lin Hsien-t'ang sent his eldest son to study at Cambridge University in England, and in 1927 thought it wise for himself to leave troubled Formosa for a time. After three months in the United States he went on to Cambridge before traveling through Denmark, Holland, Belgium, France, and Germany. On his return he took up the Home Rule problem once again.

About this time Governor-General Kamiyama and his Civil Administrator (Gotō Fumio) came under harsh attack by right-wing fanatics who alleged that they were too liberal and that the Taipei administration was not enforcing the formalities of emperor worship with sufficient diligence. A school had burned, the imperial portraits had been lost, and no one had risked his life to save them. In June 1928, both Kamiyama and Gotō were obliged to "admit error," accept responsibility, and resign.

There were more serious signs that the military and their sponsors were in the ascendency. Long-range plans for imperial expansion were being formulated at Tokyo, plans embracing regions lying far beyond Korea, Formosa, and the mid-Pacific islands. The Ministry for Colonial Development, abolished in 1898, now reappeared as a Ministry of Colonial Affairs, and the Formosan administration was shifted to its care.

A "PEOPLE'S PARTY," A NARCOTICS BUREAU SCANDAL, AND THE LEAGUE OF NATIONS

With persistent effort the Home Rule advocates won permission to transfer publication of the *Formosa Magazine* from Tokyo to Taipei, where its name was changed to *The Taiwan*

---

* Men of this expatriate group included Joshua Wen-ki Liao (M.A., Wisconsin; Ph.D., Chicago) who became a professor of political philosophy at Nanking; Thomas Wen-yi Liao (M.A., Michigan; Ph.D., Ohio State), who taught chemical engineering in China (1935–1938); Huang Chao-chin (M.A., Illinois) who joined the Nationalist foreign service; and the political chameleon and opportunist Hsieh Nan-kuang, who served both the Nationalists and the Communists in turn.

Magazine as a concession to antiforeign prejudice. It first appeared as a monthly, then as a weekly, and at last (in 1932) it
became a daily newspaper, the *Taiwan New People's News* or
Taiwan Shin Mimpō. For a time it was allowed to carry several
pages of Chinese text for the benefit of elderly persons who
read only Chinese. All Formosans associated with it were under
some degree of police surveillance, the proprietors had to accept
Japanese on the managerial staff, and every issue was scrutinized to ensure that nothing subversive or offensive to the Japanese appeared in its pages. Despite this, it reflected Formosan
opinion to an important degree. Although guarded in tone
when touching on political questions, the underlying thesis was
clear—Formosa must soon be treated on a par with the prefectures of Japan proper in economic and political matters, and the
island must be allowed to preserve its own cultural identity.
Formosans must achieve self-respect through recognition as
equals among all other subjects of the emperor.*

After returning from Europe and America, Lin Hsien-
t'ang took a bold step in helping the moderate advocates of
Home Rule found a new association, the People's Party or
Minshū-tō. Chiang Wei-shui and Ts'ai Pei-ho developed a
program with scrupulous care, writing and rewriting a platform
until it met with police approval and an organizing permit was
secured. Hope for a distinct island parliament had worn away;
what was proposed now was a compromise with emphasis upon
the need for local elective councils and assemblies whose membership would be without racial distinction or quota and whose
functions would be patterned after those in Japan proper. Except for the provincial governors, all chairmen of local units
would be elected, and all local governments would be bound by
decisions reached in the councils. Because Formosa had been
earning its own way and sending a surplus to Tokyo since
1905, the island people, through their local representatives,
must be allowed some voice in control of local budgets. Social
inequities must be overcome, the labor movement must be al-

---

* On the revival of these magazines in 1946, underwritten and edited by
the sons and nephews of the original Home Rule advocates, see *Formosa Betrayed*, pp. 218 and 313. The Minpō Press was destroyed by Chiang Kai-
shek's agents and the editor (Dr. Lin Mou-sheng) was assassinated in March
1947.

lowed to develop in an orderly fashion to protect the masses, and economic discrimination in all forms must cease.

As Dr. Chen observes in his monograph on political movements, once again the Japanese were faced with a dilemma; the Formosan demands were legitimate, and so too, were the orderly processes by which the Formosans sought to achieve their goals, but if these goals were met, and an unfettered elective system were introduced, then the Japanese minority in Formosa would be submerged.

Having secured the necessary police permits, Lin, Chiang, Ts'ai and their associates called into session the first formal, avowed political party conference in island history. As usual in all public gatherings, police agents were present to monitor the proceedings and to "maintain order."

The proposed party platform was read, section by section, and its authors and sponsors rose one after another to explain the document, citing the American program in the Philippines and the British arrangements in India. It was a formal restatement of familiar arguments.

Suddenly, on signal, the police sprang to their feet, shouted down protests, broke up the meeting, and directed the organizing committee to disband at once. The strain was too much, and faction again led to internal conflict and a damaging division among the Home Rule advocates. Chiang Wei-shui advocated a strong program in support of labor, and Ts'ai Pei-ho (always closer to Lin), urged a more moderate effort to secure the reform of local councils and the introduction of elective assemblies. Chiang, the activist, helped organize labor unions, which in 1928 were brought together to form the Taiwan Labor Federation (*Taiwan Kōyusō Renmei*). There followed a wave of strikes in Japanese-owned factories, many arrests and coercive police action. As Chiang became more openly critical of the Japanese he also made gestures calculated to win support from the Nationalist Chinese across the Strait. In 1929 he sent representatives to be present at Nanking when Sun Yat-sen's body was brought down from Peking to be placed in an elaborate mausoleum on Purple Mountain. Soon after, he devised a flag for the People's Party—an unnecessary gesture—that looked suspiciously like the Chinese Nationalist Party flag. This did the Formosan Party no good.

Lin Hsien-t'ang resigned all connections with it, and Ts'ai Pei-ho broke away to form an organization, a "League for the Attainment of Local Autonomy," devoted to the reform of local administration. Its meetings were conducted in the Japanese language and sympathetic Japanese were invited to attend. The wealthy landlord Yang Chao-chia became a cochairman and Lin became an "advisor." Chiang and Ts'ai now quarreled furiously, each repudiating the other's program, and making them the easier prey to the government's suppressive actions. The cat-and-mouse game of the policing agencies came to a dramatic pause, however, when an opportunity arose to advertise the Formosan-Japanese confrontation not only to the people of Japan proper, but to the world at large. Far away at Geneva the League of Nations Narcotics Control Commission announced an elaborate field investigation of the manufacture, distribution, control, and illicit use of drugs in Asia.

Commission members who proposed to visit Formosa in the course of their travels included Sweden's Minister to the Argentine (Commission Chairman), a Belgian, and a Czech representative, and a suitable secretarial staff. Tokyo thought the investigation in Formosa to be unnecessary, for Japan everywhere was applauded for its enlightened approach to the narcotics problem and its ready cooperation with other governments in the exchange of relevant information. The League of Nations considered Japan's annual statistical reports to be exemplary. The antinarcotics education program introduced in the Formosan public schools in the early 1920s had been hailed with interest and great approbation in other countries.

Since the investigation, however unwelcome, was unavoidable, the government prepared volumes of data, and selected witnesses to answer every query promptly so that the inquiry could be reduced to a *pro forma* affair. Six Monopoly Bureau officials, thirteen other government officers, three doctors and one "employer of labor" were groomed to give testimony.

The Commissioners spent the period February 19 to March 2, 1930, on the island. At closed sessions government spokesmen explained the organization of the Monopoly Bureau and the legal and social aspects of the narcotics control program. Three Formosan members of the Governor's Council assured the foreign guests that control policies were acceptable and effective, and that addicts now numbered fewer than fifty thousand—less than one-third the number of addicts present when the Japanese came into the island.

All went well until the Commissioners asked for a statement of popular views and a public hearing. Reluctantly the Government convened an open meeting. Soon after the opening formalities had been completed, there was a stir throughout the crowded assembly hall as someone pushed forward to hand the visitors a long document signed by Lin Hsien-t'ang on behalf of the Home Rule advocates, and by Formosan representatives of the Island's medical and legal professions.

The paper proved to be a sensational refutation of the testimony of the government's representatives and of the "three golden voices," the three Council members. The Monopoly Bureau, it said, actually promoted chronic addiction to provide excuse for continuing operations and the vaunted "opium control program" was a façade behind which the Bureau processed opium, cocaine, and their derivatives for supply to the illicit international market on a very large scale.

A prolonged and angry exchange revealed an unprecedented public concern. Reflecting this in later official reports the Commissioners noted that in fourteen other Asian countries the natives ("indigenes") either lacked interest or had been given no opportunity to testify. In Burma, for example, only six Burmese had appeared, in the Netherlands Indies only four, and in French Indo-China only one. Here in Formosa no fewer than 117 Formosans pushed forward to testify or to submit written statements.

Out of this welter of testimony the League of Nations learned that of five divisions within the Monopoly Bureau (Salt, Matches, Liquor, Tobacco, and Opium), the one processing narcotics was hedged about with great secrecy. Although the public at home and abroad had been assured that Formosa's aged addicts were disappearing and that the novice was compelled to accept treatment, in truth new licenses were issued quietly as old addicts died, and the numbers reported each year were "adjusted" to preserve appearances. Behind the cover of elaborate codes and regulations the Taipei administration was processing and exporting narcotics as an extremely profitable business.

Tokyo used narcotics as a hidden weapon wherever agents could be found to encourage addiction in areas marked for Japanese penetration. British India and Persia were the principal sources for raw opium processed at Taipei for re-export. North China and Manchuria were prime target areas. Although the poppy was not cultivated on Formosa, extensive coca plantations flourished in the highlands of Taichung and in the hills back of Taitung. The "general pharmaceutical laboratories" of the Central Research Institute made the production of cocaine and its derivatives a prime subject of experiment.

The Home Rule leaders then retold the story of the abrupt recall of Governor-General Uchida and Civil Administrator Kaku in 1924. Uchida had served as Civil Administrator from 1910 until 1915, in the heyday of Sakuma's corrupt administration, and in that period Kaku had risen to become Director of the Monopoly Bureau. When Uchida returned as Governor-General, Kaku became Civil Administrator, and the stage was set for a new "Sakuma era." Both were then suddenly compelled to resign after less than one year in office. They were found to have been shielding an illicit international narcotics traffic on the largest scale. The Monopoly Bureau (under Kaku's control) had long collaborated with a Mitsui subsidiary and with the Hoshi Pharmaceutical Company in a conspiracy to import, process, and export drugs illegally. The stakes were extremely high. Many officials had to be paid off in this delicate operation, to secure silence or favors—falsification of papers, for example—and a threat of blackmail hung over every participant. When a bitter quarrel of political origin developed within the administration—the right man had not been paid off on the right terms—the head of the pharmaceutical company (Hoshi Hajime) was exposed, arrested, and tried for having attempted to bring in 158,240 pounds of unlicensed opium, and for having arranged for the Monopoly Bureau to sell to him, as "worthless residue," certain narcotics then commanding a very high price on the international market. Hoshi had been associated with Uchida and Kaku for some fifteen years.

Since Hoshi was a civilian holding no government appointment, he was made the scapegoat and sentenced to a light prison term. Uchida was sufficiently influential to escape punishment, and Kaku was sent off to distant Geneva as an "authority on narcotics control," representing Japan at the headquarters of the League of Nations Narcotics Control Commission.

Against the background of this shabby tale, the Formosan leaders boldly warned the League Commissioners that the Taipei Monopoly Bureau continued secretly to supply world markets with illicit drugs, that the vaunted antinarcotics educational campaign in the primary schools had been abandoned, and that narcotics were being pushed covertly among young Formosans who were potential community leaders.*

Lin and his associates took care that copies of the sensational report and of their recommendations should reach metropolitan newspapers in Japan and the League Headquarters in Geneva. Angry Japanese officials realized that such harsh indictment of the Monopoly Bureau clearly implied criticism of other administrative departments and the law enforcement agencies. An important source of government revenue was threatened, and—worst of all—His Imperial Majesty's Government had been exposed to criticism and its honor impugned before the world.

Soon after the League Commission returned to Europe the Governor-General was obliged to announce modification of the opium control program with changes to include a new Opium Research Institute and Hospital. The Director would be a distinguished young Formosan, Dr. Tu Tsung-ming (Tō Sōmei). Across the world the published League report on narcotics control in Formosa studiously avoided any reference to the heated exchanges that had taken place at Taipei, nevertheless the official figures were qualified by phrases such as "The Government, in its official reply . . . ," thus suggesting that there was an alternate unofficial story. It noted, too, that the Commissioners had heard "117 unofficial witnesses" in addition to the twenty-eight put forward by the administration.[2]

This League of Nations inquiry closed an angry decade, full of kaleidoscopic confusion of leadership, shifting loyalties,

* Dr. Llewelyn Little, Chief Surgeon and Director of the MacKay Mission Hospital (Taipei), told me in 1937 that his outpatient casework with narcotics addicts indicated clearly that Monopoly Bureau drugs were made available to young men of the emergent middle class, particularly in the Hakka communities of the Hsinchu region.

organizations, names, and publications. There was underlying agreement in the fundamental desire for recognition of Formosa and of the inherent rights and interests of the Island people. This was shared by all. But on the Right those who thought self-respect and equality could be gained within the Japanese empire by full assimilation quarreled with those on the Left whose radical leaders demanded more than the Japanese could possibly concede at that time. At the center the moderates, lead steadily by Lin Hsien-t'ang, believed that free Formosan participation in an Island administration within the empire, and full elective representation of Formosan interests at Tokyo would ultimately be attainable. The strong heritage of traditional interclan, intervillage rivalries continued to be reflected in fragmented leadership and in the failure of ambitious individuals to compromise or to agree among themselves in support of a unified leadership and program. They were an easy prey to the authoritarian Japanese administration.*

* This continued to be true after World War II, and rendered the expatriate "United Formosans for Independence" impotent, thanks to personal rivalries.

9. Crises and Concessions

THE MUSHA REBELLION

*J*N MIDAUTUMN 1930, the debate generated by the League of Nations incident was overshadowed by the shock and excitement of a bloody uprising in the hills. Boundaries of the new prime forest reserve corresponded roughly with boundaries of the "temporary" reservation maintained for the unassimilated aborigines. Within this reserve, two splendid national parks had been set aside in the central ranges.* The parklands were to remain undisturbed, but the timber elsewhere was to become available for controlled and licensed exploitation. By now park rangers, police, and timbermen were pushing into every mountain gorge and high meadow.

In a mountain region back of Taichung, opened to general settlement for the first time, Musha Village became a new regional headquarters. Here several important mountain trails converged upon the terminus of a road and pushcar line leading up from the lowland, and to this station came the Taichung provincial governor with many guests, servants, and porters on the late afternoon of October 26. They were there to dedicate the new administrative buildings, and many officials had brought their wives with them, for the high slopes were ablaze with autumn color, making this a festive leaf-viewing excursion as well as an official occasion.

* Tsugitaka-Taroko N.P. (272,590 hectares, 673,670 acres), and Niitaka-Arisan N.P. (185,980 hectares, 459,557 acres). A third, smaller national park embraced a hotspring region near Taipei—the Daiton N.P. (8,265 hectares, 20,423 acres).

In the early morning of October 27, the company gathered near a flagstaff to hear the governor's address and to shout "Banzai!" No one noticed the absence of aboriginal women and children, or that the Formosan-Chinese porters had slipped quietly away. As the flag went up, Japanese cheers were suddenly drowned in wild shouts. Hundreds of tribesmen leaped from hiding to fall on the visitors with spears, swords, and guns.

When the aborigines had been driven off after a desperate fight, 197 Japanese lay dead, among them the provincial governor. It was soon discovered that policemen stationed at outlying watchposts had been slain on the previous evening, and that the total death toll was well above two hundred.

Army units promptly marched into the hills. After twenty days' action, it was announced that they had captured or killed a majority of the rebels, adding the unbelievable explanation that the women and children of the region had "committed suicide" by hanging themselves in their tiny huts. The huts therefore had been burned.

Investigation disclosed that a young Taichung Normal School graduate named Moldanao had planned and directed the attack, recruiting 375 men from nearby villages having a total population of about 1,500. He had been opposed, at first, by another well-educated youth whose Japanese name was Hanaoka Ichirō, but when Hanaoka failed to dissuade his fellows from this hopeless action, he joined them. Although for a time both leaders eluded capture, in the end they and their families committed suicide or were hunted down and killed.

The Musha Rebellion shook confidence in the Japanese policing agencies. Their elaborate networks of controls and spies had failed to alert them, and the suggestive evidence that there was an understanding between the Musha tribesmen and the local Formosan Chinese was particularly unnerving. Home Rule leaders and the People's Party had recently urged the government to adopt a more lenient and progressive attitude toward the mountain people—a first hint that the two subject peoples might draw together in a common cause.

The metropolitan press elaborated stories of the rebellion in gruesome detail, dwelling upon the savage character of military reprisals and creating such nationwide revulsion and criticism that the Governor-General and the Civil Administrator were compelled to "accept responsibility" and resign in January 1931.

Editorials across the country reviewed the causes of bitter discontent in "Japan's Ireland." The mountain people complained that they were paid wages even lower than those earned by Formosan-Chinese coolies, and that conditions of compulsory labor under police supervision had become intolerable. Policemen were no longer being trained for special mountain duty and the ordinary police agent was indifferent to the problems of language and local customs in the varied tribal regions. None remained long enough on one assignment to establish rapport with the people whose lives they supervised with absolute authority. The most bitter complaints had to do with sex. Too many policemen demanded the services of attractive girls at the mountain stations and then left them to move on to new assignments in other regions. The official story had it that Moldanao had become passionately offended when a policeman contemptuously refused to share the "double cup" used at local wedding feasts, but the popular story had it that his sister had been ravished by a policeman.

At Tokyo opposition party leaders and liberals demanded a thorough review and moderation of policing policies in the colony. The Government responded by appointing as new Governor-General a career specialist in police administration. On taking up his duties on January 16, 1931, Ōta Masahiro made it clear that he proposed to break forever any lingering spirit of rebellion. He first took careful note of immemorial blood feuds in the hills and then divided the central mountain tribes and subgroups into "protected tribes" and "allied tribes." The hamlets and houses of the "protected" natives were searched rigorously and all weapons confiscated. Arms were then issued to their traditional enemies, the so-called allied tribes, after which Ōta's men looked the other way.

There are no reliable figures on this extermination campaign, but the number of "protected" men, women, and children slaughtered between January and May was conceded to have been in the thousands. Official attempts to censor news dispatches merely spurred reporters to comb the island for reports and stories filled with lurid detail. Publication led to sensational debates at Tokyo concerning "human rights" and the rights of the hapless mountain people. An embarrassed national administration was told that its own armed forces in Formosa were the true barbarians, with an oblique reminder that they were operating as His Majesty's troops.

In the midst of this, on February 24, 1931, the People's Party met at Taipei again to review events of 1930—including the "narcotics affair" and the Musha incident—and to consider future programs. At that time the Party had seventeen branches and some eight hundred active members scattered across the island.* All members associated with Lin's "League for Attainment of Local Autonomy" had been read out of the Party and its platform had been rewritten in the previous week to call for "the unity of propertyless people" everywhere. Chiang Wei-shui had moved far to the left.

As this meeting began, Governor-General Ōta's agents broke in, arrested many, and ordered the People's Party to disband forthwith. Chiang and his chief associates were held in prison overnight and then released; harassment continued. Many of his followers left the Island for self-imposed exile. The Government increased restrictions upon foreign travel and made it difficult to secure permission to study overseas. All communication between the expatriates and their families at home were closely watched. In October, Dr. Chiang died, it was alleged, of mistreatment at the hands of the police, becoming a martyr in the eyes of the public.

The unfortunate and ineradicable factionalism among Formosan leaders and the sensational events of 1930 and 1931 could not wholly conceal the development of an islandwide sense of Formosan political identity versus the Japanese administration. This growing unity of interests was fostered by the well-developed communications network within the island, the common primary school system, interdependent economic in-

* The American Vice Consul (Charles S. Reed), reported: "The Minshu-tō is composed of Formosan-Chinese from all walks of life and all degrees of education. Among the leaders of the Party are lawyers, physicians and businessmen, some of whom attended colleges and universities in the United States. Although opposed to the Government on all questions, this Party is especially denunciatory of the policy of opium control." [1]

terests, and even the new lingua franca, elementary Japanese, in which all younger members of the Hakka, Hoklo, and Cantonese Chinese could communicate with one another, and with a rapidly growing number of aborigines able to speak Japanese.

Japan was planning new continental adventures. It became clear to the highest authorities at Tokyo that some substantial concessions would have to be made in the colony to reduce tensions there. While moving Japanese forces into China, as the military proposed to do, the government could risk no chance of an uprising in Formosa.

On March 2, 1932, Governor-General Ōta was recalled. It had been decided quietly to meet several basic demands of the moderate Home Rule leaders. The year 1935 was chosen as the time in which to create local provincial assemblies and to establish elective councils at the provincial level. Much had to be done to prepare the way.

A "FRIENDS OF THE MASSES" CONSPIRACY

While Ōta's soldiers were campaigning so effectively in the hills, the last serious anti-Japanese conspiracy, undetected, was maturing in the lowlands. To pick up the story we must go back a little to the late 1920s, when two immigrant Chinese wood-carvers joined forces with a fortune-teller named Sung Sung (So So) to form a club named innocently enough the "Parents' Society" (*Fubō kai*). It was designed originally to fleece superstitious country people who frequented the Hsinchu temple at which the three men were employed. By 1929 some three hundred gullible farmers and village shopkeepers were contributing to it. Although the police looked into it as they looked into all associations, the agents planted among the membership detected nothing subversive in its simple operations.

In that year, however, a Hsinchu native named Ts'ai returned to Formosa after seven years in China. He had taken an economics degree at Peking University and had held some minor posts with the Nationalist Party Government until ill health forced him to go home for a long convalescence. He had been stirred by the great nationalist movement on the continent and was filled with "dangerous thoughts." These he began to share with sympathetic friends. At some point he and the fortune-teller Sung Sung agreed to bring about the restoration of Formosa to China, setting the years 1935–1936 as the target date for a general rebellion.

Others were quietly drawn into the plot. For a long period the leaders escaped detection, successfully gathering and concealing weapons with great ingenuity. As the conspiracy gained momentum, the so-called Parents' Society became directly involved. Many people knew the secret, police agents discovered what was going on, and in September 1934, the government struck hard.

Four hundred and twenty-five persons were arrested. After prolonged investigations and trials, 316 prisoners were declared to have been innocent dupes and were freed, under strict surveillance. For the others—109 persons—the sentences were harsh: the leaders were executed, and the rest given long terms at hard labor.

The Japanese were deeply disturbed by evidence of discontent at all levels of Formosan society, and by the link with events in continental China. It was found, for example, that the majority of people under arrest were illiterate countryfolk—farmers and day laborers who had been persuaded that supernatural forces would drive the Japanese from the island—but no fewer than ninety-two had been educated in the public elementary schools, and at least one-fourth had also been privately educated in the Chinese Classics. Only five had finished middle or higher school courses. Clearly something had to be done to reeducate the rising generation and much had to be done to destroy any lingering sense of identity with continental China.

THE MANCHURIAN AND SHANGHAI "INCIDENTS," 1931–1932

Changing policies in Formosa reflected Japan's changing international position. The decade following World War I had brought disappointment, frustration, and anger. Feeding on this, the military were again in the ascendency at Tokyo, and Japan had decided to go it alone.* The white man would be

* Despite London's earlier, secret promises, at Versailles, Japan had been refused clear title to Germany's Pacific islands and was obliged to accept only a League of Nations mandate. Tokyo then behaved as Washington subsequently behaved in Micronesia under a United Nations mandate or trustee-

compelled to give up his privileged position in Asia, and Japan would assume leadership among the Asian nations.

England was unmistakably determined to block Japan's economic operations in China. The growth of Soviet strength in Siberia and the Maritime Provinces threatened Japan's industrial investment in Manchuria, and the Chinese were showing signs of pulling themselves together under a new, intensely nationalistic leadership. They were adopting Wei Yüan's advice that "There are two methods of attacking the barbarians, namely, to stimulate countries unfriendly to the barbarians to make attack upon them, and to learn the superior skills of the barbarians in order to control them." [2]

Thousands of young Chinese had gone abroad to acquire these "superior skills," Dr. Sun Yat-sen among them. Sun's young aide Chiang Kai-shek had gone repeatedly to Japan and had graduated from the best military academy at Tokyo. When the aging Dr. Sun began to look to Moscow for help, he sent Chiang to Russia to observe totalitarian army, party, and policing organizations, and at the time of Sun's death (1925), more than one thousand Russian "advisors" were assisting the new Nationalist Chinese Army and Party. Tokyo watched all these activities with grave concern.

The close alliance between the Russian communists and the Nationalist party (the Kuomintang or KMT) continued until the Party's bitter factional struggle led on to the Great Schism of 1927. Chiang and his associates moved into the Yangtze Valley and occupied the coastal provinces. Soon after occupying Shanghai Chiang sent his elder son, Ching-kuo, off to Russia where he was to remain seven years, marry a Russian wife, and work for the Soviet government. Meanwhile the older Chiang pensioned off his own first wife (Ching-kuo's mother) to

---

ship after World War II, taking exclusive control and using the islands for secret military purposes. London and Washington refused to write a "racial equality" clause into the Versailles Treaty, a grave offense to Japanese sensibilities. At the Washington Naval Conference (1921–1922) the two democracies obliged Tokyo to accept a humiliating 5–5–3 ratio in naval strength, and England, at Washington's insistence, abandoned the Anglo–Japanese Alliance that had been Japan's pride for twenty years. To cap these incidents, the American Congress in 1924 formalized racial discrimination in the Oriental Exclusion Act, a gesture interpreted as a show of contempt for the entire Japanese nation.

make way for a marriage alliance with the Soong-Kung family, representing the most important banking, commercial, and industrial interests in China at that time. Henceforth he would protect and advance Soong-Kung interests within China while the principal members of that extraordinary family in turn supplied funds and matériel for his military ventures in China, and exploited their worldwide economic and religious connections to secure international recognition and support for the Nationalist regime. This was a formidable alliance.

Tokyo saw that successful unification of China by the Chinese would threaten all foreign interests within the country. If Japan's dream of imperial expansion through Manchuria into Mongolia were to be realized, the drive there would have to be undertaken before the road was blocked by a resurgent China, by Russia, or by an alliance between the two.

Overriding all civilian opposition at Tokyo, Japan's Kwantung Army in South Manchuria contrived the Mukden Incident of September 18, 1931, and in January 1932, the Imperial Japanese Navy attacked Shanghai, the very heart of China's industrial and commercial life. On March 9 the Army announced the birth of a new nation, the puppet state of Manchukuo. Chiang Kai-shek signed the Tangku Truce in May, leaving Japan dominant along the coast southward from Shanghai. There the Japanese Navy in effect became custodian of Japan's long-established special treaty privileges. Although the Navy and Japan's southern expansionists were jealous of the Army's vastly enlarged authority in Manchuria and North China, the national economy was not yet strong enough to support military operations on two fronts; hence realization of Kodama's dream of empire in Southeast Asia had to be postponed.

With these developments on the continent, Formosans in China were caught between two worlds, the world of old, backward China and the world of dynamic, ambitious Japan. Thousands of expatriates in Shanghai, Foochow, Amoy, and other large cities found themselves in a most difficult position. Traditional Chinese prejudice toward "barbarian" Formosa was reenforced by a belief that the island people had become too Japanized. Many expatriates who refused to live under direct Japanese rule on Formosa nevertheless found it advantageous to retain Japanese passports and to register at the Japanese coastal consulates. Some were agents in Japanese pay—including not a few criminals who at Taipei had been given a choice between imprisonment on Formosa or employment as narcotics peddlers or *agents provocateurs* in China. Others were merely businessmen who seized the advantage of dual citizenship in a region in which Japan enjoyed special treaty rights. But as the Chinese felt that they had become too Japanized, many Japanese officers from Japan proper looked upon them as "too Chinese" and somewhat suspect because they had chosen to leave Formosa.

Formosan business men and students going back and forth could not ignore the contrast between impoverished, backward China, and the island of Formosa, with its rising living standards and well-regulated public services. Formosan clubs, societies, and brotherhoods in the Chinese cities brought them together for social and economic purposes, and wherever they met, these sharp contrasts were discussed.

Into this Fukien region, in 1934, Chiang Kai-shek sent his colleague General Chen Yi as "Chairman of the Fukien Provincial Government," beginning a career in association with Formosa that was to lead on to his death on a Taipei racecourse, in 1950, at the hands of Chiang's executioners.*

GENERAL CHEN YI IN FUKIEN—THE FORMOSAN VIEW

General Chen and his Japanese wife—a former geisha—settled down near Foochow in 1934 and for seven years thereafter played a most ambiguous role in Sino-Japanese relations. Patriotic Chinese students had launched a nationwide boycott of trade with Japan, provoked by the Manchurian and Shanghai

* Chen Yi (1883–1950), had been five years old when Chiang was born nearby in Fenghua District, Chekiang Province. On graduating from the Japanese military academy in the year of Chiang's enrollment there (1907), he returned to China, followed in due course by Chiang. Both men engaged in obscure underworld activities in Shanghai until the younger man, attaching himself to Sun Yat-sen, began to rise to prominence in the Nationalist Party movement. Chen, however, established no close personal relationship with Sun, was never well known to foreigners in China, never pretended to be a Christian and cultivated no friendly advocates in the Christian missionary community. For a time Chen held a military command under the weak but legitimate Chinese government at Peking. Betraying that regime at one point he enabled Chiang easily to take Shanghai, securing that essential power base and the enormously useful alliance with the powerful Soong Family. In reward the Generalissimo made Chen successively Director of Arsenals in the

incidents; nevertheless, the leading industrial and commercial interests of Shanghai continued to trade with unscrupulous industrialists in Kobe, Osaka, and Yokohama. Amoy and Foochow served as side doors into China through Japan's "special sphere of interest." Japanese ships were frequently in these waters and Chen and his wife maintained the appearance of cordial social rapport with the admirals and captains of the enemy's ships. It was assumed by many that the Chens were stationed at Foochow to protect clandestine trading interests.

Chen Yi was identified with the powerful Pai Chung-hsi and the so-called Political Science Clique in the government and Party organization. The Generalissimo, as usual, placed his own trusted agents near Chen to keep an eye on him, and Soong took care to surround him with men who would provide a proper management of the enormously rewarding overseas trade. Soong protégés represented the China Merchants Steam Navigation Company and the Communications Ministry in Fukien; Yen Chia-kan, outstanding among them, served as "Reconstruction Commissioner," Board Chairman of the Bank of Fukien, and Finance Commissioner of Fukien Province.

General Chen had been sent into Fukien to "reconstruct" the province following collapse of a local independence movement in 1933. It had been led by men who rejected Chiang Kai-shek and the Nationalist Party leadership. They were destroyed and the province was ruled thereafter with great severity. Yen Chia-kan and the other young civil officers from Shanghai thereupon developed what they chose to call "necessary state socialism," a euphemism for a system of state monopolies designed to wring a maximum return from the local economy. Soong's protégés controlled communications, shipping, and provincial finance, and it was widely believed that in return for military and police protection of these overseas trading interests, General Chen himself had been given a free hand to

---

War Ministry, Administrative Vice-Minister of War, and Political Vice-Minister of War, positions concerned with the flow of military supply from the great cities to the outlying provinces, and each offering superb opportunities for collusion with bankers, industrialists, importers, and shipping interests— all fields dominated by the Kungs and the Soongs.

squeeze the local economy—the Fukien people—for the benefit of the Nationalist Army and himself.*

The traditionally restive Fukien people objected to the presence of Chen and his Japanese wife, bitterly protested the monopolies, and denounced the continuing trade with the enemy. Gendarmes imprisoned critics, executing many, and forced many others to leave Fukien. Chen's police were especially notorious for brutal treatment of demonstrating and rioting students in the larger towns. Scores of Formosan expatriates decided that life under the Japanese was the lesser evil and returned to their island homes. Fukien was the "face of China" seen from across the Strait, and Chen Yi's abusive policies brought the entire Nationalist Chinese establishment into disrepute on Formosa.

Expatriate Formosans in China's larger cities joined in criticizing the Fukien administration. Groups ranging from colorless social clubs to ardent political associations began to speak out; some supported Chiang and the Nationalist Party, and some called for a new Leftist revolution. Japanese agents in China kept close watch on all overseas Formosan activities and were not pleased when a Formosan "Anti-imperialist League" in Shanghai began to distribute pamphlets calling for popular rebellion in the island. This provided excellent excuse to justify suppression of the People's Party at Taipei, and to increase pressure upon all advocates of Home Rule.

KŌMINKA—A NEW JAPANIZATION PROGRAM

When Japan's armies were in full control in Manchuria and Jehol Province, north of the Great Wall, preparations were made for a drive southward to set up puppet regional governments in North China and to squeeze Western competitors out of the Yangtze Valley and Shanghai. Military action must be anticipated along the Fukien coast at some time, and the reac-

* Several of these Soong agents followed Chen to Chungking and then accompanied him to Formosa in 1945, where "necessary state socialism" promptly provoked the uprising of 1947. Yen Chia-kan was always present in the background, more powerful than the governors, until he himself became Governor of Formosa, and ultimately Vice-President and Premier of Nationalist China.

tion on Formosa had to be considered. Hard-line chauvinists advocated a tough no-nonsense policy at Tokyo and Taipei. They would treat the island-colony as a permanently subordinate possession, inhabited by non-Japanese subjects and destinued always to be held under rigid military administration. The great corporate interests—the sugar, pineapple, mining, and lumber industries—joined in advocating firm authoritarian controls, for they wanted only a docile labor force.

Thoughtful Japanese leaders, however, knew that Formosa had moved a long way from traditional China and believed that in another generation or two the island people could be assimilated to Japan proper as the Okinawans had been assimilated after 1878. The conflict between advocates of these two points of view produced profound inconsistencies of decision in the bureaucratic agencies at Tokyo and Taipei between 1932 and 1945.

Adoption of suppressive policies—the chauvinists' "hard line"—might lead to islandwide disaffection and even rebellion, and this Japan could not afford in the midst of a great campaign to win native support throughout colonial Asia. Nor could Tokyo risk rebellion in Formosa while engaged in military operations along the Fukien coast. On the other hand, adoption of the full Formosan Home Rule formula was not possible; there was no precedent for a colonial Formosan parliament differing in any way from prefectural assemblies elsewhere in Japan, and the idea of a permanent Formosan cultural subdivision within the empire ran counter to the concept of the nation-family, united under His Majesty the Emperor.

A compromise was found in an "assimilation program," to which was given the name Kōminka. This meant, in effect, complete assimilation, "union with the emperor's people," or "changing into imperial subjects" by adopting Japanese ways and becoming acceptable as "true Japanese." It was a modern version of the ancient Chinese formula for civilizing barbarians, adapted to Japanese use. On the political level there was a token concession; prefectural "advisory councils" were created in which half the membership was elected by popular vote and the other members were selected and appointed by the local governor. Tokyo took great care to allow no elective offices to be established on an islandwide basis.

Advocates of the Kōminka policy believed that in due course Formosans could be made to substitute one culture for another throughout the colony, but ultranationalist critics considered it a contradiction of terms to suggest that aliens anywhere could become "true Japanese." They treated the Kōminka program therefore as something put forward by impractical and possibly dangerous liberals. Entrenched bureaucrats and business managers were irritated by the idea that Formosans must be treated as equals under the law. Proponents of Kōminka, to be sure, too often mistook form for substance, vigorously enforcing an exterior conformity of manners, customs, clothing, and language without realizing how deep was the resentment generated by a forcing process.

Thus Formosans often found themselves caught between rival forces. Each measure approved by Tokyo with a view to mollifying Formosan leaders and relieving tension within the island was met by countermeasures devised by the entrenched conservatives at Taipei. Policing became an obsession with the Old Guard, who mistrusted the relative liberalism of these new policies. After 1932 the social control duties of the police force were increased and the number of disciplinary agencies multiplied to an absurd degree. There were civil police, gendarmes, regular and secret naval police, harbor police, railway police, economic police, and "thought" police constantly on the prowl, vying with one another to prove that they were foremost in protecting the true Japanese interest and the imperial polity.

Japan's deep sensitivity to the issue of racial discrimination prompted exploitation of the "Oriental versus Caucasian" theme in Tokyo's bid for Asian leadership among the colonial subjects of England, Holland, France, and the United States. It is not surprising therefore to observe that one of the first Kōminka measures was designed to reduce the sense of racial discrimination in the colony.

Legal bars to marriage between Japanese and Formosans were removed, many long-standing unions were recognized at last, and children of mixed marriages no longer suffered legal disabilities.

But social integration was not something to be accomplished by legal fiat; it was one thing to announce the inauguration of a new era of social equality, and quite another to overcome established prejudice. Many Japanese and Formosans had long since established good working relations, partnerships, and friendships, but the marks of social separation lingered on. Certain areas of Taipei city remained predominantly Japanese in character and others were distinctly Formosan Chinese. Theaters, parks, tennis courts, public swimming pools, restaurants, hot springs, and beaches, though technically open to all, were in practice frequented predominantly by one or the other of the two cultural groups. It was a matter of personal preference, not of law.

Japanese and Formosans alike found a useful area of compromise by adopting Western ways, modified by either Formosan or Japanese taste. Very prosperous Formosans often chose to live in Western-style houses, with one or two Japanese-style mat-floored rooms in the living quarters and perhaps a Japanese-style garden on the grounds. Prosperous Japanese, on the other hand, lived in Japanese-style houses with a Western-style room attached, in which stood an upright piano, a table covered with tasseled green baize, and Western chairs. The Formosans tended to adopt Japanese ways, but except for certain delicious foods, the Japanese almost never adopted or adapted Formosan-Chinese cultural elements. One rarely saw a Formosan wearing a Japanese kimono, although the cheap wooden footgear, the *geta*, were popular, and no Japanese could be seen wearing Formosan-Chinese clothing. In the towns Western-style uniforms and dresses were in general use as a matter of compromise, economy, and convenience; in the countryside the farmer and the day laborer continued in the old traditional Chinese modes of dress, and country houses were little changed.

KŌMINKA AND THE ABORIGINES

An attempt to assimilate a subject people to the master race and culture had no precedent among the colonial powers in Asia. Britain, France, and the Netherlands were content to train an élitist native group in their several possessions; the United States was about to withdraw from the Philippines. In contrast, Japan determined to absorb the inhabitants of Formosa. The complex effort to substitute Japanese for Chinese culture was a formidable task in the lowlands, among the older Formosa-Chinese people. For those born in the nineteenth century it was not really possible to undergo the transformation. In the mountains, on the other hand, the Japanese made more progress. The Malayo-Polynesian tribesmen possessed a much less sophisticated culture and the rewards for cooperation with the Japanese were more obvious.

The Kōminka program as it was applied in the hills was in effect a modifed version of Dr. Gotō's original control and assimilation policy, based on education and now brought up to date. Tensions eased, and the Musha Rebellion proved to be the last significant act of group resistance. The special territorial boundaries were strictly patrolled, to be sure, but they began to be pulled back to reduce the total "prohibited" area as rapidly as the tribesmen and the mountain hamlets could be prepared for admission to the general island economy. Taipei urged the Japanese and Formosan Chinese to accept the hill-people as equals and as fellow subjects. A campaign carried on in the press and in the schools directed the public to cease speaking contemptuously or carelessly of the aborigines as "savages" (seiban-jin) and to refer to them henceforth as the "Takasago people" (Takasago-zoku), thus reviving the old seventeenth-century name for the island.

Substitution of the Japanese language for diverse aboriginal dialects became a matter of first concern. By 1935 no fewer than 552 police posts and stations were established among the unassimilated people. Some were merely rough blockhouses to shelter armed patrols at night, and others—the larger stations— usually consisted of a log blockhouse and jail, a small Shintō shrine, a schoolroom or two, and the policeman's residence, which served also as a hostel for visiting officials and certified travelers. Some large stations at important trail intersections boasted a simple clinic, a vocational craft shop, and a small store where hides, cloth, sennit, basketry, carved wooden objects, coarse tobacco, peanuts, and other small products of local manufacture could be exchanged for iron pots, knives, matches, oil, and salt.*

* In 1942, when the aboriginal territory represented about 44 percent of Formosa's total area, the mountain police stations numbered 479, a reduction

A policeman's life in the high interior was rough, solitary, and dangerous; his first duty was to instill awe and dread of imperial authority, represented in his uniform and sword, and next, to inculcate respect for all Japanese persons, institutions, and objects. He was required to become teacher, doctor, and general counsel for all the tribesmen in his district, and if he were married, his wife was expected to assist him in the classroom, the clinic, and the hostel. He served as the government's eyes and ears, reporting upon a great variety of subjects. His notes on sickness, births, and deaths supplied the public health and census records at Taipei, and his rainfall records, earthquake data, and natural history notes ultimately served the interests of the power industry and the forest service managing timber reserves. The policeman was primarily a disciplinarian, but beyond that he was Taipei's most direct and important link with the mountain people occupying half the total island area.

One by one, aboriginal families dwelling in the remote interior were obliged to move down to clearings assigned to them conveniently near police stations, and each was given assistance in building a standardized hut near a suitable water supply. The old independent hunting economy had been shattered forever, and each relocated family was obliged to supply itself principally from lands assigned to village use, cultivating a few sweet potatoes, a little coarse tobacco, peanuts, or ramie, and some newer food plants introduced by the Government's agents.

Not all the varied tribal people could be made over into useful citizens at an equal pace; just as the American Indian tribal orders have shown varied skills and degrees of adaptability, so, on a smaller scale, the natives of Formosa began to be absorbed into the larger community. It was found that the high mountain tribesmen—the Bunun and Atayal people—were generally unfit for either confining indoor work or outdoor tasks requiring monotonous repetition of a work pattern. They were superb woodsmen, however, employable in forest conservation projects requiring scouts to patrol the high watersheds in all weather.

---

of 73 during the preceding seven Kōminka years. The social service facilities had increased to include 180 educational units, 42 clinics, and 111 trading posts.

The settled Ami people, agriculturalists along the southeast coast, were long since classified as assimilated, and by 1935 some ten thousand members of the Paiwan group in the southern hills had been accepted and classified as ordinary subjects. The Yami tribesmen, who numbered only about sixteen hundred and lived in isolation on the small island of Botel Tobago, were deemed to be quite beyond hope of full assimilation. Their rocky islands had no resources beyond the local roots, plants, fruit trees, goats, pigs, and fish needed to sustain them. It was therefore decided to preserve Botel Tobago (Kō-tōsho) as an undisturbed anthropological reservation. A steamer called there once or twice a month to deliver supplies to the small police outpost—a residence, a clinic room, and a schoolroom in which a few bright Yami boys were taught a smattering of elementary Japanese. Visitors were few and were very carefully screened. Occasionally a botanist, zoologist, or anthropologist secured permission to accompany inspectors sent down periodically from Taipei.

By 1939 the Bureau of Education at Taipei reported some twenty thousand Takasago youths at school. For the first time in history members of all the subgroups and tribal divisions possessed a common language—Japanese—with which to communicate among themselves and with the Formosans and Japanese. To speed assimilation, educational tours were arranged for groups of tribesmen who were escorted into the larger towns to see the wonders of urban life and civilization, and promising boys and girls were enrolled in lowland primary and middle schools. Some then went on to the normal schools or to the "short course" offered at the Taipei medical school.

Headhunting was sternly condemned and suppressed, although it was extremely difficult for the older Bunun and Atayal warriors to give up the tradition and the ritual. A visiting European forestry expert was told (in 1934) that the going rate for a Formosan-Chinese head at that time was four times the value placed upon a Japanese skull, thanks to the centuries-old tradition of conflict with the bordermen, but that there was then no demand whatsoever for Caucasian trophies. Nevertheless, until the outbreak of World War II the Japanese and Formosan policemen rarely traveled alone and never unarmed in the high country. A great wariness marked all intercourse, and many monuments along the mountain trails provided grim reminders of an earlier day. Throughout the decade of the 1930s policemen and forest workers occasionally disappeared or were found dead, the victims of a quarrel or of a ritual killing, yielding a head for some old man's secret trophy shelf hidden in the forest.*

As part of the Kōminka program the Taipei bureaucrats required every household in Formosa to maintain a proper Shintō altar (the *kamidana*) upon which to display emblems of the Sun Goddess and her latest descendent, the Emperor Hirohito. To an old jungle-fighter the little disc of shining metal representing the mirror of Japan's Three Sacred Treasures, was indeed a poor substitute for a nicely bleached skull, but the younger, educated tribesmen were beginning to be embarrassed by these lapses into old practice. In the lowlands as in the mountains, Japan's first problem was to secure not only the acquiescence but also the loyal cooperation of the younger generation before the colony was put to the test of a general war with China.

* On hiking through the high country in the period 1937–1940, friends and I saw that every tribesman met along the trails was expected to step aside, bare his head, and bow respectfully. It was evident that the older Atayal and Bunun tribesmen looked upon our police escorts with deep hostility.

10. Accelerated Change on the Eve of War

*W*ITH solemn condescension Tokyo announced that His Majesty had been pleased to grant the privilege of elective government in the colony, to be inaugurated in 1935. Nothing in the official statements gave the least hint that the "imperial gift" had been wrung from the Government by the Home Rule leaders after twenty years of ceaseless agitation.

Although the offering proved to be form with little substance, it was at least a first definite move in the right direction. Lin Hsien-t'ang neither expected nor received credit for the gain, and the Home Rule Association had to be content without recognition for the part it had played in bringing about the concession. The arrangements fell far short of the Home Rule ideal of an islandwide elective body with authority to send representatives to the Diet in Japan proper. The importance of the announcement lay in recognition of the *principle* of representative government for the colony.

Assemblies were to be created in each province, county, and town, with half the membership to be elected by popular vote and half to be appointed by the provincial governors. These new bodies were to discuss and act on the local budget, certain local tax matters and a few unimportant administrative questions. The provincial governor, a Japanese, would hold the veto power in all deliberations.

It was an arrangement obviously designed to favor the Japanese, nevertheless it was a major concession. Since all hopes of an islandwide assembly were lost, Lin Hsien-t'ang and twenty-nine associates on September 2 quietly dissolved the old association for the establishment of a parliament. The People's Party had been forced to disband and Chiang Wei-shui was dead. This left only the League for Attaining Local Autonomy (the Home Rule Association) to lead and council the new electorate.

Voting qualifications for the first election limited the franchise to males at least twenty-five years of age who had suitable property qualifications and had been approved after review of that all-important dossier at the local police office. Candidates for office were carefully screened, and every pamphlet, public comment, and speech was scrutinized for taint of "dangerous thought." The police, in effect, set up and managed the elections, although with reluctance, for they had been ordered by Tokyo to make concessions of which they did not approve.

As the first election day approached, excitement ran high. Approximately 187,000 Formosans met the voter qualifications, and of these, it was reported, no less than 96.7 percent went to the polls. In the Hsinchu and Gilam areas—predominantly Hakka regions—the voting records were said to have been an astonishing 99.0 percent of the qualified and registered electorate. That the rigged system was unfair was at once apparent. One hundred and seventy-two persons were now ready to meet in the assemblies, but of these one hundred and nine were Japanese, and only sixty-three were Formosans. Further, the government had *appointed* sixty of the Japanese, and only twenty-six Formosans. In other words, only thirty-seven Formosans in all had actually been *elected* to office.

The police were relieved to have the elections go smoothly; contrary to Japanese fears and expectations, the assemblymen behaved themselves. Clearly Japanese-Formosan relations were improved, and as Lin had anticipated, once the elective principle had been established, gradually very real concessions began to be made. Wide experience at the polls was in itself important.

As usual, there was a price to pay. In September 1936, the new Governor-General, Admiral Kobayashi Seizō, advised Lin to disband the League "now that its objective had been achieved," and in the following year, on the occasion of the second biennial elections, the League leaders announced a "voluntary" dissolution. They had held out as long as they could. With this, the last of the six Home Rule Movement organizations disappeared. Their demise was inevitable on the eve of war with China, but their evolution was instructive. As Dr. Chen has summarized it, the first two had pursued the idea of social, political, and economic equality with the Japanese in Japan proper, and three had advocated some form of Home Rule. The dream of an Island legislature or parliament had to be given up, but the concession of elective local representation, however limited, was at last secured, and a precedent established. One organization—the Culture Society—by eschewing "politics," had managed to survive, strengthening the Formosan-Chinese sense of identity and self-respect.

Tokyo refused to entertain the idea of an island-wide assembly, fearful that it might become the power base for ambitious local leaders; nevertheless Taipei was directed to broaden the elective base by liberalizing property qualifications for voter registration in the second election period (1937). The Governor-General's Advisory Council was to be enlarged to number forty members, seventeen of them to be Formosans.

After the third biennial election (1939), when 286,700 Formosans registered, no fewer than 3,014 Formosans held *elective* office in the city, county, and provincial assemblies. The police force, too, was signing on Formosan recruits in the hundreds. The Japanese had discovered that concessions, however mild, paid high dividends. The Formosans on their part were becoming familiar with all the devices of political campaigns and electioneering—posters, pamphlets, campaign rallies, and influence-peddling—elements of training and experience that ultimately were to form a frame of reference for future (post-Surrender) demands and expectations.

THE FORTIETH ANNIVERSARY CONFERENCE, 1935

While the ordinary policeman and the grade-school teacher were fostering the Kōminka assimilation program, officers in the higher ranks of government were considering Formosa's economic and military potential for a future war. The fortieth year of Japanese sovereignty was celebrated with great fanfare.

As usual, an elaborate exposition at Taipei and lesser exhibitions and ceremonies elsewhere were accompanied by a series of economic conferences. National scientific and cultural societies were invited to meet in Formosa. The anniversary provided an excuse to refurbish Taipei, develop broad avenues, boulevards, and bridges, and to construct new parks. New and larger shrines exalted State Shintō, and near the site of the old Chinese administrative yamen—Liu Ming-ch'üan's headquarters—a handsome civic auditorium was built to accommodate conferences, concerts, banquets, and exhibitions. Parts of the old Chinese building complex were transferred to the enlarged Botanical Garden and to the zoo. Tourists were urged to come down from Japan proper to see for themselves the achievements of four decades of hard work and large investment in Treasure Island. Leading artists from Tokyo presented concerts and dramatic entertainment, and for those who liked the outdoor life there were new golf courses, new hotspring resorts, and new hiking trails laid out through the nearby hills and mountains. Tourists were encouraged to visit the Arisan forests and to climb the highest peak in the Japanese empire, Mount Niitaka.

The celebration served as an excuse to bring together many high officers of state in a festive atmosphere. There were a few foreign guests as well, and among them the Formosans were astonished to see the notorious General Chen Yi, Governor of Fukien. Chen rode in ceremonial processions and on one occasion addressed the Formosan people, congratulating them for progress achieved under imperial Japanese administration.

About sixty thousand continental Chinese—the majority of them from Fukien—lived and worked on Formosa in 1935 under an arrangement of temporary entry permits. The majority were unskilled laborers recruited for seasonal employment on sugar plantations and tea gardens, or for work in the mines. There were also many who had signed up with the Foochow and Amoy labor brokers in an effort to escape the pressures of Chen Yi's regime and the exploitation of his "necessary state socialism."

Behind closed doors, some of Japan's leading authorities in technology, economics, and administration were meeting with admirals, generals, and senior colonial administrators to design a program serving Tokyo's top-secret plans for imperial expansion—a renewed drive into continental China and an advance to the south.

Conference leaders were expected to prepare proposals and plans for an advanced base ready to process raw materials flowing back from Southeast Asia and the Indies. The Western powers were to be dispossessed and the European colonies brought under the umbrella of Japan's own Monroe Doctrine for East Asia. The slogan "Greater East Asia Co-Prosperity Sphere" had not yet been devised for propaganda purposes, but the fundamental decisions had been made. Formosa's future role was well defined.

The 1935 conference was the latest in a logical series of decennial meetings. The first and second (in 1905 and 1915) had elaborated overall agricultural programs for sugar and rice; the third (in 1925) had brought in the era of light industry related to processing of local products such as chemicals for agricultural use, bagasse pulp from the cane fields, industrial alcohol, and forest products. This fourth meeting (in 1935, known as the Tropical Industrial Research Conference) produced blueprints for an industrial structure designed to receive and process iron ore, bauxite, crude oil, and rubber from Malaysia and the Indies. All were essential industrial supplies, to be semifinished in Formosa and there stockpiled until shipped onward to Japan's great industrial centers. Local labor was comparatively cheap, power sources lay near the ports and industrial sites, and the island's forward position halfway between Japan and the tropics shortened the turn-around time for ocean freighters.

In short, the Kodama Plan was about to be realized. Formosa would become Japan's southern industrial frontier, roughly analogous to the great industrial base being developed in Manchuria under Kwantung Army supervision. In Formosa the Imperial Navy would play a dominant role: the continental clique and the southern clique each had its sphere of influence assigned to it.

The new industrial program required larger power resources and better port facilities. As of 1934, 11 government power installations and 139 private generating plants were soon to be supplemented by new units below Sun-Moon Lake, and new installations harnessing rivers in the gorges back of Hualien on the East Coast. A great new multipurpose dam pro-

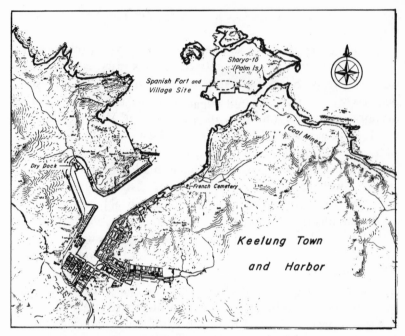

FIGURE 5. *Keelung in the twentieth century.* The Japanese enlarged and deepened Keelung harbor, sheltered from all but direct north winds. Spain occupied Palm Island from 1628 to 1642 and the Dutch held the Spanish forts from 1642 until 1668. England, the United States, and France each considered taking Keelung because of the coal mines nearby. Commodore M. C. Perry in 1854 proposed settling Americans there to support a joint Sino-American economic development program. French Foreign Legion units occupied Keelung in 1884–1885. Approximately 80 percent of the city was heavily damaged or totally destroyed during World War II.

posed for Shih-men (Sekimon) in the northern hills would supply water for irrigation as well as power. New steel mills, oil refineries, bauxite (aluminum) processing plants, and chemical industries were to be built conveniently near the ports.

Three artificial harbors were projected to relieve overcrowding at the older ports. One (Beiron) near Hualien would serve new East Coast industries; Gosei in Taichung Province would serve as a new outlet for sugar, rice, pineapples, and other agricultural products of the western lowlands, and Toshien, an anchorage just north of Takao, was to be developed to serve the Navy and the new petroleum refineries nearby.

All senior Conference participants were agreed upon the ultimate goals of this ambitious program, but there were many sharp conflicts of policy concerning details, priorities, and the like. Some leading economists felt that Formosa was being pushed too hard and that a heavy industry schedule was premature. Military men wanted sugar production reduced and the rice acreage increased to supply the immense quantities soon to be needed for the projected China campaigns. When Conference members from Japan proper proposed importing cheaper Korean labor, the Taipei administrators objected strongly that Koreans were less tractable than Formosans, and that the presence of many Koreans on the island would retard the Kōminka assimilation program just then beginning to show some success.

A façade of ceremonial display hid the serious long-range portent of the 1935 Conference and these conflicts were never made known to the public. The meetings adjourned, the Conference was proclaimed a success, and the participants returned to their usual activities. Soon after General Chen Yi returned to Foochow the Nationalist Chinese Government enlarged its Consulate at Taipei and the most cordial official relations appeared to prevail in the Strait.

Under Japanese provocation, however, Chinese nationalism grew stronger throughout China, and students in all provinces led in expressing anger and frustration that the Chinese government could not or would not do more to block Japan's economic and military penetration of the continent. Student strikes and violent demonstrations advanced the general boycott of Japanese goods with telling effect upon Japan's total commerce with China, but in Fukien Chen Yi and his associates continued to keep the doors open to Japanese trade and to put down student protest with brutal action.

Thoughtful observers were disturbed by a significant change that took place at Taipei on September 2, 1936. Admiral Kobayashi Seizō, becoming Governor-General, ended seventeen years of civilian administration. To be sure, this was represented publicly as a routine appointment, for Kobayashi was on the Navy's "retired list," but in fact it reflected a decision to prepare the colony for an approaching crisis in Sino-Japanese relations and for a thrust to the south.

FIVE HUNDRED THOUSAND FORMOSAN STUDENTS
IN THE SCHOOLS

The new Governor-General was an enlightened and moderate officer, a man of outstanding professional achievements. The Admiral had served his country well at Washington, London, and Geneva, had been Navy Vice-Minister at one time, and was a member of the Supreme War Council when he retired from active duty to take up the governorship.

There were more than one thousand primary and higher primary schools in operation about the time Admiral Kobayashi reached Taipei. To raise a wall between the oncoming generation and old China, Tokyo was pouring money into the Formosan school system. Traditional and sentimental ties with the continent had to be broken, the Japanese language had to take the place of Chinese dialects, and young Formosans were to be made to think of themselves as Japanese subjects at all times. Between 1934 and 1937 the total annual appropriation for education in Formosa nearly doubled, rising (in yen equivalents) to about US $9,000,000. This was a spectacular annual sum for an Asian colony and so small an area; in terms of money spent for education per capita this far exceeded anything then known in the provinces of China.

The national government provided subsidies for school construction and staff salaries while town, county, and provincial governments on Formosa were expected to underwrite continuing administrative costs. Enrollments were increased as rapidly as classrooms could be provided, dormitories were built for pupils living at great distance from an elementary school, and special classes were arranged at remote settlements. Free railway and bus passes enabled children to attend schools in urban centers.

Attendance at the country schools continued to be fitful and seasonal, however, for many farm families could ill afford to forego the labor of more than one child—usually the eldest son—and the government was not yet prepared to introduce and enforce a system of universal compulsory education. Slowly the system grew into an organization including sixty-three elementary vocational schools, plus secondary agricultural schools, industrial institutes, and commercial middle schools.

Night schools were opened for junior clerks and office boys who could not attend regular daytime sessions. The law required factory owners to provide vocational and "cultural" courses in company schools if more than a specified number of employees were in the low school-age categories.

It was a saturation program at the elementary and higher primary school level. Formosan parents complained that the government merely wanted children to read and obey orders, for beyond the higher primary level the road to higher education became steep and rough. Although there were more than one thousand primary and higher primary schools, there were only thirty middle schools at the next higher level, and of these, fifteen were not much more than finishing schools for girls. At the beginning of the "China Incident" (1937), when more than five hundred thousand children were in primary school, only 4,117 Formosan students were registered in higher institutions on the island. With opportunity so limited, the competition for admission to the middle and higher schools was grueling; every student had to pass through what was known as "examination hell." If the student could not afford to go on to Japan proper to school he was obliged to apply for admission to the local normal schools, a higher commercial or technical college, or the preparatory school for the local university.

Enrollment statistics advertised the inequalities of the system, for as the Formosan population approached five million, and the Japanese on Formosa numbered fewer than three hundred thousand, Japanese students continued to form the overwhelming majority in the better schools—the First Middle School, the Higher School, the Higher Commercial College, and the University. These were "élite" schools; elsewhere in schools without prestige and in all the agricultural schools and the special medical short-course institute, Formosan students outnumbered the Japanese by three to one. This meant that in the age-group of most ardent dreams and ambitions—the years fourteen to nineteen, when nothing seems impossible—the young Formosan first began to feel the sharp edge of discrimination and to take it as a very personal matter. He might lead his class throughout the year, only to find his name sometimes listed third or fourth on grade-sheets posted at the end of the term. Many Japanese teachers recognized and deplored such discriminatory practice but were obliged to conform to an unstated and therefore technically "unofficial" policy.

The Taihoku Higher Commercial College provided a remarkable window through which to see something of a larger world beyond Formosa and beyond Japan. It had been founded in the early 1920s, brought to college level in 1927, and by 1937 was fully developed to support Japan's grandiose program for the economic conquest of South China, Southeast Asia, and the Indies. Courses in commercial geography, commercial law, accounting, and foreign languages prepared the student for employment in Japan's great commercial and industrial combines engaged in foreign operations. Japanese was the language of instruction, a course in "ethics" was expected to strengthen the "true Japanese spirit," and the military training program produced reserve officers. On entering college each student was obliged to choose a language specialty—English, French, Dutch, Malay, Thai, Indonesian, or one of the South China dialects. The faculty included Japanese professors holding degrees from Japanese, American, or European universities and foreigners were employed to instruct in the advanced language courses. An excellent library supplied newspapers and magazines from Japan proper, the United States, Hongkong, Canton, Manila, Saigon, Bangkok, Singapore, and Batavia (Djakarta). Occasionally summer cruises to the south were arranged for outstanding students, who traveled aboard Japanese freighters, and Japan's noted banks and commercial houses annually recruited promising seniors for overseas employment.

Formosan students usually stood high on the class-ratings in foreign language courses; they had been bilingual throughout their lives, and had had at least five years of English before entering college. A full command of a Formosan-Chinese dialect and of Japanese, plus competence in English, gave them a decided edge in linguistic studies. Many Formosan students looked forward to overseas employment as a possible avenue of escape from the local disabilities and humiliations of second-class citizenship at home.

Higher Technical College graduates had somewhat less attractive prospects: they could expect immediate employment as surveyors, engineering technicians, chemists, and the like, but so long as they stayed on the island they had little prospect of advancement to managerial or policy-making positions in private industry or in the public communications services.

The higher preparatory school for the liberal arts and sciences—the Taihoku Kōtō Gakkō—could be likened to an exclusive American junior college. It had been organized for the Government in 1927 by Japanese professors who had done graduate work in the United States, and through them the influence of the American prep school was reflected in the excellent physical plant: a well-planned campus embracing dormitories, classrooms, laboratories, a large gymnasium, pools, playing-fields, a theater-auditorium, and an excellent library of some forty thousand volumes in the Japanese, Chinese, English, and German languages. The students were youths of superior scholastic standing, the sons of well-placed Japanese officials, teachers, doctors, technicians, and businessmen, plus a few Formosans who had proved themselves outstanding in the competitive examinations.

At the colleges of literature, politics, and science of the Taihoku Imperial University (the research institution projected by Dr. Gotō at the turn of the century and established in 1927), the emphasis was upon research in tropical medicine, tropical agriculture, and the economics, languages, and sociology of South China, Southeast Asia, and the Indies—the great target area. By 1939 the physical plant included appropriate laboratories, classrooms, and a modern library building holding more than 400,000 volumes, of which 160,000 were in the Western languages. But in that year, when the faculty and staff assistants numbered 708, the undergraduate students numbered only 283. Of these only 90 were Formosans, the great majority (75) registered in the School of Medicine.

Formosan students encountered little academic discrimination in Japan proper. There the individual from the colony was lost in a sea of Japanese fellow students. Many Formosan families made great sacrifices to send able and ambitious students to Tokyo, Kyoto, or Osaka. Some two thousand young Formosans were enrolled at university level in Japan proper in 1939, and of these at least one-fourth were at medical schools, with law and economics following next in favor.

Given the Kōminka program objectives, it followed that private schools were not looked on with favor by the administration and were kept under close surveillance and heavy pressure. Christian and Buddhist mission schools under Japanese management numbered seventeen, and had a total enrollment of about five thousand. They could be kept in line without great difficulty, but the Christian mission schools under foreign management created embarrassing problems. They were not prepared to install the imperial portraits and conduct the ceremonies of emperor worship without protest, and this in turn involved "dangerous thoughts" and skeptical attitudes toward State Shintō and the Shintō mythology. Only eighteen of the old Chinese classical schools remained in 1939, and all who enrolled in them were obliged also to satisfy the standard State school requirements.

With the advent of the second war with China, the educational programs in all schools of Japan and at all levels were subjected to grotesque distortion as the extremists, at the bidding of the military, attempted to prepare the nation for the conquest of Asia and a great confrontation with the West. The students of Formosa—and of Korea—had much less reason to accept the nationalistic ideology and "imperial polity" than had any of their Japanese schoolmates.

THE YOUNG FORMOSAN'S DILEMMA

Formosans in the rising generation were crossing an ideological frontier as real and as important as the physical frontiers crossed by immigrant ancestors in the seventeenth and eighteenth centuries. Every schoolboy in the empire was obliged to learn the pious exhortation "Boys, be ambitious!," but in the colony, students frequently gave this a bitter negative twist, saying that for them it should be "Boys, be *not* ambitious!" At the middle school level they were filled with swarming ambitions, but by the time they were ready for higher schools, they had discovered the barriers ahead; local careers were open in commerce, medicine, and law, but elsewhere there was a low ceiling in all employment. They were second-class subjects, capable of first-class performance.

Crossing the ideological frontier into the world of international science and technology began in the primary schools when teachers first took children from rural villages to the nearest large town to acquaint them with the wonders of railroads, power plants, factories, public parks, and buildings such as they had not seen before. In the middle and higher schools this process was advanced by fresh access to books and magazines, and by school excursions to Japan proper, where they toured historic sites and passed through several of the world's largest cities—Tokyo, Nagoya, Kyoto, and Osaka. Although the colonial government sponsoring this activity intended that the young Formosans should pridefully identify themselves with Japan as the leading power in Asia, it seemed curiously unaware that many keen young minds readily distinguished between modern international or Western technology and the mystical elements of the so-called true Japanese heritage.

The international or modern elements of contemporary Japanese life held the greater appeal. A well-educated young Formosan was happy to be identified with a progressive and modern Japan but remained indifferent to the so-called true Japanese spiritual tradition he was so often and so tediously called upon to admire. Every Monday morning teachers and students in Formosa were obliged to "worship from afar," bowing reverently, in unison, toward the palace in faraway Tokyo. Every household had to maintain a Shintō altar in proper order even though the family might be Buddhist or Christian or entirely without religious interest or affiliation. If members of the Imperial Family visited Formosa, as they sometimes did, the streets were cleared along the route of passage and every inhabitant standing at attention in the side-streets nearby was expected to bow respectfully until the imperial person had gone on his way. To the Formosan Chinese, all these imperial formalities were a boring and empty show. They could not truly share in the Japanese nation-family mystique and the emperor-worship cult.

Well-educated younger men and women were not much more interested in the ancient Chinese background from which the Confucian classics had been handed down. The student paid great respect to parents and grandparents and obeyed Confucian precepts governing reverent commemoration of his forebears, but as for old China and the ultimate source of these moral principles, his position might be likened to that of the average American Christian who knows and cares little about the Greek and Hebrew origins of conventional contemporary Christianity.

Contemporary China, too, was not well known and was little understood. It was difficult to keep up-to-date with the swirling politics and confusions of warlord China across the Strait. The Japanese police took great pains to restrict importation and circulation of Chinese publications in every form. All Chinese materials were censored if they came through legitimate channels. What was known of Sun Yat-sen's idealistic nationalism and the "Three Principles," and of the Nationalist party government under Chiang Kai-shek (Sho Kai-seki), had to be set against the more detailed knowledge of Chen Yi's reputation as governor in nearby Fukien.

Given a simple choice between "backward China" and "progressive Japan" in the late 1930s, an observant Formosan was strongly inclined to think of himself and of his family's future in Japanese terms, or at least within the Japanese empire frame of reference. It was not an easy choice, for the attention of the well-educated Formosan at that time was constantly drawn to the Western world beyond Japan. No province in China had such a high percentage of literate inhabitants acquainted with, and deeply interested in, foreign affairs and the Western world.

Not all the thought police on the island could curb Formosan interest in economic and political developments in contemporary Japan and the West. Hundreds of university graduates subscribed to newspapers, magazines, and technical journals published at Tokyo and Osaka, or read them at bookshops in the larger towns. The spread of literacy had prompted the growth of local publication and circulation of materials edited primarily for a Japanese-reading public. Elderly Formosans had access to this principally through the eyes and understanding of youth, and youth was interested in politics, science, and adventurous enterprise anywhere in the world. Publication in the Chinese language was rigidly supervised, and at the outbreak of the China War (1937) the Formosan *New People's Daily* (the *Shin Mimpō*) was obliged to discontinue publication of the special Chinese-language section.

It would be misleading to suggest that English might some day take the place of Chinese as a second language among the

Formosan élite, but by 1939 it had become what might be called an "auxiliary language," as a growing number of younger Formosans continued to study and use English after leaving the classroom. Every graduate from the middle and higher schools had been required to submit to at least five years of English instruction, and it may be safe to say that each class produced at least one or two students who grasped the essentials of this difficult language and maintained some interest in reading beyond the compulsory five years of hard labor. As late as 1940 the annual English-speaking contest at the capital was considered a high point in the local academic year and entrants from the leading schools were judged usually by the British or American consuls and other English-speaking residents. By the end of the Japanese era more than fifty thousand Formosans had passed through the middle and higher schools (required to take English along the way), and thousands who had gone on to universities in Japan, China, and the West had been required to study English, French, or German.

In school textbooks and in the general news media, the orientation beyond Japan was toward the United States and Europe. Solemn portraits of British, German, and American literary figures looked down upon the student from classroom walls and world maps on the wall emphasized, in color, Japan's position vis-à-vis the West. Textbooks in the Japanese and English languages carried the basic stories of European explorations, of the discovery of America, Columbus and the Indians, Washington and the American Revolution, Lincoln and the Civil War, and every schoolboy knew the fateful story of Commodore Perry and his Black Ships of 1853.

Formosan students knew a great deal more about the United States and the British Empire than British or American students knew about Formosa. An analysis of newspaper coverage and radio programing in Formosa for the period 1935–1940 showed that in total time and space devoted to foreign affairs, the United States came first, well ahead of news coverage of China, next door.*

* In 1937, for example, my students asked me to explain a Japanese-language newspaper map illustrating the popular and electoral voting patterns in the American presidential elections of 1936. On another occasion, a blind masseur asked for further information concerning the New Orleans Mardi

The range of specialized publications in Formosa included at least two journals in Braille. There were seven daily newspapers and at least thirty-eight periodicals published locally to supplement the flow of printed material from Japan. A few had been published continuously since the days of Kodama and Gotō, but the majority made their appearance after 1930 and after the Kōminka program was well under way. For many years it had been thought necessary for prestige purposes to send manuscripts to Japan proper for publication, but as press facilities were enlarged and improved, substantial books began to bear the Taipei imprint. A general bibliographical record shows that, beginning about 1920, there was an annual increase in the number of Formosan names appearing on the author-title lists and in periodical tables of content. Catalogs of the annual art exhibits reveal a steadily enlarging Formosan participation.

Something was in print for every taste and interest, with periodical titles ranging from the *Taiwan Police Review* to the *Museum Bulletin* and the *Taiwan Art News*, and from the *Taiwan Automobile Club Journal* to the *Friends of Social Enterprise* magazine. Every phase of agriculture, public health, education, and industry had its own journal; there were journals devoted to the aborigines and to the interest of alpine clubs and mountain climbers. There was even a journal devoted to fire fighting and the welfare of firemen. Many were of only the slightest value, but they reflected the insatiable Japanese interest in the printed word, and spread before the literate Formosan an extraordinary range of reading matter, available continuously at the public libraries, the bookstores, and newsstands.

The radio—a form of official journalistic enterprise—provided daily broadcasts loaded with "improving" informational programs. Local broadcasting had been inaugurated in 1928, and a decade later more than fifty thousand receiving sets were licensed and registered with the police. The majority were owned by Japanese families, but loudspeaker systems installed in public parks, markets, and popular temple courtyards served the masses.

Gras, of which he had read in his Braille books. Studies of Formosan news media were made at Washington during 1942–1943 in support of wartime psychological and propaganda campaigns.

Young Formosans were in touch with the modern world through Japan, through the schools, the press, and the cinema. Their grandparents' tales of the late nineteenth century inadvertently served to strengthen Japanese propaganda concerning "progressive Taiwan." During the decades of Chinese civil war Tokyo carried forward the modernization and development of the island-colony. A well-educated Formosan had only to look across the Strait to make significant comparisons. For example, in 1931 the whole of continental China had fewer than 9,400 miles of railway track, whereas small Formosa was served by 2,857 miles of public and private railroad. In 1934 Tokyo opened radiotelephone communication with Taipei, and inaugurated an air service by way of Okinawa for officials traveling between the national capital and the colony. This service was extended to cities around the island and opened to the public in 1936. Twenty-one regularly scheduled shipping lines touched Formosa, some calling on round-the-world service and some limited to round-the-island operations. Telegraph and postal offices served every town and many villages, and there were 21,000 telephones in operation. Island power plants were generating nearly as much electric power as the total produced in all of China. No provincial area on the continent enjoyed such public services. This was the infrastructure of a modern economy.

While the ordinary peasant was unaware of these statistics, he was keenly aware of public health services in every town and of the schools in every village. When the population was approaching five million, some five hundred thousand pupils were enrolled, and by 1945 the number had risen above nine hundred thousand. Each primary school child returned to his home in the afternoon carrying some imprint or impression of "progressive Japan." Older youths and girls at middle and higher school levels were conscious and often resentful of their position vis-à-vis Japanese classmates and the school administrations. The number of abortive middle school student "plots" uncovered by the police in this decade reflected this deep ideological conflict and led to harsh punishments.

The number who sought to go to the continent for higher education increased noticeably. By 1939 Formosan students in China for the first time equaled the number at school in Japan proper. To counter this trend, the government reduced all Chinese elements in the public school curriculum, and increased the "patriotic" emphasis. Toward the very close of the Japanese era more than one thousand ordinary primary schools and ninety primary vocational schools were in operation. Some twenty thousand students were enrolled in higher primary courses and eighteen thousand youths attended business schools. Baron Gotō's old dream of educating the aborigines was being realized at one hundred and forty-eight special institutions.

FORMOSA AND THE PHILIPPINE COMMONWEALTH

News of the nearby Philippines was of high interest. The year 1935 that brought Japan's grudging concession of local elective assemblies in the Formosan towns and provinces had brought Commonwealth status to the Philippines and opened a decade in which the Filipinos were expected to prepare themselves for independence in 1945. Washington was about to lay down the White Man's Burden. Political and economic expediency in the Depression years had dictated the American decision to withdraw; nevertheless, Formosan students and leaders innocently looked on it as "American idealism" and President Roosevelt's statements were discussed as Woodrow Wilson's had been at the close of World War I. They were genuinely stirred by the spectacle of voluntary American retreat from the Philippines and by Washington's effort to prepare the people for unfettered self-government.

The Filipinos, whose ancestors were close cousins of the Formosan hill people, now had a President of their own choosing, Manuel Quezon, who worked with an American High Commissioner during this transition decade. Quezon, who had fought the Americans on behalf of the short-lived Philippine Republic in 1898, invited a retired American general to assist him in creating an army and defense program for the new government. This was Lieutenant General Douglas MacArthur, USA, Retired, whose father, General Arthur MacArthur, had directed the American campaign to destroy the first Philippine Republic.

While the Formosans wondered if they might one day win self-government, the Japanese on Formosa had quite other reasons for keen interest in the great change in the Philippines. American withdrawal was neatly paving the way for the Philippines to join in the New Order in East Asia and to enter the Greater East Asia Co-Prosperity Sphere.

In midyear 1937, a noted Stanford University geologist visited Formosa. Since he was then in his eighty-first year, Dr. Bailey Willis had himself carried across the high central mountain trails in a basket-chair, and it may be that the Japanese authorities, somewhat disarmed by this, did not take him very seriously. Willis made a spectacular photographic record of the interior ranges and noted many things in the lowlands that were military rather than geologic in nature. Going on to Manila, he reported on the essentially military character of Formosa's developing ports and harbors. The Commonwealth government then asked him to make an aerial reconnaissance of Luzon and to advise it on the development of a geologic service.

From his seat in the bubble-domed nose of an army plane, Bailey Willis looked down on the beaches, bays, and promontories of the great island, and on returning to Manila asked the purpose of roads he had observed leading inland from isolated beaches toward Luzon's few highroads. When he was told that they were being built by Japanese timber concessionaires, he urged a quiet investigation.

11. Formosa and the "China Incident"

JAPANESE officers exploited the "Marco Polo Bridge Incident" of July 7, 1937, as an excuse to enter North China in force. This new Sino-Japanese conflict was not called a "war," although it was destined to continue for eight years and to cost millions of lives. Under terms of the American Neutrality Act, a formal declaration of war would have compelled the United States government to cut off supplies to both China and Japan, and it would have disrupted the Nationalists' side-door trade with Japan as well.

Tokyo offered many justifications for the new aggression, sometimes calling it a crusade against communism, sometimes a campaign to reorganize ancient China under a more progressive leadership, and sometimes a crusade to rescue fellow Asians from wicked Western imperialism. Under any banner it was a "sacred war," carried on in the name of the emperor whose Formosan subjects, like all others, were expected to support it without question.

The "China Incident" created a very real dilemma on the island, for it emphasized a generation gap growing wider under the effect of the Kōminka program. Although grandparents remembered the hard conditions that had prevailed before 1895, they tended to idealize "Old Country" traditions in retro-

spect and to deplore changing standards among the young. Formosans of middle age—say those born between 1885 and
1915—were cynical, knowing by experience that Tokyo's
promise of "Asia for the Asiatics" meant Asia for the military
and the ruling classes in Japan. For the young school-age Formosan, born after 1920, the "Old Country" was remote, and
the Kōminka program encouraged him to think of himself as a
modern, up-to-date person, obliged to put away "backward" or
slightly ludicrous Chinese customs.

Young Formosans, drilled to conform to mass behavior
patterns and to accept "slogan thinking," were encouraged to
feel pride as members of the winning team—the Japanese team.
The Imperial Army and Navy displayed themselves with impressive pageantry, and for a brief time after July 7, 1937, the
controlled news media made it seem that the Japanese forces
were sweeping everything before them, and were everywhere
welcomed in North China as "liberators," winning the hearts
and the minds of the people.

Looking toward China, the young Formosan saw General
Chen Yi and his associates carrying on business as usual in
Fukien nearby, and filling the jails with student leaders who
demanded a total break with Japan and a truly national effort to
resist the invader. Looking toward Japan proper he saw a nation mobilizing every material resource and every able-bodied
person to "serve the emperor." Beginning in midyear 1937, an
immense stream of military traffic moved westward through
Japan to the ports facing the continent. Every Japanese village
was gripped with war fever, a sense of supreme dedication to
the national service. Each community was called upon to sacrifice lives that Japan might survive in a hostile world.

The full pressure of mobilization was felt throughout the
Japanese prefectures many months before it was directly apparent in Formosa. Taipei moved cautiously, not yet sure of the
temper and sympathies of the Formosan Chinese. The principal
visible signs of war in the autumn of 1937 were farewell ceremonies for Japanese reservists leaving Keelung to join regiments
in Japan before shipping out to the battlefront in North China.
Labor conscription had not yet begun, rationing was not yet a
burden, and the movement of troops through Keelung and
Takao did not assume dramatic proportions until the conquest

of Canton took place in late 1938. The entire island lay under limited martial law and the larger towns and ports were technically in a state of partial alert at all times. Military air activity increased week by week and month by month as the Japanese forces moved into the Yangtze Valley and down the coast.

Defense exercises, mock attacks, and occasional air-raid drills at night were staged to remind the public of a "national crisis." Foreign residents—I among them—were obliged to observe the blackout regulations but were not called out to participate in neighborhood maneuvers. These, the Japanese residents took very seriously. Formosans living in the Banka and Twatutia quarters, on the other hand, tended to treat the practice alerts and blackout periods as occasions for larking in the street arcades behind the blackout curtains and opportunities for baiting the nervous and preoccupied Japanese policemen.

Three months after the invasion of North China the agitated Chinese Consul General at Taipei urged his fellow countrymen to leave the island, and begged the American Consul, as a "friend of China," to provide transportation for them all. He declined. The number of registered alien Chinese laborers and merchants at that time exceeded sixty thousand.

Although a mass exodus would seriously affect the local labor market the Japanese government placed no obstacle in the way of a general withdrawal. The Chinese Consul General and his staff pulled down the Nationalist flag and sailed away, leaving their countrymen to shift for themselves. Soon some forty-six thousand sailed away to Amoy and Foochow. About fourteen thousand remained at work, willing to take the risks of war.

Occasionally Japanese officials assured foreign residents that all serious danger of local rebellion had long since passed but, in doing so, sometimes inadvertently betrayed a marked degree of uncertainty and uneasiness within the Japanese community. What would Formosan reaction be if the far-away "North China Incident" became a general war affecting Fukien and the Strait nearby?

The test came on the crisp, sunny morning of February 18, 1938, seven months after the Marco Polo Bridge affair. At eleven o'clock a brief series of shattering explosions shook the air, suggesting military exercises of unusual scale somewhere in the northeastern suburbs. Military planes rose from the Sung-shan Airfield in that quarter and streaked westward. This in itself was not unusual, for there was heavy military traffic on that field every day. But two hours later the city sirens sounded an alert, the streets were promptly cleared of all ordinary traffic, civil defense wardens and policemen sped back and forth, and military trucks began to roll in from the barracks area. Troops took up positions along the main avenues, machine-gun emplacements suddenly appeared at the principal intersections, and sandbagged, barbed-wire barriers were hastily thrown up before important buildings in the central administrative district.

Taipei was gripped with excitement. No one seemed to know what was taking place. At two o'clock there was great relief when the sirens sounded all clear and the troops began to withdraw from the streets, leaving only strong guards around the principal buildings. The city was swept by rumors as darkness fell, but neither the police nor the air-wardens could explain the midday alert and movement of the troops.

Before dawn next day every barricade had been removed, and the guns, bayonets, and barbed wire had disappeared. A crisis had passed; a brief official statement said only that on the preceding day a Chinese Nationalist plane "piloted by Russians" had dropped a stick of bombs near the Sungshan Airfield, and that as it was driven back across the Strait it had attempted to bomb the Hsinchu oil refinery, without success.

Although there was no official explanation of the long delay in sounding the air-raid alert, it was learned later that the intervening hours had been filled with tense consultations leading to a decision to admit the attack, but first to take every precaution against a Formosan rising. Since the Formosans had been quite as astonished as the Japanese by this raid, foreign residents questioned the reliability of Japan's elaborate counterintelligence network within the island, and dismissed the "Russian pilot" detail as a face-saving gesture; no Japanese officer could admit that a *Chinese* pilot had successfully penetrated Formosa's defense system without warning.*

This February 18 Incident was a minor affair—a few For-

* Only later it was learned that Chiang Kai-shek at that time was indeed employing a large "volunteer" Russian air group—an example of "barbarians" retained to fight other "barbarians" on China's behalf.

mosans killed or wounded and a few houses smashed—but for the first time in history the imperial Japanese domain had been subjected to an airborne attack by an alien force. The significance was not lost among young Formosans of college age who promptly collected and kept as prized, secret souvenirs small fragments of metal picked up at the Sungshan site. Here was a hint that Japan was vulnerable.

"SPIRITUAL MOBILIZATION" AND ANTIFOREIGN PROPAGANDA

As the Chinese Nationalist administration retreated far inland to Chungking, Japan set up puppet governments at Peking and Nanking, and by the end of 1938 the principal cities along the China coast were occupied. Occasionally Chiang's armies made a firm stand, but on the whole, it was a great rout; millions of Chinese refugees streamed westward to the inland mountain barriers and provinces beyond the Yangtze gorges. Losses of life and property were beyond calculation wherever Japanese or Chinese armies passed. But in Fukien, Chen Yi and his men continued in apparently cordial and certainly profitable intercourse with the Japanese.

On Formosa the government exploited every propaganda device to whip up enthusiasm for the war and to make every sacrifice seem ultimately worthwhile. Japanese youths called up for military duty and Formosans conscripted for labor service were sent off with banners flying and *banzai* shouts. Propaganda films, executed with consummate skill, were of two kinds. Those designed for entertainment stressed the theme that Japan was obliged temporarily to hurt China in order to bring about reform and modernization, to rescue the Chinese people from "gangster rule," and to secure China from the predatory Western imperialists or from communism. The "newsreel" films stressed Japanese heroism in action, military victories, and the warm welcome with which the common people of China were alleged to greet their deliverers. The latest and largest mechanized weapons were displayed dramatically in city parks, and now and then a public military funeral was staged to dramatize the glory of death on behalf of the emperor. An announcement of the fall of any town in China became an occasion for lantern parades and fireworks in Formosa.

In this way, year after year, primary school children and youths in their early teens were exposed to a steady drumbeat of propaganda encouraging them to identify themselves with the winning side in this Asian contest. Throughout Japan and Formosa the Chinese were spoken of contemptuously as *Chankoro*,* an epithet on the level of the offensive American slang terms *Chink*, *Jap*, or *Frog*.

An extraordinary number of blindly emotional patriotic "Emperor's Service" slogans and organizations appeared. Some were legitimate service groups working with the Japan Red Cross, for example, but many were dubious enterprises or had little to contribute to the war effort. All had to be tolerated if they solicited contributions in the name of patriotism. Few persons were bold enough to turn away the importunate solicitor, and a voiced objection by any Formosan could bring around the thought police at once.

The nuisance of disorderly and unofficial street-side solicitation was overshadowed by a systematic exploitation of the economy through competing government agencies. Japanese extremists charged that Formosans were living too well and too comfortably while "true Japanese" in the home prefectures were suffering deprivation. Japanese conscripts who came down to subtropical Formosa from chronically impoverished northern prefectures were astonished and angered by the apparent plenitude of food available to the common people in the colony. Having been thoroughly indoctrinated with anti-Chinese propaganda, they saw the Formosans only as "Chankoro" and not as fellow subjects of the emperor.

In 1938 special laws and regulations began to press the island economy for heavy extra contributions. New taxes, preemption of land for military use, and a relentless exploitation of the hokō, the Youth Corps, and the scores of occupational associations and cooperatives extracted an immense total "patriotic donation" of money, materials, and labor. In one week a farmer might be required to contribute a water buffalo to the Army, and in the next, representatives of the Navy might call upon him to donate pigs, poultry, grain, or garden

* From the Chinese *Chung-kuo jen*, literally, "Man of the Middle Kingdom." Young Formosans revived the term in 1946, applying it to the incoming Nationalists.

produce. When the nationwide precious metal collection campaigns began, Formosan women were obliged to hand over bracelets, rings, and other trinkets highly prized as traditional forms of small savings for the family. Hoarding was strictly prohibited, rationing enforced, and any who violated the innumerable economic control regulations were accused of lacking the "true Japanese spirit" and penalized accordingly. When it was first decreed that coarse grains must be mixed with fine white rice, the Formosans, having an abundance of rice at hand, often ignored the rule. Soon the economic control police were entering homes unannounced at mealtime to inspect dinner tables and kitchen pots. If they discovered irregularities, the thought police soon followed to examine the state of "patriotism" in the family.

Many Japanese were deeply disturbed by overzealous efforts to advance an assimilation program that generated needless antagonism. Officious policemen sometimes stopped elderly Formosans on the street, berated them for wearing traditional Formosan-Chinese jackets and trousers, and concluded the tirade by snipping off Chinese-style buttons or otherwise damaging the "un-Japanese," hence unpatriotic, dress. Japanese extremists editorialized with harsh criticism of Formosa's traditional architecture, domestic housing arrangements, and food, calling them "uncivilized" and "filthy" because they, too, were un-Japanese.

The catalog of extremist nonsense seemed endless. Some officials were obsessed with the language problem, convinced that any effort to learn a smattering of Japanese—*kokugo*, the "national language"—could be taken as evidence of sincerity, loyalty, and patriotism. A massive adult education program marked the effort to transform older Formosans into "true Japanese" overnight. At its peak nearly one hundred sixty thousand bilingual younger people were drafted to instruct adults brought together in small groups at temples, town halls, and classrooms. A system of rewards was devised to encourage attendance and to speed linguistic assimilation. If every member of a family could speak even a few words of Japanese, a small emblem or marker was issued for display at the house gate and household members thereafter enjoyed small official favors in local affairs. An important step was taken when it was decreed that henceforth all representatives in the ho and kō units must be able to speak Japanese, and that all candidates for office in social and economic organizations and in the local assemblies must be able to speak it very well. This at once penalized the older generation and shifted active community leadership to younger people.

Some patriotic gestures and projects were patently absurd. For example, the government one day announced a "God Ascension Week" during which old Formosan household gods were exchanged, with great ceremony, for Japanese Shintō symbols, and Shintō rituals replaced traditional Formosan household rites. The gilded god-figures, emptied now of spiritual content, were gathered together and shipped away to the anthropological museum at the Taihoku Imperial University. The public was assured that old Formosan deities had been transformed, becoming guardians (*kami*) in the Shintō pantheon.

As part of an empire-wide spiritual mobilization campaign, new occasions were found to require school children to worship from afar, bowing in unison toward the distant imperial palace. Old Shintō shrines were refurbished and enlarged, and new shrines were constructed by "voluntary labor." *

Formosans remained supremely indifferent to Shintō doctrines and rituals. Compulsory attendance on public occasions and the maintenance of a Shintō altar in every house was a nuisance to be borne without protest.

The police censors, closely watching the traditional Chinese theater, in 1939 thought it necessary to suppress altogether the extremely popular puppet shows. It had been realized, at last, that under the guise of ancient Chinese stories, the puppeteers were caricaturing Japan and the Japanese armies in China in hilariously bawdy fashion, and were holding the Japanese government up to ridicule. To take the place of the Chinese puppets, the Japanese introduced their own traditional itinerant "picture theaters" (*kamishibai*), consisting of cardboard

---

* At this time a beautiful eighteenth-century Formosan temple, the Kiemtan-ssu (Kentanji) standing on the banks of the Keelung River, was torn down by the government to make room for extensions of the Taiwan Grand Shrine enclosure, overlooking Taipei, and for secret construction of underground headquarters for the Taiwan military high command, deep in the hill beneath the Shrine.

scenes, displayed one after another with a storyteller's running commentary. By tradition these were fairy tales and children's stories having no appeal to adults, but now they became lurid picture-stories of Japan's glorious campaigns in China, and (after 1939) fearful tales of the wicked Western powers encircling and threatening Japan. These recitals were accompanied by dire warnings to be alert to the danger of the lurking foreign spy.

FOREIGNERS AND JAPAN'S OBSESSION WITH SPIES

Japan's obsession with spies and spying reached an extreme in the colonies. A very old national tradition of domestic spying was here resurgent in acute form. Before the Restoration each of the 272 feudal territories had kept close watch upon one another, and the shōgun's government had spied upon all. After 1868 the new imperial government replaced this old *metsuke* system with an elaborate secret police organization. In Formosa, after 1895, the "spy syndrome" was intensified by realization that the unloved governing minority lived among millions of un-Japanese subjects. The self-conscious military, using Formosa as an advanced base for elaborate intelligence operations in China and the nearby Philippines, assumed that China and the United States had a network of spies in the colony.

As the continental war dragged on, Chiang Kai-shek traded space for time, while seeking American intervention on his behalf. Tokyo developed a propaganda theme that Japan was surrounded on all sides by predators, and was obliged to fight for survival. This was the "A-B-C-D Encirclement" theme, exploiting the technique of the Big Lie, repeated often enough to convince the public of its truth. The lands coveted by the military expansionists and their associates were *A*merican (the Philippines), *B*ritish (Hongkong and Malaysia), *C*hinese, and *D*utch (the Indies), hence the neat acronym.

At the time of the Munich crisis (1938), few Japanese knew what Tokyo's secret commitments were, and there was dread possibility of worldwide war. At Taipei, so far from Munich, a number of Formosans employed by foreign firms were suddenly arrested without explanation, held until Chamberlain flew home to London to announce "peace in our time," and were then released. Thereafter, all Formosans were marked men if they had lived or traveled abroad or showed interest in foreign language study, in foreign affairs, or in social intercourse with foreigners living in Formosa. Occasionally the foreign community learned that a well-educated Formosan had been suddenly wakened in the night and hustled off to China on "patriotic duty." Some simply disappeared.

Japan's armies had been campaigning in China for two years when Europe plunged into war in September 1939. This offered—or seemed to offer—an irresistible opportunity. In their narrow view of the world the Japanese generals felt they need no longer wait to "digest" occupied China before taking over the European colonies in Asia. On the contrary, the imperial armies bogging down on the vast continental war-front needed unrestricted access to the oil, metals, rubber, and rice of Southeast Asia and the Indies. From a moralistic point of view the expansionists felt that Tokyo had quite as much right to exploit Asians in Southeast Asia as had any white man from the West—more, indeed, if the "brotherhood of race" could be made justification.

Japan had little reason to trust her Axis partners; the Rome-Berlin-Tokyo Alliance was a cynical expedient, as none knew better than the men who contrived it. Hitler's "nonaggression pact" with Russia in 1939 was considered a betrayal in Tokyo, for it freed Russia to develop military strength in the Far East. Now Germany's swift conquest of France and Holland, and preparations for an invasion of England, meant that British, French, and Dutch colonial possessions might soon be controlled by the formidable Nazi partner, the quintessential racist in the West.

Extremists at Tokyo saw it essentially as "Japan against the world," and at Taipei redoubled efforts to plant in the public mind a blind mistrust of all Caucasians and of the decadent democracies. Police agencies assumed that all aliens were spies, and that all Formosans and Japanese who consorted with them were suspect. Radio and press endlessly repeated the theme; posters and films depicted the "typical" foreign spy as a sinister character, a blond Caucasian wearing dark glasses, always on the prowl for Japan's military and economic secrets. On meeting Caucasians in the street one heard primary children whisper to one another *"Supai!," "Supai!"*

In this poisoned atmosphere the chauvinists decreed that baseball could no longer be called *beisuboru* but must now be called *yakyū* or "field ball," and children's games began to center on the theme *Bei-Ei gekimatsu* or "Crushing America and England." This was the old "Yellow Peril" theme in reverse.

Each village unit and every school, factory, and substantial business establishment was expected to organize a "volunteer spy-prevention unit." Youth Corps members were given special instruction and the government organized "Spy Prevention Societies" within its own offices. Soon zealots demanded the formation of similar units in the sugar experiment laboratories, telegraph and wireless offices, radio repair shops, and photo-supply stores. Policemen were assigned to live in houses adjoining foreign properties, and servants were obliged to report on the activities and conversations in every foreign household. There seemed to be no limit to the nonsense as each policing agency attempted to outdo its rivals. For example, no foreigner crossed town by bus, rickshaw, or bicycle without an agent trailing along behind him, standing by while he shopped, or following him into restaurants and coffee shops. In the foreigner's absence his household wastebaskets might be handed over to the police to be sifted for discarded letters, clipped newspapers, and the like.

The militarists were attributing to foreigners the behavior required of Japanese nationals in many sensitive areas overseas. As the antispy campaign reached heights of absurdity, many thoughtful Japanese were embarrassed and regretful. Intelligent Formosans were bored by the shrill professional patriotism heard on every side, but it was dangerous for Japanese and Formosans alike to show any lack of enthusiasm or betray a flagging interest. Thought police agents everywhere encouraged talebearing that sometimes proved not only false, but deliberately malicious and the cause of personal disasters.

ASIAN STUDENTS IN FORMOSA: A PROPAGANDA FAILURE

Having translated the ancient Chinese Middle Kingdom idea into the modern Japanese dream of a Greater East Asia Co-Prosperity Sphere, the militarists could not look upon other Asian nations and peoples as equals. In practical application the propaganda demanding "Asia for the Asiatics" turned out to be "Asia for the Japanese."

In developing Formosa as a showcase demonstrating the benefits of imperial Japanese leadership, Taipei began to bring in scholarship students from other Asian countries and to offer shelter and subsidies to political exiles from target areas in the south. For example, in the period 1938 to 1940, two Thai students came to study the Japanese language, tropical agriculture, and the vocational training school program. A young Javan aristocrat, having the princely title Radan Mas, came of his own volition to study languages at the Taihoku Imperial University, supporting himself meanwhile by tutoring in the English, Dutch, and Indonesian languages. A fiery Sumatran rebel appeared, an exiled journalist and pamphleteer, who supported himself by teaching in the higher technical schools and preparing highly inflammatory anti-Dutch propaganda for broadcast to the Indies. His counterpart was a disgruntled Filipino who taught English and Tagalog locally while broadcasting anti-American programs to Luzon. The largest Asian group present at Taipei was Vietnamese—some forty persons attending an exiled prince who lived quietly in the suburbs awaiting the day for Vietnam's liberation from the French. The leading members of this little group were graduates of French universities.

The Thai, the Indonesians, and the Vietnamese all privately complained that they were being treated as natives of "backward countries," for Japanese officials often could not conceal a patronizing condescension toward other Asians, and it was entirely impossible for officialdom to conceal from foreign eyes the second-class status of the Formosan-Chinese people within the empire.

Preparation for the Great Southward Drive

Admiral Hasegawa Kiyoshi replaced Admiral Kobayashi Seizō at Taipei on November 27, 1940. The new Governor-General was on the Navy's active list and was ready therefore to assume control of all military as well as civil organizations at a moment's notice. Hasegawa was a man of distinguished naval service and wide international experience.* There were many reassignments of naval personnel at this time, for as the continental war was primarily an Army venture, so the thrust to the south would be principally a responsibility of the Imperial Navy. From a Japanese point of view the two great potential adversaries were the British and American fleets in Southeast Asian waters and in the Pacific, based at Singapore and at Pearl Harbor, with Hongkong and Manila (Cavite) as subsidiary outposts.

Japan's naval outposts were Makung in the Pescadores, Takao, Keelung, and Palau, east of Luzon. It was necessary now to rid Formosa of British subjects and American citizens who might be serving as hostile agents.

Along the China coast British consuls, missionaries, and businessmen watched every Japanese move southward toward Hongkong. The Fukien situation was bizarre, for General Chen Yi, his shrewd Japanese wife, and his extraordinarily intelligent young aides continued to protect the side-door commerce with Japan, secure in the patronage of interests close to the Generalissimo.

Chen, a Chekiang man, on occasion showed contempt for the Fukienese, and this led to a feud with the founder-patron of Amoy University. Tan Kah Kee (Ch'en Chia-keng) was a Fukienese émigré who lived in Singapore, a philanthropist influential in the overseas Chinese associations of Southeast Asia. At that time the financial and political support of such associations everywhere was of prime importance to Chiang's beleaguered Nationalist Government, and so when Tan of Singapore led a large delegation to China in 1940, he had good reason to expect consideration. The visiting delegation told the Generalissimo that, after touring unoccupied China, they must urge him to undertake sweeping domestic reforms in order to strengthen popular support in the confrontation with Japan. Tan added

---

* Admiral Hasegawa, age 57 in 1937, was a Naval Academy graduate (1903) and Russo-Japanese War veteran who later served on the Academy staff and as Japan's Naval Attaché at Washington. In 1932 he was Japan's Chief Delegate to the Naval Conference, then served as Navy Vice-Minister (1934) and as Commandant of the great Yokosuka Naval Yards. He was a member of the Supreme War Council at the time of his appointment to Formosa.

that he had found conditions in Fukien the worst encountered anywhere in China.

Chiang ignored these representations, and Tan, on returning to Singapore, began campaigning to have Chen Yi forced out of Fukien. Chen's influential patrons carried more weight with the Generalissimo, however, and the Chens remained undisturbed at Foochow, trading with the enemy as usual.

The Fukien ports and the Strait of Formosa were effectively in the hands of the Japanese Navy by 1940, as Kodama and Gotō had proposed that they should be. The way was open to the south. France had been overrun, Holland was devastated, and the Battle for Britain was underway. It was imperative now to gain control of European colonies in Asia before a victorious Hitler claimed them. Moreover, Washington was threatening to cut off all supplies of oil and strategic metals, so vital to Japan's total war effort. Formosa must be made ready for the supreme effort, the thrust to the south.

In a sweeping security measure Tokyo set about ridding the island of all Caucasians from, or in sympathy with, the A-B-C-D countries. Among these, the missionaries had always been most suspect, for they commanded the respect and confidence of some sixty thousand Formosan Christians and their students. A majority of the missionaries spoke local dialects reasonably well and thus were able to communicate directly with the older unassimilated Formosan generation, and it was no secret that they encouraged younger people to retain a Formosan cultural identity vis-à-vis Japan proper. Their aims were therefore basically hostile to the Kōminka objective, and from the Japanese administrative point of view, they had to be squeezed out. A multitude of new regulations were enacted to reduce the autonomy of the mission schools, hospitals, clinics, and the leprosarium near Tamsui. Doctors, nurses, and teachers tried valiantly to conform to the new rules, but found it impossible to do so without compromising Christian principles. For example, compulsory veneration of the imperial family portraits in the schoolroom could not be imposed upon the students in good faith, nor could the curriculum absorb the nationalist mythology without comment. Formosan students had to choose between Jehovah, the God of Israel, or the Sun

Goddess of Japan, the Bible, or the "Record of Ancient Matters," the *Kojiki*.

By late 1941 there was no further room for compromise and accommodation. A mass of "national emergency regulations" impeded daily routine, converts were bullied, students were subjected to intimidating and endless interrogations, and Christian work among the aborigines was altogether forbidden. Household servants had to be dismissed to spare them overwhelming trouble. With profound regret the Canadian and English Presbyterians withdrew, handing over extensive and valuable properties to Japanese and Formosan-Chinese fellow Christians. Members of the Spanish Dominican Mission managed to hold on precariously throughout the ensuing war years because of Spain's alignment with the Axis powers in Europe.

One by one the foreign teachers departed. The Dutch professor took his family back to Java and the American sailed home. The Italian professor of English and Latin and his British-born wife managed to stay on until Mussolini fell, when the little family was hustled off to a concentration camp in Japan proper. Two German teachers continued to live on quietly and obscurely in Taipei's back streets, tolerated as "Axis allies" but aware that they were unwelcome and under close surveillance.

Foreign business enterprise became hopelessly enmeshed in legal and extralegal regulations spun out by the Taipei administration. Police action disrupted daily routines when Formosan and Chinese employees were called away to prolonged interrogations. They were expected to reveal employers' trade secrets; many refused to spy upon their foreign friends and resigned as a measure of protection for their families. The foreign firms were forbidden to correspond in business codes, legitimate business secrets no longer could be kept, and competing Japanese import-export firms enjoyed unfair advantage. Foreign freighters entering port were subjected to innumerable restrictions and port fees were increased to an intolerable degree. By December 1941, foreign business was paralyzed, management and properties were entrusted to local agents and the foreign businessmen and their families had left the island. Only the consular officers remained.

Getting rid of consuls and consulates involved delicate matters of diplomacy. The Dutch agency closed when its representative, manager of the Rising Sun Petroleum Company, left Taipei. The British Consul and his staff were long under great pressure because of the intensive anti-British campaign on the continent. At times the effort to drive the British officers from their handsome Tamsui property reached grotesque and comic extremes. Each policing agency wished to gain credit by assigning men to keep check on the consular compound with the absurd consequence that the numbers of workmen pretending to repair roads and lanes nearby and the number of idle "tourists" strolling nearby to take the hilltop view, often exceeded the total staff of clerks, interpreters, and yardmen on the consular payroll. In rainy weather these ill-disguised agents all tended to bloom with identical large yellow oiled-paper umbrellas, issued from a common store; every plainclothesman assigned to shadow foreign residents was liable to become a victim of practical jokes contrived from time to time to expose him.

London valued this small Tamsui window on the Formosan scene, the Admiralty understood the strategic significance of the island, and over the years British observers had quietly built up a body of essential data relating to Formosan ports, airfields, and inland communications. His Majesty's Government gave no hint that Britain considered withdrawing under any provocation. There was a sharp decline in consular business as normal traffic with Shanghai, Hongkong, and Singapore fell off, but the British consular staff was maintained at full strength until December 8, 1941.

GETTING RID OF AMERICANS: THE MATSUO AFFAIR

For a period of forty-two years the United States and Japan had shared a common frontier in the sea channel below South Cape; nevertheless, no one at Washington seemed to take seriously frequent Japanese references to Formosa as an "aircraft carrier," "stepping stone," and "stone aimed at the south." The small American establishment at Taipei was useful as a training station at which young vice-consuls gained administrative experience far from the Consulate General at Osaka and the Embassy at Tokyo. There was little direct commerce with the United States, hence consular business was negligible beyond routine reports and the minor problems of an occasional tourist, passing businessman, or the two American evangelists associated with the Canadian Mission. Since there was no American mission establishment drawing support from American parishes there was no flowback of information to attract attention and advertise Formosa in the American mission press.

The United States government held no real estate, preferring to rent a shabby building in which the consul's family lived above the offices. Conditions for Foreign Service personnel in 1940 had not changed much at Taipei since Vice Consul Fisher made his long complaints to Washington in 1905. It was rated a hardship post and assignments were short—there were seven different officers in charge between September 1937 and December 1941.

Washington considered closing the office in 1939; the volume of business no longer justified operational costs, it was said, and neither the Army, the Navy, nor the State Department felt that it was important to keep a watchful eye on Japan's military activities here. Before a final decision could be made by all the department bureaucrats concerned in such matters, the so-called *Matsuo* case attracted brief attention.

Tokyo had decided to test stringent new national security laws. Without forewarning, one day the consulate's chief clerk, the assistant clerk, the interpreter and the rickshaw man were all seized and jailed. Matsuo Chūhei, the chief clerk, had been employed in the consulate for twenty-seven years. He had never been asked to "spy" and he had never volunteered to do so. In 1940 he had made his routine annual survey of local market opportunities for American suppliers of automotive equipment and for this he was charged with violating decrees forbidding disclosure of economic data "of a military nature." He was convicted and forthwith sent to the penitentiary for a long term at hard labor. With him went the three Formosan-Chinese consular employees, held and convicted because they refused to fabricate stories to support the trumped-up charges.

The American Embassy at Tokyo found that it could not intervene. The Consulate at Taipei had ceased to be useful; a new chief clerk (an American of Japanese ancestry) took Matsuo's place, but import-export restrictions had killed foreign enterprise, and the chilling Matsuo affair effectually closed off all important sources of commercial information.*

By late 1941 the question had ceased to be "Will Japan and America go to war?" and had become "When will hostilities begin—and where?"

* After brutal treatment the assistant clerk died in prison. The others were released in late summer 1945, all with shattered health. Matsuo crept out of the penitentiary on hands and knees, too crippled to walk upright for some weeks thereafter. Years passed before bureaucratic Washington managed to meet just claims for back salaries.

12. The Pacific War
— Early Years

1941: FORMOSA AND THE PHILIPPINES BEFORE
PEARL HARBOR

THE CHINA campaign did not progress according to Tokyo's military timetable, and as the invaders were drawn far
inland and dispersed across a vast continental hinterland,
supply problems became acute. Japan's war industries needed
oil, iron, tin, rubber, and aluminum in ever-larger quantities,
but none of these were to be found in Central China. The
nearest supplies were in Southeast Asia and the Indies.

Across the world Japan's Axis partners boasted that France
had fallen and that Britain must sue for peace, but Australia,
New Zealand, Singapore, and Hongkong assured London that
the colonies and the Commonwealth nations would carry on.
The Dutch in the Indies remained defiant, but the French at
Saigon were much less sure of themselves. Would the Vichy
Government yield Indo-China to the Nazis?

Japan had no great reason to trust her Nazi ally, the racist
Hitler, nevertheless Tokyo was pleased when the Nazi invasion
of Russia (in June 1941) drew Soviet troops from Siberia to the
European front, relieving Japan of pressure along the Manchurian borders and the Sea of Japan. The final drive southward into southern Indo-China began; Japan was about to settle
the third account—the French account—outstanding since the
Triple Intervention of 1895.

Americans at Manila paid close attention to Japan's move toward Saigon but appeared singularly indifferent to growing Japanese strength on Formosa. No particularly significant reports were sent by MacArthur's headquarters (Manila) to the Military Intelligence Division offices at Washington. In strong contrast, Japanese headquarters at Taipei and Tokyo were giving close attention to American establishments on Luzon, which lay on the flank of the advance to southern Indo-China. For Tokyo a crisis had come in July; in an effort to check Japan's occupation of French colonial territory, President Roosevelt suspended shipments of strategic materials from American ports, Britain and the Netherlands joined the embargo, and now Tokyo was denied access to those essential resources lying just beyond reach, in Malaya, Java, Borneo, and Sumatra. From the popular point of view, the A-B-C-D Encirclement propaganda had proved true.

Until this crisis, Tokyo had had considerable reason to believe that the Philippines could be brought into the Greater East Asia Co-Prosperity Sphere with little difficulty, for the United States had promised to withdraw from the islands in 1945. Many prominent Filipinos—Manuel Quezon, José Laurel, and Manuel Roxas among them—were already assiduously cultivating Japan's goodwill. The great European conflict made the future uncertain for a fledgling nation whose nearest neighbor to the north was the only industrial and military power in the Orient. The problem of future relations with Japan was a most delicate issue. Filipino leaders were encouraged to believe that if they collaborated with Japan in matters of regional economy (the Greater East Asia Co-Prosperity Sphere), and in international relations vis-à-vis the United States and Europe, they would enjoy full autonomy under their own flag—in form and appearance an independent sovereign republic, but in reality a client state in the projected Co-Prosperity Sphere.

The doctrine of Asia for the Asiatics offered a powerful emotional appeal after forty years of subservience to the United States and four hundred years of subservience to the white man. Manuel Quezon and Emilio Aguinaldo were considered direct heirs of José Rizal, martyred "Father" of the First Philippine Republic destroyed by the Americans in 1898. After forty years' effort to achieve Home Rule, the Filipinos had no desire to exchange one foreign master for another or to become a "second Formosa." Realism dictated some accommodation with the Japanese, hence the marked ambivalence in Filipino attitudes toward the United States while the Japanese military High Command perfected its plans for the attack upon Hawaii and the concurrent drive into the Philippines.

LUZON UNPREPARED

The strike at Pearl Harbor was expected to cripple the American Navy in the Pacific and to destroy American capacity to interfere with Japanese movements anywhere in Asian waters. Tokyo must have found it difficult to credit intelligence reports from hundreds of agents scattered through the Philippines—from the Japanese farmers, fishermen, merchants, and forestry experts working in Mindanao and on Luzon. Beyond doubt the United States government was not ready to defend the Philippine Commonwealth.

A basic defense plan for the Philippines had been prepared at Washington in 1921, when the question of naval rivalries in the Pacific had become acute. Then and thereafter Formosa was mentioned in the war games programs for the Central and Western Pacific, but as an objective to be taken from the Japanese rather than as a base from which Japan might attack American fleets or territories. This reflected an overweening American self-confidence and a prejudice that would concede little to the "Japs."

When the Commonwealth came into being in 1935 and Washington sent the distinguished but retired Lieutenant General MacArthur to Manila, the new Commonwealth leaders were inspired to grant him the resounding title, honors, and income of a Field Marshal of the Philippines Armed Forces—a distinction not available in the American service but in accord with his lifestyle and expectations. Many large plans were proposed, but little had been done to carry them out when the Commander in Chief of the United States Asiatic Fleet (Admiral Thomas C. Hart) transferred his headquarters from Shanghai to Manila in 1940.

The scattered Philippine archipelago was still an American possession and the United States armed forces continued to be responsible for it. Admiral Hart fully appreciated the Japanese threat from the north, and expected to coordinate military planning with the Field Marshal of the Philippines. The basic plans devised in 1921 were recast, and a new strategy outlined between January and March 1941, but thanks to traditional interservice rivalry, the American admirals and the generals at Manila barely acknowledged one another's presence, and did not come to agreement on detail.*

An overconfident Field Marshal MacArthur believed that he had the situation well in hand, but after six years at Manila, he had established no warning coastal patrols, and no effective air watch. Testifying at Washington years later, he admitted to the Congress that his forces on Luzon were relying upon "eye and ear warning" of an attack from the north. The only radar station was working only intermittently, he said, and he had faced serious difficulties in recruiting, training, and equipping local forces. These were ex post facto excuses. In brief, General MacArthur in 1941 was relying upon precisely the methods used by the sixteenth-century Spaniards in preparing for an expected Japanese attack from the north, and he was not aware, of course, of Koxinga's seventeenth-century threat that he "would lay a bridge of boats from Formosa to Manila to subdue it."

On the Formosa problem neither Admiral Hart nor General MacArthur could expect much help from Washington, had they asked for it. Naval intelligence files then held copies of occasional consular reports from Formosa, deemed of some possible military interest, and a miscellany of maps, hydrographic charts, photographs of the Formosan coasts, and pictures of Keelung and Takao taken long before the Japanese clamped strict security controls upon those ports during World War I. In the Old Munitions Building on Constitution Avenue, the Army's intelligence files on Formosa were even less well supplied. One file-folder held a nineteenth-century map of Keelung with faded photographs dated 1895, and a copy of the Kodama Report of 1905. A few consular reports on Formosa's roads, railroads, and developing industrial complex were the only currently useful items in the lot. The Army Map Service supplied

---

* I follow here the record assembled by Rear Admiral Kemp Tolley, USN, Ret., and published as "Divided We Fell" in *U.S. Naval Institute Proceedings* 92, no. 10 (October 1966), pp. 36–51.

a set of Japan's own Imperial Land Survey maps to supplement these sparse records.

Admiral Hart's Manila office lay next door to General MacArthur's headquarters; nevertheless, only by chance did Hart discover that MacArthur had formulated a new defense plan for the Philippines, had submitted it to Washington, and had received Washington's approval.

On July 27 MacArthur was recalled to active duty, promoted, and made Commanding General of U.S. Forces in the Philippines, with authorization to bring his Filipino recruits into the American Army. Altogether he had about one hundred thousand men under his command and expected a prompt addition of seventy-five thousand to be sent out from the United States. He told Washington that he expected war to come about April 1, 1942.

Hart and MacArthur were charged with defending some seven thousand islands, large and small, with a total land area of 115,000 square miles and a population of eighteen million, but they did not come to agreement on an operational plan until the last week of November 1941. In that week—on November 26—senior Japanese admirals met in Formosan waters for a final conference. Transports were standing by at Takao, Makung, and Keelung, and at Palau Island, east of Luzon. Heavy bombers and fighter-escort planes were ready in south and central Formosa. Far to the north, in the foggy Kuriles, a Japanese fleet was ready to move toward Pearl Harbor, waiting the coded signal to "climb Mount Niitaka." Since the Formosan peak was the highest in the Empire, this signal meant that the nation and the armed forces must now scale new heights.

DECEMBER 8, 1941—MAY 6, 1942

About two-thirty o'clock on the morning of December 8 (Manila time), the American Naval Headquarters at Manila intercepted word of the Pearl Harbor attack. Admiral Hart was notified immediately and the news was sent at once to MacArthur's aides. There are variant accounts, for MacArthur later wrote that he first learned of the attack when called from Washington by trans-Pacific radiotelephone. However that may be, at dawn that day, Japanese planes flew south from Formosa over the old sixteenth and seventeenth century sea routes leading to Luzon's ancient "Port of Japan" near Aparri. There, at Aparri, the radar was either not functioning or the operators were not in communication with Manila; again, the stories do not agree. At approximately nine-thirty o'clock, thirty-two Japanese bombers struck airfields in north-central Luzon. Clark Field, MacArthur's principal airbase far to the south, was alerted, planes rose, circled about, saw nothing, and returned in formation to line up neatly on the field while the crews went in to lunch.

At 12:45 P.M., the Japanese appeared overhead at Clark, and simultaneously struck at Nichols Field, near Manila. A total of 192 Japanese planes took part in these two strikes, and of these only 7 were lost. Within minutes the Americans had lost 42 bombers, totally destroyed. Many others were seriously damaged and out of service. MacArthur's air defenses for Luzon were crippled beyond recovery, and two days later the Cavite naval base was wiped out. By December 11, 1941, United States Naval forces ceased to exist as an effective military arm in Philippine waters. The archipelago was open to invasion. Six years of unproductive talk and planning at Manila had been set against forty years of secrecy, planning, and hard work on Formosa nearby. From the Japanese point of view the enormous investment in the colony had at last paid off as General Kodama had proposed that it should do.*

Naval transports from Keelung, Makung, and Takao began to put Japanese forces ashore in the Bashi Channel Islands at dawn on December 8, and on December 10 they were landing in force at Aparri. Gradually the massive and carefully planned invasion began to take form, culminating in Lingayen

* The Pearl Harbor catastrophe obscured this Philippine debacle, thus sparing MacArthur and Hart the fate of the court-martialed General Short and Admiral Kimmel. Thanks to Japanese secrecy and American unpreparedness, the Philippines' defenses had been shattered within four days, nevertheless, the stereotyped American caricature of the Japanese as a race of toothy, bowing copyists, not to be taken seriously, continued to comfort older military men and to soothe hurt vanity. For example, a noted naval historian, writing in 1963, says of the Luzon campaign that although the Japanese had been pushing the Chinese about for years, the Imperial Army had a "wholesome respect" for American forces, "something of the attitude of a bush-league team facing a national champion for the first time." Elsewhere he adds that "these orientals" had made a fetish of secrecy, and that the victory in the Philippines, as at Pearl Harbor, "was one of stealth and strength, rather than skill." [1]

Gulf when seventy-six transports came to anchor. Concurrently, twenty-four transports from Amami Oshima (the Ryukyu Islands) moved down Luzon's eastern coast and others came westward from Palau, ready to put troops ashore at the

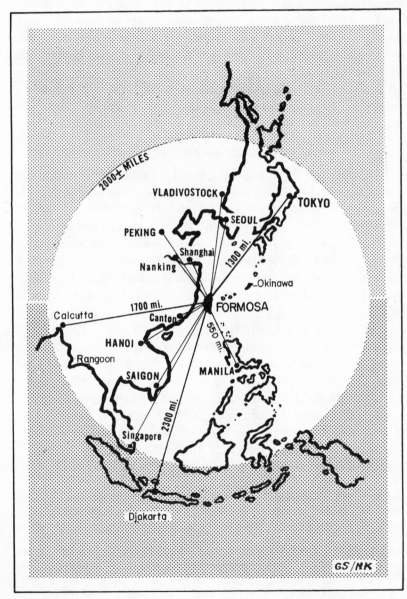

Figure 6. *Strategic Formosa: New frontiers in an air age, 1941.*

"Bailey Willis" beaches from which roads led deep into the island.*

Within three weeks the Japanese successfully carried through nine amphibious operations and the long, terrible push toward Bataan and Corregidor had begun. The MacArthurs were spirited away from Luzon under cover of darkness by a daring U.S. naval team and were soon safe in Australia where the General prepared to fight another day. The true hero of the Philippines resistance, General Jonathan Wainwright, held out on Bataan and Corregidor until May 6, 1942, when he was compelled to surrender and was taken off to a long, hard confinement on Formosa.

FORMOSA'S WARTIME ROLE WITHIN THE EMPIRE

Thoughtful Japanese were deeply disturbed by discovery that Imperial Japan was now at war with the United States, England, Holland, France, and the British Commonwealth countries, as well as with China, the most populous nation on earth. The sense of pride and elation produced by victories at Pearl Harbor and Manila could not obscure the fact that they were now at war in a new dimension, a naval war, and a deadly contest with giants of technology, commanding inexhaustible supplies.

For a few weeks popular excitement ran high. Radio loudspeakers in every village throughout the Empire blared forth the Navy's new marching songs such as "Breaking the A-B-C-D Encirclement," "The Decisive Battle for Greater East Asia," "The Naval Battle of Hawaii," and "The Fall of Hongkong." Astonishing Japanese advances in 1942 represented an explosion of national energy. By the year's end the Rising Sun flag had been carried into American Alaska (Kiska and Attu), and to Burma and the borders of India. Neither Alexander, Genghis

---

* At Manila MacArthur had made the mistake the British had made at Singapore; he had anticipated a seaborne attack coming in by the main entrance to the Bay, under the guns of Corregidor, whereas the Spanish Governor Dasmarinas long ago (1593) had conveyed a warning to Madrid that the ships of Japan "would not come to this [Manila] Bay, but that the soldiers would march here by land." [2] Dasmarinas expected the Japanese to land in the bays of Cagayan and Lingayen and had therefore established effective watch stations along Luzon's western coast, from Aparri southward to Manila.

Khan, nor Napoleon in their greatest days had occupied such far-flung territory in so short a time. Japanese naval units were in Australian waters, and landings in force had been carried through on many islands scattered across the vast Central Pacific. It was a spectacular drive to the north, the east, and the south, but the momentum was soon spent.

Formosa, on the bold frontier in December 1941, now lay far back near the heart of this great theater of operations. The island was overcrowded with men and supplies enroute to the fighting fronts. Ports and airfields were overtaxed, obliging the government to preempt large tracts of agricultural land for emergency landing strips. Civilians who had been technical specialists based on Formosa, were now sent overseas to help reorganize and manage newly occupied territories. For example, the Bank of Taiwan despatched men to manage finance and new currencies along the China coast and throughout Southeast Asia and the Indies. Technicians of the Taiwan Development Company moved out from Taipei to speed deliveries of oil, ores, and rubber to processing plants on the island. Every able-bodied man, woman, and child was mobilized to serve the State in this supreme effort, every square rod of cultivated ground was made to yield food. Transport services, power resources, and industries were strained to maximum capacity.

The decennial long-range planning conferences had prepared for this day. The Zuihō mines near Keelung—among the largest in the Empire—were producing gold, copper, and related mineral and chemical by-products. Copper taken here alone was estimated to be approximately 10 percent of Japan's total production, and the Japan Aluminum Company plants at Takao and Hualien were refining bauxite from Malaya, meeting about one-fifth of Japan's wartime needs. Formosa's sulphur, salt, petroleum by-products, pulp, industrial alcohol, and other industrial chemicals assumed great importance when declarations of war cut off foreign supplies.

Across the Strait a change took place in Fukien. When the United States declared war upon Japan, the Generalissimo was at last obliged to sever diplomatic relations with Japan. The Japanese had installed Chiang's political rival, Wang Ching-wei, at the head of a puppet government at Nanking (1939), and now it began to be rumored that General Chen Yi might go over to Wang and become an openly acknowledged collaborator. He was called to Chungking and relieved of his Fukien governorship in 1942.*

The year 1942 brought unsurpassed production records, nevertheless there were already serious labor shortages, and hard-used equipment became less and less productive through lack of proper maintenance and unskilled handling. Thousands of Formosan Chinese were conscripted for naval service or were shipped overseas to form labor battalions in Burma, Timor, Java, Malaya, and the Philippines. Many were compelled to work with continental Chinese farmers behind the lines, acting in a "workers-liaison" capacity. Hundreds of tribesmen from the central mountain ranges were sent out as scouts and porters with the Japanese troops in the jungles of Luzon, Mindanao, Borneo, and New Guinea. To raise morale on the home front and to suggest contempt for the Caucasian enemy, Tokyo sometimes announced that Takasago recruits were being employed to guard and discipline Allied prisoners.

For a time after the Doolittle raid upon Tokyo (April 1942), Formosa lived in expectation of a further punishing Allied strike; the years of "encirclement" propaganda made it difficult to believe that the enemy in reality had posed no immediate threat. During 1942 and 1943 a stream of British, Dutch, American, and Australian prisoners came in through Takao and Keelung, and were paraded ostentatiously through Taipei's streets leading out to the prisoner-of-war compounds. News broadcasts widely advertised that the largest Allied POW stockade stood adjacent to the Taiwan Grand Shrine. The Japanese knew very well that the international rules and conventions of warfare to which the United States then presumably subscribed, forbade wanton destruction of temples, shrines, churches, hospitals, and the like, hence the association here of POW camp and Grand Shrine suggested double insurance that Allied flyers would avoid bombing the wooded hill in the

---

* Chen was made Secretary-General of the Executive Yuan, working with H.H. Kung, Mme. Chiang's brother-in-law, Vice-President of the Yuan and concurrently Finance Minister. Yen Chia-kan was also called to Chungking where he continued to act as Finance Commissioner of the Fukien Provincial Government until 1944. He became Procurement Director of China's War Production Board and a key man in handling American aid to China.

northern suburbs. Under that hill, as noted earlier, deep in a hive of subterranean offices, the Japanese High Command had established its secret Formosan headquarters.

Throughout 1942 Tokyo boasted that His Majesty's forces had shattered the A-B-C-D Encirclement conspiracy and that the white man would never again make slaves of Asians. The hardships and sacrifices of war would prove to have been worthwhile; prosperity would soon come to Greater East Asia, thanks to Japan's self-sacrificing leadership.

This propaganda line seemed plausible enough until a change began to be felt in Formosa in 1943. Serious economic difficulties could no longer be concealed, and clandestine radio reception stimulated disquieting rumors that all was not going well on distant frontiers. The "liberated" peoples—the Filipinos, the Malays, the Indonesians—were not cooperating wholeheartedly with the self-styled liberators, impeding the swift exploitation of resources in the tropical south. Although Japanese forces won the naval Battle of Savo Island in the Solomons, the United States Marines retook Guadalcanal and neutralized Rabaul nearby, checking the Japanese advance toward Australia. In 1943 the tide began to turn.

"CHINA'S DESTINY" AND THE CAIRO DECLARATION

At Chungking, on March 10, 1943, Chiang Kai-shek published a treatise entitled *China's Destiny*, spelling out his theory of the State. This became at once a school textbook and required reading for all members of Chiang's Party and Government. In this the Generalissimo developed his curious personal interpretation of Chinese history and his dream of China's future in world affairs. Here was the authentic voice of the new Chinese nationalism and a vision of a "Greater Reich," a *Chinese* Reich, the old Middle Kingdom in modern terminology.

According to the Generalissimo's argument, language, race, and traditional culture give China territorial and political rights which the New China must assert. The great continental river basins are described as the heartland, with Formosa, the Pescadores, Manchuria, Inner and Outer Mongolia, Sinkiang, and Tibet as indispensable strategic outlyers ("fortress areas") essential to China's security. A second, revised edition of *China's Destiny* promptly added the Ryukyu Islands (Okinawa) to these outlyers. According to Chiang, Formosa and the Pescadores had been "opened" originally by the Han Chinese empire builders some two thousand years ago, then lost to the Dutch, "recovered" by Cheng Ch'eng-kung (Koxinga) the loyalist, and lost again to Japan in 1895. Text and maps made clear the Generalissimo's determination to control peripheral areas to which Chinese had migrated long ago. Stripped of rhetorical nonsense about the ancient Ch'in and Han empires, *China's Destiny* in effect called for restoration of the more recent Ming and Ch'ing empires, cloaked in "republican" terminology; Japan's Greater East Asia Co-Prosperity Sphere would become a *Chinese* sphere, and the Western powers would enter Asia hereafter on sufferance.

In late November 1943, President Roosevelt summoned the Chiangs to Cairo to meet with him and a (reluctant) Prime Minister Churchill in an endeavor to generate inspiring propaganda during the darkest weeks of the European war. Churchill took a poor view of the Chiangs as partners and of China as a "great power," but Roosevelt was determined to keep the disgruntled Generalissimo and Madame Chiang in the war, if possible. The United States Navy was gathering strength for a great drive across the Pacific to Formosa, the Fukien coast, the Ryukyu Islands, and Japan itself. It was of prime importance to keep Japan's forces fully occupied in the wasteful continental venture, pinned down far inland. On the other hand, the Chinese people were desperately weary. While Chiang waited for the barbarians to destroy one another, there was growing danger that his Nationalist Party and Army organizations might not survive the strain. Wang Ching-wei, the second-ranking officer in the Nationalist regime, had broken away, and others might follow him.

The Cairo Declaration was designed to give China (and the Generalissimo) face before the world. The fateful document, issued on December 1, 1943, promised that Formosa and the Pescadores would be returned to the Republic of China upon Japan's defeat, together with other territories such as the Kurile Islands, allegedly stolen by Japan.*

* The Kuriles had been acquired by Japan through friendly treaty with Russia in 1875; the United States had never questioned the legitimacy of Japan's sovereignty in Formosa until this Cairo Declaration was published.

By now Tokyo had transferred responsibility for the Formosan administration from the Ministry of Colonial Affairs to the Home Ministry, a move designed, perhaps, to please the Formosans, but also intended to impede foreign discussion of Formosa as a postwar *colonial* problem.

About this time the U.S. State Department established a Territorial Studies Committee to consider postwar problems in occupied areas and regions subject to transfer of sovereignty. Memoranda concerning Formosa were discussed, but there is no public record that these were given more than cursory attention; sometime before March 27, 1943, President Roosevelt had already determined Formosa's fate. Between the Cairo meeting with Chiang Kai-shek and Japan's formal surrender—an interval of twenty-one months—no one appears to have given the President cautionary advice on the subject. His jaunty self-assurance that he knew "how to deal with China" seems to have precluded any serious effort to introduce reservations to ensure that Allied and Formosan interests were preserved and guarded through a transition period. Formosa's traditional relationship to the continent, the effect of the extraordinary "Japanese half-century," and the island's exposed position on the Western Pacific frontier, taken together, created a special "Formosa problem" requiring special policy consideration. The armed services saw this, but from beginning to end the State Department assumed the policy position that Formosa was just another Chinese province, infested temporarily by the enemy.

This was not surprising, for with one unfortunate exception, not one man working at or near the policy-making levels in the Department of State had first-hand knowledge of the island. That one exception was Joseph W. Ballantine, Chief of the Division of Far Eastern Affairs in 1943 and later Special Assistant to the Secretary of State. Mr. Ballantine had served as the American Vice Consul in Formosa in 1912.

The wartime policy decisions were usually negative— decisions to assume no responsibility for the island's future beyond taking it from Japan and transferring it to Chinese control as swiftly as possible. The armed services, realizing that China's great domestic quarrel had not been resolved, urged caution, but at the State Department, from Pearl Harbor onward, it was as if nothing had changed on the island after 1895, or, at least, since 1912. The men who prepared "position papers" assessing potential difficulties and suggesting alternative policy options, signally failed to alert their superiors to anticipate difficulties inherent in the situation.

13. On New Frontiers Again

$\mathcal{I}$N THE opening months of 1944, Allied submarines took heavy toll of shipping between Formosa and Japan proper. Keelung and the smaller ports were sometimes overcrowded with vessels that dared not leave on schedule, and Formosan warehouses overflowed with cargo for which no ships came in. Consumers' goods were in short supply, and construction schedules everywhere were disrupted by material shortages or by fierce priority disputes concerning allocation of manpower and materials. None knew better than the Japanese admirals that events at Midway, the Solomons, and Saipan reflected growing Allied power and Japan's diminishing strength. The gravity of Japan's position was being concealed by a fog of boastful propaganda when a few farsighted leaders began to prepare Formosa for a long ordeal and the ultimate crisis.

The Imperial Navy was given full control at Taipei. Admiral Hasegawa proposed to make the island self-sufficient, ready for long isolation—the loss of all sea communication with Japan proper. To provide essential consumers' goods, he sought some diversification of local industry, but it would prove difficult to replace worn and obsolete machinery or to find sufficient skilled labor for specialized jobs. Although a revised general conscription program enabled both military services to assign Formosans to noncombatant duties hitherto reserved for "true Japanese," the High Command was reluctant to arm and train a Formosan-Chinese Home Guard.

Total food production dwindled as chemical fertilizers were no longer to be had, and the supply of field labor, too, was drastically reduced. These problems were offset somewhat by the great accumulation of stored rice and other foodstuffs waiting at the ports. There was no danger of hunger, for these unshipped grains, vegetables, and meats could be made available to the civil population. In anticipation of a prolonged siege, the military had stockpiled enough of its own supplies to feed two hundred thousand men for a minimum of two years, or two hundred fifty thousand men for eighteen months, if need be.

The civil population suffered principally through loss of public health and welfare services. A shortage of funds, supplies, and trained personnel made it impossible to maintain the smallpox vaccination services or to continue the islandwide malaria suppression campaigns. Unbalanced diets, long hours of hard work, and prolonged exposure in fields and forests not yet cleared of the anopheles mosquito meant a rapid increase in the incidence of the disease throughout the island.

In 1944, with great secrecy, a few highly placed civilians and naval officers at Tokyo began quietly to review the prospects of defeat. Rear Admiral Takagi Sōkichi assessed Japan's position at sea and concluded that Japan must find a formula for peace before the Allies brought the war directly to the home islands. He therefore recommended using the "outer territories"—Korea and Formosa—for bargaining purposes, possessions to be given up if that sacrifice would forestall direct invasion of the imperial heartland. He would have Japan reverse the role Formosa had played in 1895, when China handed it to Japan to forestall further Japanese advances on the continent.[1]

Although no hint of such shattering proposals reached the public, a sense of impending crisis pervaded Formosa, and highly placed officials began to send wives and children back to Japan proper. Many were lost on the high seas.

Washington needed detailed intelligence of the defenses, port activities, communications, and industries of Formosa. Early economic studies had revealed its important place in the total empire economy, and now the accelerating naval drive westward through the Pacific islands made it imperative to prepare for a possible invasion of Formosa and an indefinitely prolonged occupation pending Japan's total defeat. The presence of five million native Formosan Chinese seemed to offer excellent cover for properly trained agents—Chinese agents—who could be smuggled across the Strait. Washington needed data on troop movements through Formosa, notes on military construction and communications within the island, and information useful to the psychological warfare offices. The Pentagon hoped that our Chinese allies at Chungking might supply such information by sending in men who could also promote labor unrest and slowdown tactics, and who might sabotage key points in the strained economy. In other words, we needed a well-organized underground agency on Formosa, which, because of problems of race and language, only our Chinese ally might successfully supply.

But no Chinese in the Nationalist intelligence organization ventured across into the "wild beasts' cage"—at least no evidence reached Washington that such dangerous operations had been undertaken. To preserve face, Chinese generals at Chungking endorsed a series of alleged intelligence reports, and handed them to the Americans at Chungking who in turn forwarded them to Washington. Some of these remarkable documents solemnly began with the statement that China had discovered Formosa in A.D. 607. Well-known events of the decade preceding Pearl Harbor were recapitulated, with muddled dates, names, and details, and usually dressed up to tell Americans what they obviously wished to know. For example, one report asserted that huge oil reserves had been destroyed by Chinese agents in March 1938—a fantasy built on the futile attempt to bomb the Hsinchu refinery on February 18 of that year. Another told of a railway tunnel running eastward from Takao for a distance of eighteen miles to supply the airfields at Pingtung (Heitō). No such tunnel existed. There were stories of massive uprisings in the hills in 1939, and of bloody revolts in 1940, involving thousands of Formosan conscripts. There were extraordinary tales of sabotage in factories and rail yards between 1938 and 1943, and reports of a great bridge "built to lie a little under water, for camouflage." One report, giving a precise date in 1944, asserted that Keelung harbor was empty of shipping although American photo reconnaissance on that date actually showed the port overcrowded with freighters waiting to slip out to sea through the Allied submarine packs.

One report handed to the Americans at Chungking was prepared by a Formosan expatriate named Hsieh Nan-kuang, "Chairman of the Formosan People's Revolutionary Federation," and this document had serious consequences after the Surrender in 1945. Hsieh represented himself as spokesman for thousands of Formosans living in China who were—he said—eager to slip back into the island as saboteurs. They needed a large sum of money and very considerable supplies. Investigation quickly disclosed that Hsieh's "saboteurs" lived in occupied China, far beyond his reach. Nevertheless, Hsieh was persistent; as a youth in the 1920s he had quarreled with more conservative Home Rule advocates and had left the island in disgust. He dreamed of high position—perhaps the governorship—under an American occupation when the Japanese were driven out. With this in view, he handed to the Americans at Chungking a voluntary report on conditions and· personalities within the island. This was principally an enumeration of Home Rule leaders with whom he had quarreled before leaving Formosa, men who were still on the island and hence were potential rivals in an occupation period. He smeared them all, labeling some as "pro-Japanese collaborators" and others as "suspected communists." This peculiar and mischievous document was not checked out by investigators at Chungking, and at Washington copies went into the Military Intelligence files and to the Office of Strategic Services where in due course—unchecked and unverified—it became a basic O.S.S. yardstick for post-Surrender investigations.

Meanwhile China's Foreign Minister T. V. Soong (Madame Chiang's brother) spent many months in Washington. There he set in motion enquiries of a different quality and for a different purpose. The J. G. White Engineering Corporation and J. P. Morgan and Company reported on the extensive studies of the basic Formosan economy that had been made before the U.S. $22,000,000 bond issue was floated on Japan's behalf in the 1920s. From the Board of Economic Warfare, Soong's agents obtained elaborate analyses of Formosa's total agricultural and industrial organization and the mines, the forests, and the fisheries, the banks, insurance companies, and savings institutions. Soong's men were not concerned how the Americans wrested this prize from Japan, but only how swiftly and completely it would be handed over to China and to Soong's control.

THE LAST MONTHS OF WAR

American planes made reconnaissance flights over Formosa from bases deep within China. The first bombing strike took place on Thanksgiving Day 1943, at the Hsinchu airdrome, and at about this time Tokyo ordered Japan's ground forces in China to sever all rail connections leading from inland provinces to the coast, and to destroy the forward bases from which American planes were reaching out to the island. One after another the forward airstrips fell into Japanese hands, and as they drove southward toward the borders of Indo-China, the Japanese threatened Kunming, vital point on the Burma-China airlift supply route.

Washington's relations with the Nationalists were strained exceedingly in 1944. President Roosevelt demanded a greater Chinese contribution to the war effort, and Washington concluded that Chiang Kai-shek was avoiding action, "yielding space for time," in an attempt to conserve his personal forces and military stockpiles while the Allies pushed on toward Japan by sea. According to ancient Sun Tze's principle, when the barbarians had destroyed one another, Chiang would be freed to turn on his continental rivals within China itself. But Washington demanded that the Japanese armies must be pinned down in China and exhausted there while Admiral Nimitz led the American fleets to the Western Pacific frontier, to Formosa and the Fukien coast, thus cutting Japan's supply lines to the south. Roosevelt seriously considered terminating aid and supply to Chiang Kai-shek.

Tokyo was aware of these strained relations and sought to exploit them. Foreign Minister Shigemitsu Mamoru suggested that some sort of peace should be patched up with Chiang, some arrangement freeing Japan of the bleeding military commitment deep within continental China. The great threat to the homeland was coming from over the sea, from the south and east. It would be to Japan's advantage to free Chiang to confront his communist rivals. Terms for Chiang, Shigemitsu suggested, might include surrender of Formosa and withdrawal from Manchuria.

This "civilian solution" was unacceptable to the military, and nothing came of the Shigemitsu plan as the tempo of war increased. The Battle of Leyte Gulf in October 1944, brought an American victory; Luzon would now be the southern frontier, and Formosa next after Luzon.

In late 1944 a majority of Formosa's 323,000 Japanese civilians lived in or near Taipei. Some 36,000 were government employees and about 14,000 held technical or managerial positions. The military population changed from week to week as units moved through Formosa to and from the war-front, with a usual average of about 200,000 present.

Now the Taipei Government began to mobilize in anticipation of an attack and a long siege, issuing handbooks on behavior in crises, prescribing survival procedures in the forested hills, and illustrating nutritious grasses, roots, and wild fruits upon which to subsist at mountain shelters. Civil defense activities were intensified. The money presses were moved to underground shelters near Taipei, valuable industrial equipment and research materials were dispersed through the countryside, and many city dwellers went to country retreats taking their most cherished possessions. War weariness affected Japanese and Formosans alike and tensions increased.

At Shanghai Formosan expatriates were discussing what must be done if and when Japan was forced to give up Formosa. Yang Chiao-chia and his associates carefully prepared a plan for an island government of Formosa by Formosans that could fit into a federal scheme for the New China heralded in so much Allied (American) propaganda. At Chungking Hsieh Nan-kuang and Huang Chao-chin maneuvered for favor and place in the post-Surrender government that must be needed soon. Joshua Liao, who had been professor of political science at Nanking, was developing a program and an appeal to the democracies, and his brother Thomas (then working for the Japanese on Formosa as a chemical engineer) was secretly considering his role in a post-Surrender administration.

The Formosans were not fired by any emotional desire to "die for the Emperor," and the Japanese now had ample cause to regret many things in the past—the Sakuma decade, for example, the expropriations of land, police brutalities, harassment of Home Rule leaders, and the long record of social, economic, and political discrimination. It was well known that labor conscripts were still subjected to unfair treatment and segregation in the Japanese armed forces, and that in battle areas Formosan units were the first to be put on short rations, left without weapons with which to defend themselves in some situations, and sometimes the first to be abandoned in retreat. The rate of desertion by young Formosan conscripts was rising sharply; if Formosa came under direct attack and an invasion took place, Formosan loyalties would be put to the supreme test.

On December 30, 1944, Admiral Hasegawa was replaced at Taipei by Lieutenant General Andō Rikichi, Formosa's nineteenth and last Japanese Governor-General. The Imperial Navy had ceased to be an effective shield and it was assumed that when Formosa came under direct attack it would have to be defended at the beaches, in the wide plantation fields, and in the mountains. Tokyo could expect five hundred thousand Japanese to fight to the end, but what of the five million Formosans?

It was well known at Chungking—and therefore at Tokyo—that the United States Navy was preparing for the assault. In March 1944, the Joint Chiefs of Staff at Washington had directed Admiral Chester Nimitz to plan for the invasion of Formosa in February 1945, and the project had been dubbed "Operation Causeway." Formosa was to become a base for the great final drive to Japan proper, and no one knew how many months or years might be required to force a Japanese surrender. For this reason the Office of the Chief of Naval Operations trained more than two thousand officers for special duty in military government on the island.*

* The Naval School for Military Government and Administration was established at Columbia University, New York City, N. Y. Captain F. X. Cleary, USN, took charge of a training program guided by Dr. Phillip Jessup (International Law) and Dr. Schuyler Wallace (Public Administration). A Formosa Research Unit (of which I was in charge), prepared training materials, handbooks, and specialized maps for use in the School and in the field. Twenty-five officers, eight enlisted personnel, and twenty-three civilians produced nine Civil Affairs Handbooks organized on a regional (provincial) basis, and handbooks on the administrative structure. A volume on the aborigines was begun but not completed. A map series, prepared by LT Robert Blessing and based on current aerial reconnaissance photos, was designed for officers

Spectacular successes in the Central and Western Pacific enabled Admiral Nimitz to clear the way to Japan at an accelerated pace; it was proposed to bypass both Luzon and Formosa. General MacArthur insisted that he must first "return to the Philippines." This moral obligation (as he called it), a face-saving gesture, would erase memory of the fiasco of December 1941. In a decision made at Washington on October 3, 1944, Operation Causeway—the conquest of Formosa—was abandoned and plans to establish a foothold on the Fukien coast were given up. Officers were no longer trained for military government in Formosa.

With unusual candor Tokyo announced that more than one thousand American planes had struck the principal Formosan cities on November 13, 1944, and it is said that on learning of the strike the Emperor exclaimed, "So they have come at last!" Formosan skies thereafter seemed never free of hostile planes, striking from carriers in the seas nearby and occasionally from bases deep within China. Farmers heard the high drone of bombers, saw the distant explosions, and watched the smoke drifting above stricken towns. Thousands of city dwellers moved out to the hills and isolated country hamlets. At Taipei some eighteen thousand Formosans were made homeless when the government cut broad fire lanes between crowded Twatutia and the Japanese heart of the city, the jō-nai. Since the prevailing winds were from the west, however, Manka and Twatutia were spared when repeated American raids set great fires in the administrative center, that rectangular target so clearly defined by tree-lined boulevards at the heart of the city.

American forces reoccupied Manila in February 1945. The gradual reduction of Japanese resistance throughout Luzon once again placed Formosa on Japan's true frontier. General Andō prepared for a long siege; pillboxes, trenches, and elaborate barbed-wire barriers were installed along the beaches, and preparations were made to block inland roads, bridges, and

---

who would be in charge of public health, utilities, transport, policing, etc. Lt. Cmdr. Francis W. Cleaves, on leave from Harvard University, directed the location, selection, and translation of Japanese source materials upon which the Handbook texts were based.

tunnels. Every able-bodied person was expected to assist in keeping communications open until an invasion began.

Formosa suffered no threat of starvation, but the general diet was poor, rationing was sometimes unfair, and distribution schedules often disrupted. Although some nine hundred thousand pupils were now registered in the schools, attendance became irregular and unenforceable. Classes were interrupted by frequent air-raid alarms and by emergency work projects that took precedence over all other considerations. Mortality rates rose as public health services were drastically curtailed and medicines became scarce or quite unobtainable. Tuberculosis and malaria took the lives of many schoolboys and girls sent to patrol the beaches and occupy dugouts at rain-drenched watch posts in the hills.

General Andō's counterintelligence reports showed that everyone was war weary and that the Japanese on Formosa were beginning to suffer a sense of profound isolation. Their Formosan neighbors and colleagues were behaving with commendable discipline, neither eager to prepare for a last-ditch struggle nor hostile to Japanese effort to be ready for the worst. This was Japan's war, not theirs; what the immediate future held, none could know. The police reported that the hokō and the Youth Corps were cooperating satisfactorily, capturing downed Allied fliers and bringing in drifting castaways found along the shore. No Formosan dared attempt to give aid to an enemy or to conceal him. It was noted that none of the captured fliers or castaways was Chinese.*

At Tokyo the General Staff correctly assumed that Formosa was not to become a prime invasion target, for even as the National Diet considered belated political concessions to the Formosans, the greatest naval force in the world's history was gathering north of Keelung. The Battle for Okinawa, the last great battle of World War II, began on April 1.

Tokyo had decided that more must be done to ensure the cooperation of Formosans. In a dramatic bid for support, it was announced that the island would no longer be considered a

---

* The American Graves Registration Team subsequently estimated that at least 600 Allied fliers lost their lives on or near Formosa.

colony, that general elections would be held in 1945 to establish a Prefectural Assembly, and that henceforth elected representatives would represent the island in the National Diet. The lower and upper Diet chambers adopted amendments to the electoral laws on March 25, and on April 1 a solemn Imperial Rescript confirmed two ordinances issued to "improve the political treatment" of Korean and Formosan subjects. The hokō or "mutual responsibility" system was dissolved, and two days later His Majesty the Emperor named ten new members to the House of Peers.

Lin Hsien-t'ang's name led the list of new peers from Formosa. Here was the reward for thirty years' steadfast devotion to the Home Rule cause; the Association had won a battle, thanks to Lin, but this recognition came too late; Japan had lost a war.

Allied air strikes at Formosan ports, bridges, rail yards and airfields redoubled in number and weight in an attempt to paralyze all Japanese support facilities south of Okinawa. Takao and Chia-yi were reduced to smoking ruin, the heart of Taipei was burned out, and Keelung was pulverized. Although less than five miles of railway had been severely damaged, ports and anchorages around the island were choked with capsized ships, and airfields everywhere were pocked and cratered beyond possibility of quick repair. The heaviest strikes took place in May as the Okinawa battle reached a climax. On June 21 Japanese resistance on Okinawa came to an end. In eighty days of raging combat the Americans had lost 12,000 men killed and 35,000 wounded; Okinawan civilians, caught between hammer and anvil, suffered more than 50,000 casualties; the Japanese military losses exceeded 100,000.

Formosans were spared this agony; a few hundreds had died in the bombing raids and some thousands had died because of the breakdown in public health and medical services, but on the whole the civil population had come off very lightly in the ordeal. Moreover, there remained on Formosa approximately 170,000 well-rested and highly disciplined Japanese troops, waiting and ready to meet an invasion.

APPROACH TO SURRENDER: ALLIED PROMISES
AND PROPAGANDA

Although the Allies—Britain and America—had a vast naval force cruising nearby when the Battle for Okinawa came to an end, they made no move to enter Formosa. General Andō had more to worry about than a storm of fire and steel during the spring and summer months, however, for hundreds of thousands of propaganda leaflets were fluttering down across the countryside, and American broadcasts beamed to the island were being heard at many clandestine receivers. Some of the illustrated pamphlets and papers (produced in Hawaii) were addressed exclusively to the Japanese in Formosa, advising them to give up the fight before it was too late, but the great majority were designed to weaken the Formosan will to continue cooperation with the government. The five million Formosans were urged to turn upon the Japanese, sabotage the war effort, and rise in rebellion. The Allies were coming in as liberators, so the leaflets said, and Formosans were urged to cooperate during the invasion.

Every Japanese police agency drove hard to gather up these dangerous bits of paper, fluttering down like a deadly rain; there were heavy penalties for anyone who did not destroy them or promptly turn them in, and all discussion of their content was absolutely forbidden.

Formosan attention was not focused on the call for sabotage and rebellion, however, but upon the promises of postwar freedom to participate in their own island government. President Roosevelt and Generalissimo Chiang were pictured as smiling brothers-in-arms, the world's great champions of democracy. The Japanese military organization was caricatured as a hideous octopus crushing Formosa within its tentacles. The Four Freedoms of the Atlantic Charter were quoted, and the text of the Cairo Declaration was cited as a guarantee that "stolen" Formosa would be returned to the motherland, the Republic of China. In April, May, and June this propaganda began to emphasize the importance of the United Nations, and there were pledges and glowing promises that a New China was about to emerge with American help and that a new era of democracy was about to dawn for Asia.

To Lin Hsien-t'ang and his older colleagues it all seemed familiar; Woodrow Wilson's moving principles were being rephrased, and the United Nations, with full American support, was about to take the place of the old League that had faltered when the United States failed to join it, and had been destroyed when Japan's delegates walked out in 1932.

In July came news of the Potsdam Conference and the Ultimatum, reaffirming the Cairo pledges. On August 6 and 9 came the world-shattering strikes at Hiroshima and Nagasaki, and on August 13 a thousand planes flew over battered Tokyo.

Then came Emperor Hirohito's astounding decision to surrender lest the nation be totally destroyed. In calling upon his subjects to face the inevitable and accept defeat, he compared his position to that of his grandfather, the Emperor Meiji, at the time of the Triple Intervention, saying "As he endured the unendurable, so must I, and so must you." Terms used in the Rescript addressed to the service ministers are of peculiar interest. In directing the armed forces to lay down their arms he said ". . . we are about to make peace with the United States, Britain, Russia and Chungking . . ." * Japan was not surrendering to "China" but merely to Chiang's organization, propped up in Chungking by Washington.

On August 14 fifty thousand radios carried his voice into every Formosan town and district meeting place, and to every village square. There would be no bloody invasion, no fighting along the shores and in the hills—no "second Okinawa." For everyone on the island the news came as a great relief. For the Japanese it was stunning, an incredible blow, ending all the years of hard work and sacrifice in a bitter and unprecedented defeat. Here in Formosa they were no longer masters, for the island was no longer theirs.

Five million Formosans heard the emperor's capitulation with strangely mixed emotion—a compound of relief, elation, and uncertainty. It meant, at least, the end of fifty years of humiliating status as second-class subjects; they would no

---

* Butow, Robert J.C., *Japan's Decision to Surrender*, p. 208. In Japanese the reference was made to "Ei, Bei, Ro, narabi ni Jū-kei . . ."

longer be required to bow before the emperor's portrait and the policeman's box. Henceforth the farmer could plant and harvest whatever he chose to have on his own land, and he would sell or withhold his crop as he pleased. He might even recover lands he had lost to the great Japanese corporations in past years or to the government during the years of war. It would no longer be necessary to work without reward on a thousand special projects for the Japanese State. All these and many other thoughts crowded the minds and the conversations of Formosans during the days following the astounding broadcast from Tokyo.

For a few days General Andō had to cope with two dissident groups unwilling to accept the prospect of total surrender. One group of young officers proposed, without success, to organize a local resistance on the grounds that the emperor had been forced to make the surrender broadcast against his will. Another group proposed to back several wealthy pro-Japanese Formosans in a bid for Formosan independence. This, too, failed.

At Chungking, far away, T. V. Soong's men moved into action. On August 20 the government promulgated *Articles Governing the Organization of the Governor General's Office in Taiwan Province*, and on August 29, General Chen Yi was appointed "Administrator General of the Taiwan Provisional Government." When the Chungking office of this "provisional government" started operations on September 15, there were the familiar faces of the old Fukien organization, most of them active or former members of Soong's China Merchants Steam Navigation Company (CMSN).*

Meanwhile Lin Hsien-t'ang and five other prominent Formosans were quite unexpectedly invited to Nanking by General Ho Ying-chin who asked them to represent the Formosan people at the formal surrender ceremonies on September 9. There, under obscure circumstances, they were inspired to petition the

---

* The commissioners-designate included Chou I-kuo (Civil Affairs); Pao Ko-yung (Industry), whose younger brother was sent to take charge of the Taiwan Liaison Office at Shanghai, located in the CMSN Building; Jen Wei-chun (Trading Bureau); and Hsu Hsüeh-yu (Communications). The appointment of Hsu caused such an outcry of protest that Yen Chia-kan was obliged to take Hsu's place.

Chinese government to grant Formosa a special status "in order to assure the continued prosperity of the island."

In political innocence, many Formosan leaders had assumed that at last Formosa would be governed by Formosans, and that Formosans would be elected to represent the island in the central government of the Republic of China. The accepted guarantee for this was the American presence in China. The Western Allies—and not China—had compelled Japan to surrender, and within China itself Generalissimo Chiang maintained his position thanks only to American sponsorship and American military supply. On June 26 fifty-one nations, led by the United States, signed the United Nations Treaty, and among the pledges advertised to the Formosan people, the second—derived from the Atlantic Charter—loomed most important. This was the promise that "no territorial changes will take place except through the freely expressed wishes of the people concerned." The promise appeared to be guaranteed by the most powerful and richest nation on earth.

On October 5 American planes brought in the first Chinese advance team, and on October 18, American ships brought in Chiang's 70th Army, commanded by Lieutenant General Chen K'ung-ta. On October 24, General Chen Yi and Commissioner Yen Chia-kan flew in aboard an American plane, escorted by an American colonel and the author, then an Assistant Naval Attaché from the American Embassy at Chungking. On the following day, October 25, 1945, General Andō signed the documents delivering Formosa to the Chinese.

On that day the stage was set for resumption of Formosa's long struggle for autonomy and self-government, for the uprising against continental Chinese authority in February and March, 1947, for the flight of Chiang Kai-shek to Formosa in 1949, and for the shock of the Nixon-Chou Communiqué of February 27, 1972.

Notes

CHAPTER 2

1. [Hayashi Tadasu], *Secret Memoirs of Count Tadasu Hayashi*, edited by A. M. Pooley (New York, 1915), p. 107.

2. Takekoshi Yosaburo, *Japanese Rule in Formosa, with Preface by Baron Shimpei Gotō*, translated by George Braithwaite (London, 1907), p. v.

3. Ibid., p. vii.

4. *North China Daily News* (Shanghai, 20 May 1895), editorial.

5. James W. Davidson, *The Island of Formosa, Past and Present* (New York, 1903), p. 367.

6. Takekoshi, op. cit., p. 96.

CHAPTER 3

1. H.B.M.'s Minister at Peking (MacDonald) to Foreign Office, London, April 26, 1898.

2. Hsu, Leonard Shihlien, *Sun Yat-sen: His Political and Social Ideals* (Los Angeles, 1933), p. 57.

CHAPTER 4

1. Arthur Waley, *Three Ways of Thought in Ancient China* (London, 1939), p. 217.

2. J. J. L. Duyvendak, trans., *The Book of Lord Shang* (London, 1928), p. 192.

3. Ibid., p. 194.

4. Ibid., p. 195.

5. Ibid., p. 193.

6. Ibid., pp. 14–15.

7. Ibid., pp. 16–17.

CHAPTER 7

1. Woodrow Wilson, *President Wilson's State Papers and Addresses* (New York, 1918), p. 468, Address to the Congress, 8 Jan. 1918.

2. Ibid., p. 475, Address of 11 Feb. 1918.

3. Ibid., p. 500, Mount Vernon Address, 4 July 1918.

4. Hideo Naito, ed., *Taiwan, a Unique Colonial Record—1937–8 Edition* (Tokyo, 1938), p. 76.

CHAPTER 8

1. [Lin Hsien-t'ang (Rin Kendō), et al.], "Formosan Petition—Claim for a Constitution," *Japan Chronicle—Weekly Edition* (Kobe, 26 Feb. 1925), pp. 271–272 (English text of Petition addressed to the Japanese Diet).

2. [League of Nations], *Report, Commission of Enquiry into the Control of Opium Smoking in the Far East* . . . (Geneva, 1930). Vol. I, pp. 98–101. (Map of Formosa incl.)

CHAPTER 9

1. American Consul (Chas. S. Reed), Taihoku, to Washington, 10 March 1931.

2. [Wei Yüan], "On the Better Control of the Barbarians," in *China's Response to the West—a Documentary Survey, 1839–1923*, edited by Teng Ssu-yu and John K. Fairbank (Cambridge, 1954), pp. 54–55.

CHAPTER 12

1. Samuel Eliot Morison, *History of the United States Naval Operations in World War II*, (Boston, 1947–1960), Vol. III, *The Rising Sun in the Pacific, 1931–April 1942* (1948), pp. 167–168.

2. Governor Dasmarinas (Manila) to the King (Madrid), 1593, in *The Philippine Islands, 1493–1898*, edited by E. H. Blair and James A. Robertson (Cleveland, 1909), Vol. IX, p. 54.

CHAPTER 13

1. Robert J. C. Butow, *Japan's Decision to Surrender* (Stanford, 1954), p. 14.

Bibliography

Bibliographies

Extensive European-language bibliographies include Henri Cordier's *Bibliographie des ouvrages relatifs à l'île Formosa* (Chartres, 1893), a work reproduced also in Clément Camille Imbault-Huart's *L'Île Formose, Histoire et Description* (Paris, 1893). William Campbell's *Formosa Under the Dutch* (London, 1903), includes an important bibliography, brought down to date of publication. Nothing on this scale appeared again in the European languages until Father José-María Álvarez published his three-volume work entitled *Formosa: Geográfica e Históricamente Considerada* at Barcelona in 1930. Several volumes of the United States Navy's eleven-volume Civil Affairs Handbook series concerning Formosa carry useful bibliographical references to the Japanese era. These were published at Washington in 1944 and are listed here in the Bibliography. For Japanese materials, see the *Taiwan Bunka Tenkan* (Bibliography of Taiwan Materials) published at Taihoku in 1934 by the Taiwan Aisho Kai (Taiwan Booklovers' Society), Francis W. Cleaves' *Analytical Notes on Scanned Bibliography* (New York, 1944–1945), and G. H. Kerr's *A List of Formosa Materials in the Japanese Language* (Taihoku [Taipei], 1946) with important annotations by Gengo Suzuki.

Japanese Materials

The principal government archives and libraries on Formosa survived the air raids of 1944–1945 and passed into continental Chinese hands in comparatively good condition, but thereafter some major libraries and many smaller institutional and private collections were heavily damaged or entirely lost when carpetbagging new custodians sold books and archival materials in bulk to local pulp and paper mills, pocketing the proceeds.

Historical notices published in the Japanese language between 1895 and 1945 included elaborate compilations and critical studies of

Chinese materials relating to Formosa's past. These provide a background against which to measure the extent and rate of change after 1895. For example, the archivist Ino Yoshinori compiled and edited source materials under the title *Taiwan Bunka Shi* (A History of Taiwan Civilization), a three-volume work totaling 2,885 pages, well illustrated, and published in 1928. The *Taiwan Dai Nempyō* (Taiwan Chronology) published at Taihoku in 1925 by the Taiwan Keisei Shimpō Sha, provides a detailed record of administrative and economic change during the first thirty years of Japanese rule. The later years of the Japanese Era became noteworthy for the number of annuals, yearbooks, guides, professional journals, and research reports issued by the government, by public bodies and associations, and by private research organizations. The *Taiwan Jijō* (Conditions in Taiwan), published annually from 1914 until 1944, and the *Taiwan Jihō* (Current Review of Taiwan), a monthly published from 1919 until 1945, were particularly noteworthy journals to which leading authorities contributed reviews, analyses, and statistical data.

It should be noted that from 1946 onward a wide range of Japanese materials began to be translated into Chinese, and reissued at Taipei or elsewhere, but sometimes without acknowledgement of the true history of the material. Occasionally this has led to the confusion and embarrassment of foreign students undertaking research programs in postwar Formosa.

Educational, cultural and intellectual development in the Japanese era is reflected in the numerous publications of literary associations, art clubs, and other private groups producing well-illustrated annual exhibition catalogs, journals, and finely designed books to which Japanese and Formosan artists, poets, and essayists contributed. Nishikawa Mitsuru's Masō Press publications series was especially noteworthy.

The present review is based largely upon research and translation done at the wartime U.S. School of Military Government and Administration at Columbia University. (See footnote, p. 227, and F. W. Cleaves' *Analytical Notes on Scanned Bibliography*).

BIBLIOGRAPHY

Akizawa Usen. *Taiwan Hisshi* [Brigands of Taiwan]. Taihoku, 1923. 340 pp.

Alip, Eufronio M. *Japan-Philippines Relations—Historical, Political, Social, Economic*. Manila, 1938. 26 pp.

Álvarez, José-María. *Formosa: Geográfica e Históricamente Considerada*. Barcelona, 1930. Vol. 1, 568 pp.; vol. 2, 466 pp. [Bibliography, vol. 2, pp. 445–466].

["An Occasional Correspondent"]. "The Japanese in Formosa." *China Mail*, Hongkong, 22 June 1901, p. 5.

Anon. "Die Erforschung des Tschinwan Gebietes auf Formosa durch die Japaner." *Globus* 70 (Braunschweig, 1896):93–98.

Anon. *Shina Jihen Yonnen Shi* [Four Years of the China Incident]. *Taiwan Jihō* 23, no. 8 (Aug. 1941):82–89.

Anon. *Taiwan Tembō* [From the Taiwan Viewpoint]. *Taiwan Jihō* 23, no. 5 (May 1941):146–150.

Aoki Shigeru. *Jūmoku to Seiji* [Trees and Politics]. *Taiwan Jihō* 23, no. 7 (July 1941):112–119.

Asaka Teijiro. *Taiwan Kaiun Shi* [History of Taiwan's Sea Transport]. Taihoku, 1941. 517 pp.

Campbell, William. "The Island of Formosa: Its Past and Future." *Scottish Geog. Mag.* 12 (Edinburgh, 1896):385–399.

Chang Han-yu and Ramon W. Myers. "Japanese Colonial Development Policy in Taiwan, 1895–1906." *Journal of Asian Studies* 22, no. 4 (Aug. 1963):433–450.

Chavannes, Eduard. "Les Résultats de la Guerre entre la Chine et le Japon." *Ann. Géographie* 5 (Paris, 1896):220–223.

Chen Chen-hsiang. *Geographical Atlas of Taiwan.* Taipei, 1959. 144 pp. [Japanese materials, reworked]

Chen, Edward I-te. "Formosan Political Movements under Japanese Colonial Rule, 1914–1937." *Journal of Asian Studies* 31, no. 3 (May 1972):477–497.

———. "Japanese Colonization in Korea and Formosa: A Comparison of the Systems of Political Control." *Harvard J. Asiatic Studies* 30 (1970):126–158.

Chiang Kai-shek. *China's Destiny and Chinese Economic Theory.* Chungking, 1943. [Unauthorized translation by Philip Jaffe, London, 1947, 347 pp.]

Cho Seki [Shih Hai-wei]. *Taiwan no Nenchū Gyōji* [Annual Observances of Taiwan]. *Taiwan Jihō* 23, no. 7 (July 1941):128–131.

Clark, J. D. *Formosa.* Shanghai, 1896. x1 + 213 pp. Maps.

Cleaves, Francis W. "Analytical Notes on Scanned Bibliography" [relating to Formosa]. Trans. Section, Research Unit #2, U.S. Naval School of Military Government and Administration, Columbia University, 1944–1945. 105 pp. Ditto. [See also from same source "List of Books and Articles Translated from the Japanese," 11 pp., Ditto]

Colquehon, Archibald R. *The Mastery of the Pacific.* London, 1897. Chap. 15, pp. 358–378. [On Formosa and Japan]

Davidson, James W. "Formosa under Japanese Rule." *Trans. & Proc., Japan Society, London* 6 (1902):30–53. Illus. [Pamphlet reprint, 1903]

———. *The Island of Formosa, Past and Present.* New York and London, 1903. 720 pp. Illus.

[Duyvendak, J. J. L., trans.] *Kung-sun Yang: The Book of Lord Shang, a Classic of the Chinese School of Law.* Translated from the Chinese with Introduction and Notes by J. J. L. Duyvendak. Chicago,

1963. 360 pp. [London edition, 1928, is entitled *The Book of Lord Shang.*]

Ebihira Shiki. *Musha Tōbatsu Shashin-chō* [Photo Album of the Musha Incident]. Taihoku, 1931. Text, 33 pp.; photos, 87 pp.

[*El Correo Sino-Annamita: Correspondencia de las Misiones del Orden de Predicadores en Formosa, China, Tung-king, y Filipinas*]. 33 (Manila, 1905): *Letters of* F. Giner, 20 Jan. 1905, pp. 7–10; P. Prat, 20 Feb. 1905, pp. 16–24; J. Sasián, 8 Mar. 1905, pp. 16–24; Á-M. Rodríguez, 27 May 1905, pp. 637–654. [Toroku incident], mission statistics following p. 654.

Fairbank, John King. *China: The People's Middle Kingdom and the U.S.A.* Cambridge, 1967. "Communist China and Taiwan in U.S. Foreign Policy," pp. 49–71; "Taiwan: Myth, Dream and Nightmare," pp. 72–79.

Fernandez, Elías. "Resena histórica de la prefectura apostólica de Formosa." *Analecta Fratrum Praedicatorum* 17 (Rome, 1925): 560–567.

Fischer, Adolf. *Streifzüge durch Formosa.* Berlin, 1900. 382 pp. Maps, photos; drawings by Wada Eisaku.

Foster, John Watson. *American Diplomacy in the Orient.* Boston, 1903. p. 341.

Franck, Harry A. *Glimpses of Japan and Formosa.* New York, 1924. Chaps. 20–32, pp. 141–235.

Fujino Shijin. *Nippon Hyaku to Shi no Kasei to Shōbo Setsubi* [Fires and Fire-fighting Facilities in One Hundred Japanese Cities]. Tokyo, 1928. Pp. 217–225.

Fujisaki Seinosuke. *Taiwan Zen-shi* [A Complete History of Taiwan]. Tokyo, 1928. 960 pp. Map, photos.

―――. *Taiwan Shi to Kabayama Taishō* [The History of Taiwan and Admiral Kabayama]. Taihoku, 1926. 960 pp.

Fujishima Gaijiro. *Taiwan no Kenchiku* [The Architecture of Taiwan]. Tokyo, 1948. 222 pp.

Goldschmidt, Richard Benedict. *Neu-Japon: Reisebilder aus Formosa, den Ryukyuinseln, Korea, und dem Südmanschurischen Pachtgebeit.* Berlin, 1927. 303 pp.

Gordon, Leonard. "Formosa as an International Prize in the Nineteenth Century." Ph.D. dissertation, University of Michigan, 1961. 336 pp.

Gotō Shimpei. "Manifesto to the People of Fukien." *China Mail,* Hongkong, 19, 22, 25, 26 June 1901. [Editorial comment 22 June, p. 4]

―――. "The Administration of Formosa (Taiwan)." In *Fifty Years of New Japan,* edited by Okuma Shigenobu, vol. 2, chap. 28, pp. 530–553. Translated by Marcus B. Huish. New York, 1909.

Grajdanzev, Andrew. "Cultural Policy in Taiwan and the Problem of Kominka." *Pacific Affairs* 14, no. 3 (New York, 1941): 338–360.

————. "Formosa (Taiwan) under Japanese Rule." *Pacific Affairs* 15, no. 3 (New York, 1942):311–324.

Han Li-wu. *Taiwan Today*. Taipei, 1951. 162 pp.

Haruyama Yukio. "Taiwan no Inshō" [Impressions of Taiwan]. *Taiwan Jihō* 23, no. 8 (1941):10–17.

Hasegawa Kinosuke. "Taiwan no Hōko Arisan" [Arisan, Treasure-house of Taiwan]. *Turisto* [The Tourist] 6, no. 6 (1918):30–42.

Hashimoto Hakusui. *Higashi Taiwan* [Eastern Taiwan]. Taihoku, n.d. 417 pp.

Hoshi Tametaro. *Gunsei no Shinzui—Chihō no Riso to Genjitsu* [Essentials of *Gun* (County) Government—The Ideal and the Reality of Local Government]. *Taiwan Jihō* 23, no. 10 (Oct. 1941): 2–10.

Hsieh Chiao-min. *Taiwan—Ilha Formosa—A Geography in Perspective*. London, 1964. "The Japanese Industrial Period," chap. 13, pp. 162–183.

Hsieh Nan-kuang. The Formosan Revolutionists League. Chungking, Aug. 1943. 8 pp. Mimeographed. [A fictitious "intelligence report" prepared for the U.S. Army]

Hsu, Leonard Shihlien. *Sun Yat-sen: His Political and Social Ideals*. Los Angeles, 1933. Pp. 56–58.

Hsu Shu-hsi. *China and Her Political Entity*. New York, 1926. "The Japanese War [1894–1895] and Its Consequences," pp. 150–22.

Ide Kiwata. *Nanshin Taiwan Shikō* [Brief History of Southward Advancing Taiwan]. Tokyo, 1943. 412 pp.

Ishidō Shigeyori and Morita Masao. *Taiwan Kōmin Hōkō Tokuhon* [Principles of Loyalty (to the emperor) for the Taiwanese Reader]. Taihoku, 1941. 278 pp.

Ishii Shinji. "The Island of Formosa and Its Primitive Inhabitants." *Trans & Proc., Japan Society, London* 14 (1916). Reprint, 24 pp. 16 pls.

Iwao Seiichi. "Nanyō no Nihonmachi to Taiwan" [Japanese Settlements in the South Seas and Taiwan]. *Taiwan Jihō* 23, no. 8 (1941):50–74.

Jansen, Marius B. *The Japanese and Sun Yat-sen*. Cambridge, 1954. "1900: Waichow and Amoy," chap. 4, pp. 82–104. [Formosa as a base for the proposed occupation of Fukien]

[Japanese Govt., pub.]. *Eisai Nempō* [Annual Health Report]. Tokyo, 30 July 1940. Pp. 108, 266–267; Tables 25, 84. [Data prepared by Bureau of Public Health, Ministry of Public Welfare]

————. *Shokuin Roku* [Register of Civil Servants]. Tokyo, 1943. "Taiwan Sōtoku-fu" [Government-General of Taiwan], pp. 218–231.

————. *The Special Population Census of Formosa, 1905*. Tokyo, 1909. 210 pp. Diagrams, maps. [A compendium of data gathered between 1895 and 1905, summarized in the first complete decennial census]

Johnston, Rev. James. *China and Formosa, with the Story of a Mission.* New York, 1897. Chap. 9, pp. 161–180; "The Story of the Formosa Mission," chaps. 16–17, pp. 301–331.

[Kaizō-sha, pub.]. *Nihon Chiri Taikei* [Outline of Japanese Geography]. Vol. 11. *Taiwan.* Tokyo, 1931. 368 pp. Illus.

Kataoka Iwao. *Taiwan Fūzoku Shi* [Record of Taiwanese Manners and Customs]. Taihoku, 1921. 1,184 pp.

Kazuyama Eiichi. *Taiwan no Rōdō Shin Taisei Mondai* [On the Question of a New Order for Labor in Taiwan]. *Taiwan Jihō* 22, no. 12 (Dec. 1940):42–49.

[Kerr, George H., comp.]. "A List of Formosa Materials in the Japanese Language." Taihoku, 1946. 107 pp. Legal mimeo. [Annotated by Professor Suzuki Gengo]

Kerr, George H. *Formosa Betrayed.* Boston, 1965; London, 1966. Chaps. 1–3, pp. 1–79.

———. "Formosa: Colonial Laboratory." *Far Eastern Survey* 11, no. 4 (23 Feb. 1942):50–55.

———. "Formosa: Island Frontier." *Far Eastern Survey* 14, no. 7 (11 Apr. 1945):80–85.

———. "Kodama Report: Plan for Conquest." *Far Eastern Survey* 14, no. 14 (18 July 1945):185–190.

———. "Some Chinese Problems in Taiwan." *Far Eastern Survey* 14, no. 20 (10 Oct. 1945):284–287.

Kimura Kowashi. *Kodama Kotarō Taishō* [General Kodama Kotarō]. Taihoku, 1944. 279 pp.

Kinebuchi Yoshifusa. *Taiwan Shakai Jigyō Shi* [History of Social Work in Taiwan]. Taihoku, 1940. 1,250 pp.

Kirjassoff, Alice Ballentine. "Formosa the Beautiful." *Nat. Geog. Mag.* (March 1920):246–291. Photos.

Kirk, William. Social Change in Formosa. *Sociology and Social Research* 26, no. 1 (1941). Reprint. 26 pp. [Based on a Consular report prepared by J. K. Emmerson, Taihoku, 27 Nov. 1939]

[? Kodama Gentarō]. *The Kodama Report: Translation of Japanese Plans for Aggression, 1902.* Institute of Pacific Relations, New York, 15 Sept. 1945. 32 pp. [Trans. from *Journal des Débats* (Paris), 11–13 Jan. 1905]

Koizumi Tetsu. *Bankyō Fubutsuki* [Customs and Things Observed in the Aboriginal Territory]. Tokyo, 1932. 332 pp. Illus.

———. *Taiwan Dōzoku Shi* [Record of Local Customs in Taiwan]. Tokyo, 1933. 332 pp.

Komatsu Tosaburo. *Genka no Jikyoku to Taiwan no Chii* [Present Situation and Position of Taiwan]. *Taiwan Jihō* 23, no. 10 (Oct. 1941):127–130.

Kurozawa Heihachirō. *Nan-shin-ron to Taiwan* [Taiwan and the

Southern Advance]. *Taiwan Jihō* 23, no. 10 (Oct. 1941): 130–132.

Kuwada Rokurō. *Hontō-jin no Kai-sei ni tsuite* [On Changing Names of the Formosan People]. *Taiwan Jihō* 23, no. 1 (Jan. 1941): 14–19.

Kuzue Ryūzō. *Taiwan Keizai Shin Taisei Zuisō* [Random Thoughts on the New Economic Order in Taiwan]. *Taiwan Jihō* 23, no. 11 (Nov. 1940):22–31.

Kyu Ei-kan [Khu Eng-han]. *Dakusui-kei* [The Dakusui River]. Tokyo, 1954. 218 pp. [Novelized memoir of wartime and postwar Formosan student life]

Lamley, Harry J. "The 1895 Taiwan Republic—A Significant Episode in Modern Chinese History." *Journal of Asian Studies* 27, no. 4 (Aug. 1968):739–762.

———. *The Taiwan Literati and Early Japanese Rule, 1895–1915: A Study of Their Reactions to Colonial Life and Modernization.* Ph.D. dissertation, University of Washington, 1964. 530 pp.

[League of Nations]. *Report of the Commission of Enquiry into the Control of Opium Smoking in the Far East—Reports to the Council I.* Geneva, 1930. Pp. 98–101.

———. *Report on the Conference on the Suppression of Opium-Smoking Convened under Article XII of the Geneva Opium Agreement, Bangkok, 1931.* Geneva, 1932. P. 51. [See also annual League reports to 1940]

Liao, Joshua W. K. "Formosa Speaks." In *Formosa under Chinese Rule*, edited by F. W. Riggs. New York, 1952. Appendix 5, pp. 187–191. Reprinted as a pamphlet, Hongkong, 1950, 59 pp.

———. "*Quo Vadis Formosa?*" Reprint, n.d., from *Bul. de l'Université l'Aurore* (Shanghai) 7, no. 1. 22 pp.

Liao, Thomas W. I. *Formosanizumu* ["Formosanism," i.e., separatism]. Tokyo, n.d. 230 pp.

———. *Inside Formosa.* Tokyo: 1st ed., n.d., 76 pp.; 1960 ed., 64 pp.

[Lin Chin-fa, comp.]. *Taiwan Kanshin Nenkan* [Yearbook of Officials and Notable Men of Taiwan]. Taihoku, 1933. 3rd. ed. 285 pp.

Lin Fo-shu [Lim Put-chhiu]. *Tō-a Kyōei-ken to Taiwan no Kaihen-sei* [The East Asia Co-Prosperity Sphere and the Reorganization of Taiwan's Economy]. *Taiwan Jihō* 23, no. 5 (May 1941): 2–8.

Lin Hsien-t'ang. "A Brief Record of My Career." Tokyo, 1952. 2 pp. Typescript memo.

Lin Hsien-t'ang [Rin Kendō], et al. "Formosa Petition—Claim for a Constitution." *Japan Chronicle—Weekly Edition*, Kobe, 26 Feb. 1925, pp. 271–272.

Ludwig, Albert Phillip. *Li Hung-chang and Chinese Foreign Policy, 1870–1895.* Berkeley, 1932. 134 pp. [Europe's reaction to Japan's advance]

243

McCordock, R. Stanley. *British Far Eastern Policy, 1894–1900.* New York, 1931. "England Fails to Save China," chap. 2, pp. 76–141.

McGovern, Janet B. Montgomery. *Among the Headhunters of Formosa* [in 1916–1918]. London, 1922. 220 pp. Illus.

Makio Tetsu. *Taiwan Kiristo-kyō Dendō Shi* [History of Christianity in Taiwan]. Taihoku, 1932. 134 pp.

Masuda Fukutarō. *Taiwan-tō Jin no Shūkyō* [*Religions of the People of Taiwan*]. Tokyo, 1935. 101 pp.

Mitchell, C. A. *Camphor in Japan and Formosa.* London, 1900. Pp. 29–55; 60–66. Maps. [Memoir of an investigative trip, 1897–1898]

Mitsunaga Shizō. "Taiwan." In *Shimbun Sōran* [General Survey of Newspapers]. Tokyo, 1938. Pp. 421–435.

Miyakawa Jirō. *Taiwan no Nōmin Undō* [Taiwan Agrarian Movements]. Taihoku, 1927. 324 pp.

Miyauchi Etsuzō. "Taiwan-hokubu no Banzoku ni tsuite" [Concerning the Aborigines of Northern Formosa]. *Jinruigaku Zasshi* 49 (Tokyo, 1934):64–70. [Report of the 10th anthropological survey]

Miyazaki Naokatsu. *Jibyō Shin no Shōten* [Ascension of the Enshrined Gods]. Taihoku, 1942. 111 pp.

Mizutsu Yakichi. *Hontō Naigai no Keizai Jōsei ni tsuite* [On the Internal and External Economic Situation of Taiwan]. *Taiwan Jihō* 23, no. 10 (Oct. 1941):16–22.

Mochiji Rokusaburō. *Taiwan Shokumin Seisaku* [Colonial Policy in Taiwan]. Tokyo, 1911. 612 pp. [Details of early Japanese administration compared with European colonial administrations in Asia] Abridged ed., 1921, 242 pp.

Morison, Samuel Eliot. *The Rising Sun in the Pacific, 1931–April 1942. History of the United States Naval Operations in World War II,* vol. 3. Boston, 1963. Pp. 168–183.

Morita Shunsuke. *Kokumin-gakkō Rei to Taiwan Shotō Kyōiku Gimu-sei* [The National Schools Law and Compulsory Elementary Education in Taiwan]. *Taiwan Jihō* 22, no. 10 (Oct. 1940): 64–73.

Morse, Hosea Ballou. "A Short-lived Republic (Formosa May 24th to June 3rd 1895)." *The New China Review* 1, no. 1 (Hongkong, Mar. 1919):385–399.

Moyer, Raymond. "Agriculture and Foodstuffs in Taiwan." *Foreign Agriculture* 9, no. 1 (Jan. 1945):2–12.

Myers, Ramon, and Adrienne Ching. "Agricultural Development in Taiwan under Japanese Colonial Rule." *Journal of Asian Studies* 23, no. 4 (Aug. 1964):555–570.

Myers, W. W. "The Japanese in Formosa." *North China Herald,* Shanghai, 23 Oct. 1899, pp. 833–834.

[Naito Hideo, ed.]. *Taiwan—A Unique Colonial Record—1937–8 Edition*. Tokyo, 1938. Text, 350 pp.; photos, 202 pp.

Nakashima Eiji. *Nippon Suidō Shi* [History of the Water Systems of Japan]. Tokyo, 1927. "*Taiwan Jōsui-dō,*" chap. 5, pp. 670–681.

Nakura Kisaku. *Taiwan Ginkō Yonjū-nen Shi* [Forty Years Record of the Bank of Taiwan]. Tokyo, 1939. 418 pp.

Ng Yu-zin [Huang Chao-t'ang]. *Taiwan Minshu-koku Juritsu Hatsuansha ni Tsuite no Kenkyū* [A Study of the Establishment of the Taiwan Republic]. Tokyo, 1967. 28 pp.

Ng Yu-zin. *Taiwan Minshu-koku no Kenkyū: Taiwan Dokuritsu Undō-shi no Ichi Dansho* [A Study of the Taiwan Republic: A Facet of the History of the Taiwan Independence Movement]. Tokyo: Tokyo University Press, 1970. 280 pp. Biblio. 11 pp.

[Nihon Hōsō Kyoku]. *Shōwa Jūgo-nen Rajio Nenkan* [Showa 15 (1940) Radio Yearbook]. Tokyo, 1940. "Taiwan no Hōsō Jigyo" [The Broadcasting Business in Taiwan], pp. 290–301; [Register of organizations, personnel], p. 467.

[Nippon Dempō Tsūshin Sha]. *Shimbun Sōran* [General Survey of Newspapers]. Tokyo, 1940 ed. "Taiwan," pp. 421–435.

[Nippon Iji Shimpō Sha]. *Nippon Iji Nenkan* [Japan Medical Yearbook]. Tokyo, 1939 ed. Pp. 1299–1309; [Taiwan data], p. 1589.

Norbeck, Edward. *Folklore of the Atayal of Formosa and Mountain Tribes of Luzon*. Anthropology Papers No. 5, Museum of Anthropology, University of Michigan, Ann Arbor, 1950. 44 pp.

North China Daily News. 20 May 1895. Editorial. Shanghai.

Notestein, F. W., and Irene Tauber. "Formosa." *Population Index—1944* 10 (3):147–158. Princeton, N.J. [Analysis of prewar data]

[Ōgata Taketoshi, ed.]. *Shisei Gojū-nen Taiwan Soso Shi* [Brief History of Fifty Years from the beginning (of the Japanese Administration) in Taiwan]. Taihoku, 1944. 333 pp.

Ōgata Tarō. *Takasago-zoku* [The Takasago (aboriginal) Tribes]. Tokyo, 1942. 322 pp.

Ogawa Naoyoshi and Asai Erin. *Gengo ni yoru Taiwan Takasago-zoku Densetsu-shū* [Collection of Myths and Traditions of the Taiwan Aboriginal Tribes Recorded in the Vernacular]. Tokyo, 1935. 783 pp.

Ogawa Yoshiaki. *Taiwan Kyōiku Shi* [History of Education in Taiwan]. *Taiwan Jihō* 22, no. 10 (Oct. 1940):78–83.

Okamatsu Santarō. *Provisional Report, Investigation of Laws and Customs of the Island of Formosa, Compiled by Order of the Governor General of Formosa*. Kobe, 1902. [English text, 154 pp.; Chinese documents, 87 pp.]

Ōura Seichi. "Commentary on the Imperial Rescript Declaring War against America and England." Taihoku, 8 March 1942. 27 pp. [Typescript translation by Willard Wattles]

Oyama Tsunatake. *Mitsui Zaibatsu no Taiwan Shihon* [Capital of the Mitsui Zaibatsu in Taiwan]. *Taiwan Jihō* 23, no. 10 (Oct. 1941):56–76.

Pelcovits, Nathan A. *Old China Hands and the Foreign Office.* New York, 1948. Pp. 172, 175, 183 ff. [British views of the Shimonoseki Treaty and transfer of Formosa to Japan]

Reiss, Ludwig. "Geschichte der Insel Formosa." *Mitt. der Deutschen Gesellschaft für Natur- und Völkerkunde Ostasiens* 6, no. 59 (Tokyo, Apr. 1897):406–447.

Riggs, Fred W. *Formosa under Chinese Nationalist Rule.* New York, 1952. Appendix 5, "Formosa Speaks," by Joshua W. K. Liao, pp. 187–191.

Rin Shimpatsu. *Taiwan Tōchi Shi* [History of the Taiwan Administration]. Taihoku, 1935. "Kaku-shu no gensei" [Contemporary Administration of Each Province], pp. 321–450.

Rutter, Owen. *Through Formosa–An Account of Japan's Island Colony.* London, 1923. 288 pp.

Sano Haruo. *Shin-Taisei Josei Shokoku-jō* [The New Order, Women, and Employment (in Formosa)]. *Taiwan Jihō* 22, no. 12 (Dec. 1940):50–54.

Scheer, Otto. *Sagen der Atalayen auf Formosa.* Berlin, 1932. 71 pp.

Seguchi Tai. "Nanshin no Kyōten Taiwan" [Taiwan as a Base for Southern Advance]. In *Chuō Koron* (Tokyo, July 1940), pp. 188–197.

Shibuya Naganori and Matsuo Kō. "Taiwan no Kakyō" [Overseas Chinese in Taiwan]. In *Taiwan Keizai Nempō* (Taihoku, 1943): pp. 401–444.

[Shinko-sha, pub.]. *Taiwan. Nihon Chiri Fūzoku Taikei* [Outline of the Geography and Customs of Japan], vol. 15. Tokyo, 1931. 425 pp. Illus.

Stöpel, Karl Theodor. *Eine Reise in das innere der insel Formosa und die erste Besteigung des Niitakayama* (Mount Morison) [in 1898]. Buenos Aires, 1905. 106 pp.

Suzuki Masuto. *Shōwa Jūgo-nen ni okeru Taiwan Sōtoku-fu Kansei Kaisei ni tsuite* [On the Organizational Changes in the Taiwan Government General in 1940]. *Taiwan Jihō* 23, no. 2 (Feb. 1941):54–67; no. 3 (Mar. 1941):8–16.

Suzuki Seiichirō. *Taiwan Kyūkan Kankon Sosai to Nenchū Gyōji* [Old Customs and Annual Events in Taiwan]. Taihoku, 1934. 521 pp.

[Taichū Prov. Govt.]. *Taichū-chō Riban Shi* [History of Administration of the Aborigines of Taichu]. Taihoku, 1914. 395 pp.

———. *Taichū-shū Yoran* [Taichu Province Survey]. Taihoku, 1929. 170 pp.

[Taihoku-dō Bunten]. *Nanyō Shigen Shiryō Tokushu Mokuroku* [Catalogue of Books Concerning Resources and Development of the Southern Region]. Taihoku, 1941. 61 pp.

Taira Teizō. *Nanshin Seisaku Shiken* [Private View of the Southward Advancement Policy]. *Taiwan Jihō* 23, no. 8 (1941):2–9.

[Taiwan Aisho Kai]. *Taiwan Bunken Tenkan* [Bibliography of Taiwan Materials]. Taihoku, 1934. 51 pp.

[Taiwan Govt. Genl.]. (Publication by government agencies, or directly sponsored by the G.G. In addition, many associations, e.g., the Forestry Association, received government subsidies, but published autonomously.)

Progressive Formosa. Taihoku, 1926. 108 pp. Illus. [English text]

Report on Control of the Aborigines of Formosa. Taihoku, 1911. 44 pp. 100 photos, charts, maps. [English text. Issued by Bureau of Aboriginal Affairs.]

"Riban Shikō" [Draft History of Pacification of the Aborigines]. MS. 340 pp. Taihoku, n.d. Prepared in Central Police Office.

Rinji Taiwan Kyūkan Chōsa Dai-ichi Chōsa Hōkoku-shō [First Report of the . . . Provisional Committee for the Investigation of Social Manners and Customs in Taiwan]. Kyoto, 1903. Pp. 144–170 [On traditional Chinese land policies]

Shina Jihen to Kakyō [The Sino-Japanese Incident and Overseas Chinese]. Taihoku, 1939. 216 pp. [Issued by Taiwan Development Corp.]

Shiseki Chōsa Hōkoku [A Report on Historically Noteworthy Places]. Taihoku, 1936. 74 pp. 32 pl.

Taiwan (Formosa): Its System of Communication and Transport—A Report to the International Postal Union. Taihoku, 1929. 50 pp. Illus. [English text]

Taiwan Banzoku Kanshū Kenkyū [Study of the Customs of the Aboriginal Tribes of Taiwan]. Taihoku, 1915–1921. 8 vols. Illus., maps.

Taiwan Chihō Keisatsu Jitsumu Yōran [Outline of Local Police Duty in Taiwan]. Taihoku, 1923. 183 pp. [Issued by the Police and Prison Wardens Training School]

Taiwan Gakuji Nempō [Taiwan Educational Affairs Annual]. Taihoku, 1940 ed.

Taiwan Genjushu-zoku no Genshi Geijutsu Kenkyū [A Study of the Primitive Arts of the Taiwan Aborigines]. Taihoku, 1944. 412 pp.

Taiwan Jihō [Current Review of Taiwan]. [A monthly, issued by the Dept. of Information, Taihoku. Articles cited elsewhere under authors' names.]

Taiwan Jijō [Conditions in Taiwan]. Annual. Taihoku, 1939 ed., 774 pp.: pp. 1–32 (Land, Population); pp. 45–68 (Administrative Agencies); pp. 69–84 (Legal System); pp. 85–120 (Police); pp. 121–134 (Justice, Penal System); pp.

135–168 (Shrines and Religions); pp. 209–244 (Social Education); pp. 245–300 (Social Welfare); pp. 301–328 (Health); pp. 329–726 (Economic Affairs—all aspects); pp. 727–742 (Research Agencies); pp. 743–757 (Important Cities, Places of Interest, Old Sites).

Taiwan Meishō Kyūseki Shi [Places and Scenes of Historical Importance in Taiwan]. Taihoku, 1916. 626 pp.

Taiwan Nōji-hō [The Taiwan Agricultural Review] 36, no. 12 (Dec. 1940):1–216. "Shōwa Jūyon-nen Taiwan Nōgyo Nempō" [Annual Report of Taiwan for 1939].

Taiwan no Kōgyo [Manufacturing Industries of Taiwan]. Taihoku, 1937. 152 pp.

Taiwan Shashin-chō [Photograph Album of Taiwan]. Tokyo, 1908. Text 5 pp.; 100 photos; maps. [Issued by Documents Section, Govt. General Secretariat. Captions in Japanese and English.]

Taiwan Shūkyō Chōsa Hōkoku-sho [Research Report on Taiwan's Religions]. Taihoku, 1919. 184 pp.

Taiwan Tetsu-dō Ryokō Annai [Taiwan Railway Travel Guide]. Taihoku, 1932. 375 pp. Maps. [Handbook on local topography, customs, developments, prepared by Railroad Dept., Bureau of Transportation]

Taiwan Tōchi Gaiyō [Summary of Administration in Taiwan]. Taihoku, 1945. 506 pp. [Detailed review, prepared between 14 Aug. and 26 Oct. 1945, to facilitate transfer of authority to incoming Chinese]

[Taiwan Gunshirei]. "Taiwan Tobatsu Senseki Gairon" [General Survey of Subjugation Conflicts with the Taiwan Natives]. MS. 155 pp. [Prepared by Taiwan Army Headquarters; copied at Taipei, 1945]

[Taiwan Jiyū Genron Sha]. *Taiwan Toji Kankei Gikai Shinshiboe Roku* [Record of Diet Speeches Concerning the Administration of Taiwan]. Taihoku, 1928. 352 pp.

[Taiwan Keisei Shimpō Sha]. *Taiwan Dai Nempyō* [Taiwan Chronology] Taihoku, 1925. 153 pp.

[Taiwan Keizai Nempō Kankō Kai]. *Taiwan Keizai Nempo* [Taiwan Annual Economic Report]. Tokyo, 1943 ed.

[Taiwan Kyōiku Kai]. *Izawa Shuji Sensei to Taiwan Kyōiku* [Professor Izawa Shuji and Education in Taiwan]. Taihoku, 1944. 162 pp.

———. *Taiwan Kyōiku Enkaku Shi* [History of Education in Taiwan]. Taihoku, 1939. 1,098 pp.

[Taiwan Peoples' Representative Govt. Assoc.]. *Constitution and By-laws of the Taiwan People's Representative Government Association*. Taipei, 1946. 26 pp.

[Taiwan Ringyō Kai]. *Taiwan no Ringyō* [Taiwan Forestry]. Taihoku, 1935. 116 pp. [Issued by the Taiwan Forestry Association]

[Taiwan Tsūshin-sha]. *Taiwan Nenkan* [Taiwan Yearbook]. Taihoku. [Annual, 1924–1944, with varied pagination]

Takahama Saburō. *Taiwan Tōji Gaishi* [Brief History of Government in Taiwan]. Tokyo, 1936. 408 pp.

Takahashi Kamekichi. *Gendai Taiwan Keizai-Ron* [Discussion of the Economy of Contemporary Taiwan]. Tokyo, 1937. 634 pp.

Takasu Kōya. *Taiwan Keisatsu Yon-jū-nen Shiwa* [An Account of Forty Years of the Police in Taiwan]. Taihoku, 1938. 473 pp.

Takekoshi Yosaburō. *Japanese Rule in Formosa, with Preface by Baron Shimpei Gotō.* Tokyo, 1907. 342 pp. Illus., biblio. [Japanese ed., 1905, 534 pp.]

Takeuchi Kiyoshi. *Jihen to Taiwan Jin* [The (China) Incident and the Taiwanese]. Taihoku, 1940. 290 pp. 25 photos.

Tamagna, Frank. "Papers on Finance in Taiwan." New York, 1944. 53 pp. Mimeographed. [Prepared in the Federal Reserve Bank for the Naval School of Military Government and Administration, Columbia University]

Tamate Ryōichi. *Satō no Taiwan ni mo Kippu-sei* [A Coupon System Even in Sugar-producing Taiwan]. *Taiwan Jihō* 22, no. 9 (Sept. 1940):88–91. [On Rationing]

Tamiya Ryōsaku. *Hontō Shakai Seisaku no Ichi Kadai* [One Theme in the Social Policy in Taiwan]. *Taiwan Jihō* 23, no. 4 (Apr. 1941):10–22.

Tanaka Zenryu. *Taiwan to Nampō Shina* [Taiwan and South China]. Tokyo, 1913. 376 pp. [Historical Relations with Fukien; Koxinga]

[Teikoku Hoki Shuppan K. K.]. *Genko Hōki Zensho* [Compendium of Laws and Regulations Now in Force]. Tokyo, 1904–1937. 27 vols. [All titles re Formosa (Taiwan) listed in the *I-ro-ha Betsu Sakuin* (Index Volume)]

[Terry, Phillip, ed.]. *Terry's Guide to the Japanese Empire, including Korea and Formosa.* New York, 1914. "Formosa (Taiwan) and the Pescadores," chap. 7, pp. 761–791.

Thompson, Laurence C. "Notes on Religious Trends in Taiwan." *Monumenta Serica* 23 (1964):319–350.

Togo Minoru. *Taiwan Shokumin Hattatsu Shi* [History of Colonial Development in Taiwan]. Taihoku, 1916. 122 pp.

Tomita Yoshiro. "On Rural Settlement Forms in Taiwan (Formosa), Japan." *Proc. 5th Pac. Sci. Cong., Canada.* Vol. 2. Toronto, 1933. Pp. 1391–1395.

Trautz, Frederick Max. *Japan, Korea and Formosa.* Berlin, 1930. 256 pp. [A photographic record]

Tu Tsung-ming [Tō Sō-mei]. *Statistical Studies of Opium Addiction in*

Formosa (Second Report). J. Med. Assoc. Taiwan 34, nos. 6–7 (June–July 1935):91–114; 131–150.
[U.S. Govt.]. *Diplomatic and Consular Correspondence*
  A. *Microcopied records, National Archives, Washington, D.C.*
      Despatches from United States Consuls. Tamsui FM 117, Roll 1 (22 July 1898–7 Aug. 1906).
      Diplomatic Despatches [from U.S. Ministers abroad]. *China* FM Roll 101, (11 Oct. 1895–29 Apr. 1896).
  B. *Published documentary records, Department of State, Washington, D.C.*
      Papers relating to the foreign relations of the United States, 1943. Vol. 3 (The Far East), pp. 35–38. Memorandum of conversation by the Secretary of State [with the British Foreign Secretary and others] on 25 Mar. 1943, reporting, *inter alia*, President Roosevelt's proposal to return Formosa to China.
      Papers relating to the foreign relations of the United States, 1944. Vol. 5 (The Far East), pp. 1266–1274. Memoranda on postsurrender Formosa policies exchanged by the Inter-Divisional Area Committee on the Far East with (a) the Civil Affairs Division, War Department, and (b) the Occupied Areas Section, Navy Department, in June, July, and September 1944.
  C. *Unpublished miscellany* (Consular Reports from Taihoku unless otherwise noted).
      Cameron, C. R. "Narrative Report on Inspection Trip to Taiwan," 7 Sept. 1939. 6 pp.
      DeVault, Charles L. "Regulations Governing Immigration of Chinese into Taiwan," 16 Dec. 1925.
      Emmerson, John K. [1939]: "Regulations Governing Student Tours of the Philippines," 19 July; "Taiwan and Expansion to South China and the South Seas," 10 Aug.; "All-Taiwan Anti-British Meeting," 18 Aug.; "Anti-British Agitation in Taiwan," 22 Aug.; "The Industrialization of Taiwan," 16 Sept.; "Promulgation of Ordinance to Control Taiwan's Sugar Industry," 5 Oct.; "Kominka, or the Japanization of the Formosan People," 27 Nov.; "Investigation of Taiwan by Japanese Bankers," 4 Dec.
      Ketchum, John B. "Alleged Activities of the Japanese in the Philippines," 21 Feb. 1933. "Railway Conditions in Taiwan," 28 Aug. 1934.
      Maney, Edward S. "Rural Electrification in Taiwan," 24 June 1935. "Revolution . . . and Return to China Plotted in Taiwan . . . The Secret Society "Shuyu-Kai" (Mass Friends Society) Incident." [Translation,

with comment, of *Taiwan Nichi-Nichi Shimbun* article of
19 Oct. 1936; report dated 22 October]. "Alleged Plot
to Foment a Revolt in Taiwan by Certain Formosan
Chinese," 23 Oct. 1936.

Nicholson, M. R. "A Report on Japan's Use of Formosans in the Narcotics Traffic in China." Shanghai,
20 Mar. 1939, U.S. Treasury Attaché.

Reat, Samuel C. "Taiwan Government Reports (including 'The Arisan Railway,' issued by the Arisan Forestry Bureau," 8 May 1913.

Reed, Charles S. "Current Affairs Report," Taihoku, 10
March 1931.

Rice, Edward E. "Summary Report on Conditions along
the Fukien Coast," Nanping, Fukien, 2 Apr. 1942.

Rowe, Alvin T. "Report on the Official Japanese View
of Local Reactions to the Sino-Japanese Conflict," 20
July 1937.

Warner, Gerald. [Taihoku, 1937]: "Report on Regula-
tions Forbidding Re-entry into Taiwan of [continental]
Chinese Who Depart Therefrom," 26 Nov. [1938]:
"The Air Raid on Taiwan" [18 Feb., with press pho-
tos], 25 Feb. and 1 March; "February Developments in
Taiwan," 3 Mar.; "Taiwan Development Company's
Five Year Development Plans," 26 Mar.; "Railway,
Bus and Pushcar Transportation in Taiwan in the Fis-
cal Year 1937," 26 Apr.; "Electric Power in Taiwan,"
16 Sept.; "Formosan Employees of Foreign Firms
Drafted during Munich Crisis," 3 Oct.; "The Sino-
Japanese Conflict," 1, 3, 13, and 29 Oct.; "Labor
Problems in Taiwan," 10 Nov. [1939]: "Taiwan's
Arable Land, Land Values, Farm Population and Ag-
ricultural Production in 1938," 24 Jan.; "Electric
Power Developments in Taiwan—2nd Report," 9
June.

Yuni, William R. "The Overseas Activities of the Taiwan Development Company during 1937," 14 July
1938. "Railway and Highway Transportation in Taiwan," 23 July 1938.

[U.S. Govt.]. *United States Relations with China, with Special Reference to
the Period 1944–1949.* Dept. of State Publication 3573, Far
Eastern Series 30 (Aug. 1949). 1,054 pp.

[U.S. Govt.]. *World War II Intelligence Data* (Field reports, research,
publication).

A. *Basic Reports.* Radio broadcast intercepts, captured documents and diaries, POW interrogation records, and information digests prepared in the Pacific Ocean area and Al-

lied field offices were used at Washington in preparing aerial reconnaissance programs, bombing objective folders, and propaganda, e.g., William Acker's "Prospectus for a Leaflet Series to be Used in First Stage Psychological Warfare in Taiwan (Formosa)," Washington, 1942.

B. *Civil Affairs Handbooks.* An illustrated series designed to guide officers assigned to occupation duty on Formosa was issued by the Office of the Chief of Naval Operations, Washington. Handbooks Nos. 1 to 9 were compiled in Research Unit #2 (Formosa Research Unit), Naval School of Military Government and Administration, Columbia University.

  1. *Taiwan (Formosa).* OPNAV 50E–12. 15 June 1944. 198 pp.

  2. *Taiwan (Formosa)—Taihoku Province.* OPNAV 13–27. 1 Nov. 1944. 209 pp.

  3. *Taiwan (Formosa)—Shinchiku Province.* OPNAV 13–25. 15 Oct. 1944. 110 pp.

  4. *Taiwan (Formosa)—Taichu Province.* OPNAV 13–26. 15 Oct. 1944. 235 pp.

  5. *Taiwan (Formosa)—Tainan Province.* OPNAV 13–28. 1 Oct. 1944. 106 pp.

  6. *Taiwan (Formosa)—Takao Province.* OPNAV 13–22. 1 Oct. 1944. 110 pp.

  7. *Taiwan (Formosa)—Karenko and Taito Provinces.* OPNAV 13–24. 1 Oct. 1944. 101 pp.

  8. *Taiwan (Formosa)—The Pescadores Islands.* OPNAV 13–21. 1 Sept. 1944. 39 pp.

  9. *Japanese Administrative Organization in Taiwan (Formosa).* OPNAV 50E–14. 10 Aug. 1944. 71 pp.

  10. *Taiwan (Formosa)—Economic Supplement.* OPNAV 50E–13. 1 June 1944. 127 pp. [with selective bibliography]. [Prepared by Far Eastern Unit, Bureau of Foreign and Domestic Commerce, Dept. of Commerce, for Occupied Area Section, Chief of Naval Operations]

  11. *The Fishing Industry in Taiwan (Formosa).* OPNAV 13–29. 1 Nov. 1944. 32 pp. [with bibliography]. [Prepared by Supply and Resources Service, Office of Economic Programs, Foreign Economic Administration, for Military Government Section, Central Division, Chief of Naval Operations]

Washizu Atsuya. *Taiwan Tōji Kaiko Den* [Recollections of Government in Taiwan]. Taihoku, 1943. 402 pp.

Yamayoshi M. *A Comparative List of the Chinese and English Names in Formosa and the Pescadores—with Maps.* Tokyo, 1895. 17 pp.

Yanaihara Tadao. *Teikoku Shugi Ka no Taiwan* [Taiwan under Imperial Rule]. Tokyo, 1929. 361 pp.

Yonan [pseud.]. *Shasetsu Pikku-appu Tō-nai Nikkan-shi* [Editorial Pickup from the Island's Daily Newspapers]. *Taiwan Jihō* 23, no. 8 (Aug. 1941):102–108.

Index